CW01369349

adventures of
Hebe

adventures of Hebe

John Latham

Henry Regnery Company · Chicago

Library of Congress Cataloging in Publication Data

Latham, John R.
  Adventures of Hebe.

  1. Europe — Description and travel — 1971-
2. Yachts and yachting — Europe. 3. Latham, John R.
I. Title.
D923.L37 1976 914'.04'55 75-32973
ISBN 0-8092-8190-2

Copyright © 1976 by John Latham
All rights reserved
Published by Henry Regnery Company
180 North Michigan Avenue, Chicago, Illinois 60601
Manufactured in the United States of America
Library of Congress Catalog Card Number: 75-32973
International Standard Book Number: 0-8092-8190-2

Published simultaneously in Canada by
Beaverbooks
953 Dillingham Road
Pickering, Ontario L1W 1Z7
Canada

To Eunice

Contents

1. How It All Began 1
2. Getting Ready 12
3. Under Way 25
4. The Rhine 31
5. Kidnapped 35
6. Never a Dull Moment 38
7. The Mosel 58
8. Trier 64
9. Triptyque 75
10. France 79
11. To the Summit 89
12. Sojourn in the Vosges 99
13. *Hebe* is Winged 106
14. Marchons vers Lyon 110
15. Lyon 125
16. Avignon to the Med 135
17. Marseille 146

18	The Med	164
19	Greece	188
20	Epilogue	200

1
How It All Began

One miserable, gray, wet Sunday in February about eight years ago we were sitting around in our pjs, feeling rather heavy after a brunch of buckwheat cakes, sausage, and real Vermont maple syrup. We were engrossed with the usual pile of papers, not each other, when Eunice piped up with, "Now that's something I want to do with you!" What was that, did I hear something? "Come again," I said. She said, "Here is something I would like to do with you," holding out a beautiful color picture of Regensburg. Being somewhat of a dimwit, I had to have this explained—for example, do *what* in Regensburg that could not be done here?

Well, in the first place Regensburg is in Germany and is the uppermost seaport of the Danube and it would be fun to go foldboating down it, don't you think? Heavens no, we're too old to go traipsing around in a leaky old canvas boat, sleeping under the stars in a heavy dew, eating mulligan stew out of tin cans, and, besides, are you sure that Regensburg is on the Danube? Out came the atlas and sure enough, she was right.

That set me to thinking. The dear girl had always wanted to go to Greece and had made two attempts at getting there. The last try damn nearly cost her life, but that is another story. Then I started to ponder this suggestion—or was it a subtle direction? Mmmmm, the Danube goes to the Black Sea, and from there you can get to the Bosporus and Turkey and the Dardanelles . . . Hot damn! The Aegean and Greece.

"Soooo, my love," said I, "why don't we go first class from Amsterdam to Greece by way of Regensburg?"

Ha! Now it was her turn to be incredulous. Just what did I have on my tired, little mind this gray Sunday, and who said anything about Greece, anyway? Well, now, you've always wanted to go to Greece, right? And you just mentioned you want to go down the Danube, right? And why go halfway when we can go all the way from the North Sea to the Aegean? What, in a foldboat! No, we'll look around and get a Dutch botter or boijer or something, that's what.

That started us on our way. The rest of the day was spent poring over the atlas, looking up information on the waterways of Europe, dancing around the room like a couple of nuts, and generally enjoying the release of a great brainstorm. There were crazy moments, like "Hon, I didn't know you cared about Greece"—breathlessly. I don't give a damn about Greece, ruins, and all that rubbish, my sweet, it's just that I love you and like the idea of cutting across Europe in a boat with you and coming out in the Aegean. Why, it's like the Argonauts, only in reverse.

Also, in the back of my mind was the story Negley Farson had once told me about how, back in the twenties, he and his bride made this trip alone in a twenty-odd-foot sloop, and what a wonderful yarn he made of it in his book *The Way of a Transgressor*.

The next day we went into action. The first call was at the German consulate, mistake number one. Yes, there is a Danube. Also, a Rhine and Main. Canals? No. There were some. Yes, but not now, nein! Maybe someday they will be rebuilt? Ja. Stuttgart to Ulm? Not yet. Frankfurt to Regensburg? Nein. What now, you Dummkopf (me, of course)?

So I went to the New York Yacht Club, and, with the librarian, Mr. Hori, went through the files and exhumed all titles that had to do with the Rhine, Main, and Danube. There was precious little, but Mr. Hori got very interested in the project and offered to do some research on his own, such as writing various yacht clubs along the proposed route. Through him we began a lengthy, interesting correspondence with the Düsseldorf Yacht Club, which also seemed to take a personal interest in the idea. In spite of that, however, we could not get charts or detailed data on currents, locks, and canals. This must have been due to a language barrier or poor interpretation of my correspondence. However, neither they nor Mr. Hori lost interest, and some information started to build up.

From the harbor master of Stuttgart, we heard that charts were not necessary for the Rhine, Main, or Neckar rivers since the markings were clear and the buoy system complete. He suggested that we obtain a copy of Weska. This is an annual calendar, or "Eldredge," if you will—the full title of which is "Westdeutscher Schiffahrts-und-Hafenkalender"—published by Binnenschiffahrts-Verlag G.m.b.H., Duisburg-Ruhrort. The cost is nominal, and we found it invaluable. All barge captains carry it. It contains all pertinent information with respect to such things as bridge clearances and width and depth of locks. It is in German, but you'll get used to it.

At about the same time, Eunice wrote a friend in Brunswick, Germany, who is in the publishing business, requesting as much information as possible. In return we received a map of all the inland waterways of Europe, published by W. Seghers in Antwerp, Belgium. Soon afterward, mail began to pour in from all branches of his family imploring us to stop by for a visit—or maybe they could go along part of the way, ja? (I forgot to let you know that Eunice had spent some time in schools in Germany, when her father, a professor, was on sabbatical leave. Also, for the same reason, she had some schooling in France. As a result, she has warm contacts in both countries and speaks both languages fluently—a great help, believe me.)

Now all this was well and good, but what do we do about a boat? A very good question. First, we got in touch with all our friends in the yacht-brokerage business. We told them what we needed and how much we might consider paying. Unfortunately, friend or no friend, a sellers' market means that everybody sits on his thumbs and nothing gets done. There were few vessels available for the price we set and fewer for the job to be done. But there were a couple of brokers who really tried hard to dig up some old buckets that might do the job. One of them came close to making a deal; the boat was just what we wanted. However, the owner, through some hassle with a previous bidder, withdrew her from the market.

At about the same time, a friend of ours leaving for Europe on business was having dinner with us when he made the most awful mistake of inquiring if there was anything he could do for us while there. From then until flying time we let him have it! He got the message and became almost as enthusiastic as we were. When he returned he had a long list of yachts, hookers and such to leave with us, and also a promise that a list of offerings would be forthcoming from his contact in Amsterdam. And it came!

We looked it over and groaned. It was much too good and *the* one in particular was obviously beyond our means—why do yacht brokers always leave off the price? Damn it all, not everyone is a Morgan and some people *do* have to be concerned with price, even if it is a boat.

After a few days of mulling over the temptation, I decided to write the contact in Amsterdam and inquire how much asking, please, your bucket the *Hebe*. I knew it was beyond our reach, but I just had to ask, because ever since I read the book *The Night Life of the Gods* by my old friend Thorne Smith, I had been secretly in love with the goddess Hebe. And here she was on the block and I had to save her for revelry with me! I did not tell Eunice about this straight off because she thinks there is no other woman.

After several endless days of pins and needles and adding up my net worth, walking the poodles—who are the stars of this tale—and talking gibberish to them and the night at large, I received a letter from Amsterdam. With some trepidation I opened it, read it, reread it, and finally sat down in a sweat. This character is a vile, loathsome thing, I thought. He has put the price just within grasp, or bargaining range. He is a fiend and I shall have nothing to do with him. Somehow or other, this came up at dinner that evening—innocently, of course—and before you knew it Eunice and I were in earnest about the possibilities.

Progress came to a halt. No more news from the brokers —nothing new on the route. The time had come to speed things up. If we went to Europe we could look over everything ourselves. So one night I said, "Sweetheart, you need a rest. You need to travel and get all those agency cobwebs out of your mind. Besides, it is going to be Amanda's birthday soon, and you are her godmother and should be there to look after her spiritual education, just as you promised in church at baptism. What I propose is a quick trip to Holland, Germany, and England. I have had a cache of dough put away for this meander, and, as a matter of fact, it just so happens that we have reservations to leave for Amsterdam on October 1, 1968."

Upon landing at Schipol Airport, we fell in love with Amsterdam, and all of Holland, immediately. The airport is a gem. The atmosphere seemed to greet us warmly. We took the bus into town and settled in at a small hotel called the Centraal that used to be quarters for Olympiads! Considering our goal, that seemed like a good place to start.

We had a wonderful time taking in all the free goods KLM offers, and then some. We did the canals, the restaurants, museums, churches, and landmarks. If you're Eunice, this sort of thing has to be done first if you're going to get anything else done. Don't get me wrong though, she is great fun to be with. A little research goes a long way, she always says. Some mornings I thought we had researched rather too well.

After a few days of reveling in all our leisure and window shopping, we put in a call to the fiend and offhandedly told him that we were in town, and, if he could make it convenient, that we might be able to look at *Hebe*. He was equally diffident and allowed as how (in Dutch, of course) perhaps something could be arranged. He would call later, perhaps.

True to our indifference to him, we set forth to visit old friends in Blaricum, a beautiful suburb of Amsterdam. We spent a delightful day with the Warnings at the local art museum donated by none other than Singer (sewing machines), walked over the surrounding heath, and were driven through the dike country where old customs still prevail. I inquired of Hans if he knew where to get charts. He suggested that we try the ANWB (Algemene Nederlandse Wielryders Bond), the automobile club. Simple as that, and, do you know, that is where we got them! ANWB puts out magnificent charts of all the waterways of Holland and parts of Germany, Belgium, and France. They are inexpensive and detailed.

When we returned to the Centraal there was a message from the man saying that he would be at the marquee at 8:30 in the morning, which he was. It developed into quite a day. We were driven to this boat and that and to the Royal Yacht Club in Muiden, and you might just know it, almost every boat we were shown was designed by you know who. Very late in the day, we arrived at the DeVries Lentsch yard in Nieuwendam, and there she was, *Hebe,* all covered with hair . . . moss, that is.

She was tied up to a broken barge and could be boarded only by walking a "tickly-bender" type gangplank. In spite of the moss, she had charm and pretty much everything else we wanted. I prayed that my short breath did not give away my emotions. Gad, three double cabins, a stainless galley, stall shower, twin diesels, etc., etc., tabernacles, stainless rigging, lifelines, teak decks, teak house, picture windows, a bowsprit you could dance on, walk-in engine rooms . . . Forget it, chum, wake up and look away! The owner, or representative of the estate, was aboard and seemed like a nice guy, but he was busy with his accountant . . . I suppose figuring out how much they could get out of these Americans. As a matter of fact, when we all went ashore, before parting, he asked almost that—what was our bid? We reckoned as how *Hebe* might be salvaged and when we got to it we would enter a bid, if interested, all of which went over like a lead balloon.

The next day the agent called and said he would like to drive us to the Zeelands where he had uncovered a few boats that might be of interest. We accepted at once and set off in his ailing Simca. The trip was truly exciting. What the Dutch are doing there is almost unbelievable except that it happens right before your eyes; dikes and reclaimed land begin to appear slowly, but positively, right there in front of you. Perhaps you have read something about the Delta Works.

We stopped at an attractive village called Middelharnis and looked over a few more hookers. The contrast with *Hebe* was enough to make you spew, which I damn near did. There was no comparison, and the asking prices were like Nevins in the dear old U.S. So, the rest of the day was spent pleasantly eating at a nice hotel on the banks of a canal, and then a tour of Rotterdam and a stop for dinner at a historic roadhouse in Leiden. We told our friend we would drop him a line and thanked him for a really lovely time. Almost liked him that day.

That stop at a historic roadhouse the night before almost did us in. They must have served some historic old victuals because the morning found both of us giving it all back to history. We were so sick, I couldn't face a drink for days.

Upon recovery, we decided we should visit a pal or two in Geneva, and so we hopped aboard a plane with the explicit understanding that old pal would meet us at the airport. Of course, there was no pal, and it was bucketing rain. We telephoned. He was in bed . . . a great party last night, should have been along, take a bus, meet you at the nearest saloon. Well, he and his charming wife did just that and took us to the best lunch we ever had, with a breathtaking view of Lake Geneva that I'll take to the grave.

You might just as well know that the weather during the entire tour was absolutely foul until we got to London. Flying to Geneva was hair-raising. . . . No wonder Eunice bought a jug of brandy en route. Right outside our window you could see a jagged peak of the Alps, and then we dove into the clouds and saw nothing until we were on the ground. Thank God for brandy and St. Bernards.

Back to Amsterdam that evening and off to Hamburg the next morning. What a city! This was old stuff for my bride, but poor ole me had never been anywhere but Staten Island and London. Gads, lads, this is the place. Canals, boats, yachts, scenery, everything. German food heavy? Forget it. It's wonderful. And do they sail! Every day, Lake Alster was carpeted with class sailboats, regardless of weather, and they can give lessons to many on spinnaker jibes, believe us.

Back in the sabbatical days when Eunice was a student in Hamburg, one of her classmates was Etta Blohm. It seemed likely that we could get all the navigation information on the inland waterways, including charts, from them, and so we asked Christian, her husband, if he could manage. Certainly Blohm & Voss should have access to all this data, and we will be happy to provide. That Christmas he wrote, "Sorry, not available." If the Germans don't know, how do we find out? We'll tell you later.

There is a good publishing house in Hamburg specializing in water travels, charts, and things nautical. No information on what we wanted there.

To hell with it, let's visit. And we did. Wonderful, wonderful friends of Eunice's—with whom she went to grammar school and suffered some of the early days of Hitler's rise to power (another story) — her English teacher, and German teacher, too, all entertained us as if we were royalty.

While in Hamburg, we did not forget the other part of our mission . . . boats that could carry us through Europe. We looked around, up and down the Elbe, all to no avail. The food and the scenery and the hospitality, however, wherever we travelled, more than made up for the lack of available boats.

As we took off for London, I drafted a letter to the fiend in which we made a bid for *Hebe*.

Arriving in London we were greeted by our friend Mary, who just has to do everything possible to amuse, entertain, and care for you. Mary is a Mississippian who worked with Eunice in UNRA and later married Fred, an Englishman who was killed in that inexcusable plane crash at the London Airport. Amanda is their daughter and she was away in school so we were unable to see after her spiritual needs, though we did speak with her by phone.

It was a beautiful day, the first London had seen since we had left New York and one of the few we had seen. Everything was still green — and warm, including the people.

We visited all around, and in Sussex we had a fondue with our friends, the Dekkers. Bertus Dekker is Dutch and was part of our underground in the search for a boat, and he married a Bennett, a name to be conjured with in England when it comes to boats. Even with this combination we were unable to find a suitable boat.

We were having lunch at Mary's on our last day when John Bennett arrived a bit late with the news that Jackie had married Onassis. Well! This called for more of the excellent wine Mary was serving. Later, at the airport, before we took off, the news was confirmed.

Back in New York at our dusty apartment we said to each other, "My, but that was fun, but we still have no boat, caravel, bark, or canoe, and further, we don't know which way we are going or how." As we fell asleep I mumbled, "Never fear, lass, the fiend will come up with a riddle . . . might even come up with a route."

And riddle he did. In two weeks we heard that they enjoyed meeting such naive Americans, and that since we were so charming and really loved boats, *Hebe* could be had if we came up with a bid of $10,000 more than our original offer. Cripes, in the old days I could have had *Hebe* for a dollar or two, plus three gins for Thorne!

Well, you live and learn, they say. But never, really. Weeks of negotiating ensued, with the obvious result that our bid was accepted, subject to the usual Lloyd's survey. You can get trapped on this one, friends, and we did. I suppose Lloyd's will sue me, but, children, get a good old experienced hand on this one, for sure as you are born you will get screwed, without love. Better still, get a survey done by ANWB.

It was early in the year and nothing could be done on *Hebe,* since she had not been put under cover and the winter in Holland was severe. We decided to use the time to determine our route and to get all other pertinent information.

I called on all the tourist bureaus (no consulates!) for the countries we would pass through if we went via the Danube. Everywhere the greetings were pleasant, enthusiastic, and inviting. We learned that there are no special papers required other than usual boat papers and passports. Except for Austria, a visa is necessary, but this is no problem. It is possible to get visas at the border or, if you wish, to send your passport to the consulate or embassy involved and it will be arranged. The latter is recommended. Hungary posed a small currency problem, but I understand that this has been eliminated. The Romanians were a joyful lot, and some of them wanted to come along if we did, in fact, go down the Danube. The Bulgarians were cooperative, but drab. In their own land, I suppose they would be hellers.

All this seemed so easy. So, why not try the German tourist office? I did and immediately realized what a complete, utter ass I had been. They had all the answers, or almost all. They not only were interested but would do all they could to help.

In the first place there is no existing canal from the Main to the Danube. When one is completed it will connect a few miles above Regensburg. The tourist office advised us to contact the Federal Railroad right down the hall, and they would try to arrange an overland carry. As for coming down from Ulm, forget it. It is a very swift river, but more important, the locks are only 12 feet wide and your vessel is 13 feet, 6 inches. That answered that one in a hurry. For more information, write the Port Captain in Regensburg . . . which we did.

Down the hall we stopped in at the railroad office. Here, courtesy is the order of the day. Also, they were interested in helping, proud of their railroad. They also handle trucking. It was their opinion that the canal had been cut through to the Danube. They had seen a news clipping on it; so had I. They would investigate all possible routes and report back within two weeks.

A few days later, a letter arrived from the Port Captain in Regensburg. If we wanted charts for the Danube, they could be purchased from a retired captain and river pilot in Vienna; he gave us the name and address. The charts are excellent, the price is reasonable, and the captain updates them every year or two as changes demand.

For charts of the inland waterways of Germany and France, he went on, you should write Motoryachtverbund in Munich. This we did. Charts are indeed available at a very nominal cost, about $3.00 a set. They are in four color and include all necessary detail. How simple when you know how! That Port Captain is a great source of information and seems to be interested in helping yachtsmen. We write to him occasionally now. He would like to see us come through Regensburg.

The railroad came back with the news that they did not have heavy enough equipment to lift us out unless we would agree to leave the Main at Aschaffenburg, several miles below the headwaters of the Main. It would be possible to put *Hebe* on a low-bed trailer there, but they would need a cradle. At the moment, they could not give us an estimate on cost because they were trying to figure out a route where ample clearance (for bridges and underpasses) was available and the roads heavy enough for them to get a permit for the load. The Autobahn was out because repairs were under way and also clearance was a problem. These fellows knew what they were doing, I thought.

Another two weeks went by and the bad news arrived. No soap. The load would be too heavy to get a permit and there was not another route that would provide the required vertical clearance. Perhaps they could be of help some other day. There was nothing to do but thank them profusely. If any of you require such service, do not forget the German Federal Railroad.

That was that—no Danube. Too bad, because a huge hydroelectric dam is being built at the Iron Gates and now we never will be able to see or go through that mighty swirl. There is to be a very modern lock operating there next year.

Now for alternate routes.

The French Travel Office in Radio City knows all the answers, and the girls are pretty. I was given a neat package of literature for yachtsmen planning to go through France. All the requirements are spelled out. Included, also, is a map showing the major water routes from Holland, Germany, and Belgium. They advised joining the Touring Club of France. An excellent idea, we discovered. They obtained the needed papers for us at no charge. Having written the proper department of the French government ourselves, we now had everything in duplicate except a triptyque, a French document of passage which no longer is required. At the time, it caused some bother. For now, suffice it to say that a triptyque meant the posting of a bond for $2000 plus a fee for paper work. It could have been handled by the Automobile Club here, providing that all the needed data about the boat were in hand. Such was not the case, thanks to the efficiency of our pal in Amsterdam, and so we decided to get the triptyque when we got to Amsterdam.

Now, everything fell into place.

We had read Irving Johnson's travels through Europe and many other books, all of which were enlightening. There is one book everyone recommends, *The Inland Waterways of France*. It is difficult to follow, but, nevertheless, full of information. We used it and recommend it.

There are many ways to get through France to the Mediterranean, all converging on the single funnel out to the sea, the Rhône. Eunice thought that the Mosel would be the most attractive route. It meant fewer locks than some ways and more than others. The fabulous wine country of the Mosel and its meanders were the final factors in our decision.

We would go from Amsterdam to the Rhine, on the Rhine upstream to the Mosel at Koblenz, then upstream to Metz and over to Nancy, through the Canal De L'Est to the Saône, thence to the Rhône and then to the Mediterranean. Wonderful. We had charts. Now to get going.

2

Getting Ready

Along about the end of the year we made a bid for *Hebe* and enclosed our check for the usual ten percent. Assuming no further problems, we figured we ought to get away early in May to take advantage of high water in the rivers even though this would add to the currents we would have to buck. We were thinking very positively for we knew that *Hebe* could handle up to 8 to 10 knots with the back of her hand. Also, we thought that May would be a magnificent time of the year to start out when the countryside would be bursting with blossoms and budding greenery and the air would be saturated with springtime fragrance.

There were many reasons why we wanted to have *Hebe*. We will tell you about them. First of all, she was an ideal boat for charter work. Three separate double cabins offered unusual privacy in a boat only fifty-six feet in length, excluding her bowsprit. Her three separate "heads" and full shower provided additional comforts not often found in a vessel of this size. The galley was up to date and would make it comparatively easy to prepare food for guests plus crew, eight people altogether. The saloon was like a "dropped living room" with large windows ahead as well as on both sides, making it bright, airy, and a comfortable haven in bad weather. Her beam was thirteen feet, six inches, not too wide for her length, but wide enough to provide extra room below. Her draft of five feet, three inches, with the centerboard up, would make it possible for us to go through any of the many canals and waterways we had in mind. She was underrigged, which would add to guests' comfort. That is, we would not have to shorten sail, which might make some guests uneasy, on many occasions; with the centerboard down, her draft would be nine feet, six inches, which should help her to bite into the wind or beat to windward, as they say, and make for stability. Finally, she was a beautiful-looking lady with gobs of deck space for all to enjoy.

In sum, she was a staunch, seaworthy, steel-hulled vessel, expertly finished below decks, with hand-polished teak paneling throughout. Under the main saloon was a huge storage area with space for all the ship's gear, luggage, cases of canned goods, soft drinks, wine, and booze. Each cabin had its own storage space, cuddies, and full-length hanging lockers. Over each bunk was a reading light.

Her large fuel tanks provided her with a cruising range of 1500 miles under power, and she carried 250 gallons, or one ton of fresh drinking water.

It was in the middle of February when we got word that *Hebe* was ours. It was fortunate that we had been doing our homework; as a result, we had a list of things to be done and checked by the yard. This was sent on to the fiend, who apparently had set himself up as the director of operations, with the request that he get firm prices on each item listed—informed him that no work would be authorized until we had the figures in hand and until the survey had been completed.

Things moved slowly now, including correspondence from the other side. Ultimately we received the list of prices. In addition, we were told that the winter continued severe, that *Hebe* could not be moved inside until the ice disappeared. (What in God's name was she doing outside, anyway?) The survey could not be made, either, until conditions improved. Also, don't worry about the payment of the balance due since this had to be done in the U.S. consulate in Amsterdam when we got over there so that we could obtain legal papers for the boat. We were stymied.

However, there were many other things to do such as making a list of gear and extra equipment to send over, getting all the needed charts, light lists, and pilot books for the Mediterranean, just as a starter. Since we were going first class we looked into things like special outdoor grills so that a varied menu would be possible. This, incidentally, proved to be a great favorite with the chef and our guests. There were a lot of other damn-fool ideas that crossed our minds and these were investigated and retained or discarded. Eventually, when we had double-checked, we decided that everything was in pretty good order.

Along about this time we heard from Dick Eames that his boat, *Andiamo,* could not be commissioned in the yard at Kaag where she had wintered because of a busy building schedule. Hank Chamberlain was going to take her over to DeVries Lentsch for the necessary work, and he would stay until the job was completed. He would be happy to watch over *Hebe* at the same time. At least this was good news.

Our agent friend in Amsterdam had nothing else to do one day because a letter arrived with the suggestion that we forego the survey, pay the unpaid balance and proceed forthwith with the work on *Hebe* just as soon as the yard could get her hauled. Well, that was certainly a gasser and it was vetoed peremptorily. Further, he went on to tell us, a complete service report had been received from the Perkins dealer with respect to the engines; and it was his opinion that there was nothing to do except change the oil and start them up. Whether to believe this was a question, but the news was beguiling and so we tumbled to it . . . a frightful error, as it turned out.

Finally, the weather relented and orders were issued to haul, scrape and paint. Some deck work was needed and this was authorized, along with the go-ahead on building in a permanent upper in the after starboard cabin. There had been a leak in the saloon on the port side and we had noticed some dry rot in the paneling. We told the broker to proceed with this repair also. Mind you, we had no survey as yet, but took the chance anyway. All this was passed on to Hank to keep him abreast of everything. Feeling reasonably secure, we proceeded to other pressing matters.

Our purchases of equipment and odds and ends were by now a formidable pile in the living room. Inasmuch as we were going over on KLM, it seemed to make sense to discuss with them the problem of moving this heap. The freight department recommended that every time we got a load together, weighing one hundred pounds or more, we should have it packaged securely, mark it "personal effects" and they would pick it up and fly it air freight to Amsterdam and hold for our arrival. In this way, there would be no problem with customs or duty. The alternatives were to try to ship everything air freight on our flight or to ship direct to the *Hebe* in transit. Neither was recommended.

Suddenly our happy little world was shattered by a letter from Hank saying that absolutely nothing was being done on *Hebe*, the broker and the yard were at odds, the survey had not been made, and I had better get myself over there as quickly as possible. After all, it's past the middle of April and *you* want to leave in early May, right?

On the way over, I had a conference with myself and conjectured that the proper approaches had not been made to those involved. This proved to be true, all around, including Hank. Gian DeVries Lentsch could not have been more helpful and obliging, and the yard superintendent, Mr. Kaiser, was understanding, cooperative, and able. The problem stemmed from the fact that the agent was trying to chisel down each job — I suppose for our benefit — and, as a result, nothing was being done. Incidentally, unknown to Hank, *Hebe* had passed her survey and work had commenced the day before my arrival.

As an example of the kind of chiseling that was fouling up our progress, let's take a look at the dry rot in the paneling. The whole panel measured about three square feet and altogether only about one foot was affected. The agent wanted to put in two patches, while the yard insisted on replacing the whole panel. They took the attitude that a patch job would look like a patch job regardless of the workmanship they put into it, and they refused to do that kind of work unless specifically ordered by us. The difference in cost was not enough to fuss about. I agreed with the yard. Later, when the final bill was presented it was almost on the button with the estimate.

I had gone to Amsterdam without letting our agent know, and it must have been a surprise for him when I called Sunday and asked him to join me Monday. At lunch I reviewed with him my observations at the yard that morning. I made it very clear as to what was to be done, how it was to be done, and that in the event of any dispute between him and the yard he was to notify me immediately by phone or telex. While his efforts to save us some money were appreciated, I reminded him of our schedule, of the time his haggling had cost us and of that old saw about being "penny wise and pound foolish."

I had left New York on a Friday evening with the idea of returning home Sunday. Hank knew I was coming and was to meet me. However, because of bad weather and other complications, the plane did not arrive in Amsterdam until late afternoon Saturday. Hank had left a message that he would see me at his hotel. I had brought a huge duffle bag along to lighten the load on the next trip, and I got it all aboard a bus and transferred to a taxi at the bus terminal. A few minutes later, I was deposited in front of one of those quaint, narrow, walk-up hotels in the Rembrandtsplein, the Greenwich Village of Amsterdam. That first flight up was a ballbuster, particularly with the duffle on my shoulder, because the stairs were very narrow and went straight up like a ladder. In the "lobby" the attendant told me that Mr. Chamberlain was in his chambers, naturally. After a few minutes, Hank and Annie showed up and gave me the whole story as they saw it. I was tired and confused. I asked them to hold my duffle bag until I came back next trip and to drive me to the Mermaid. It was too late to go to the yard, so I would rest and they could pick me up around seven and I would take them to dinner.

That night and all day Sunday was a miserable experience. I woke up about two in the morning in a cold sweat, shivering like an aspen in a high wind and obviously running a fever. At the same time, my heart was flipping around like a gaffed bluefish. I suffer from occasional attacks of fibrillation. I gobbled some pills I carry for this, piled on every blanket in the room, and waited for the sun to rise. Daylight came, but it rained all day. Hank arrived about eight for breakfast and I asked him to get me a doctor. The doctor was horrified and gave me some pills and a prescription. He said I was to take it easy and if I wanted to return to New York tomorrow it was on my head, and above all, "You idiot," he said, "if you wish to survive you'd better stop smoking those cigarettes," pointing to a

Getting Ready 17

pack on the end table. This last was a stab in the back to an old tobacco man. However, I knew he was right. Cigarettes do trigger the nerve that regulates the heart beat. And so I quit, 1100, April 19, 1969. I gave Hank my cigarettes and did as the man said — rested. My conditon probably was the result of jet fatigue, too much on my mind plus the twenty-four-hour bug.

To get back to my lunch with our agent, he seemed to get the drift. He drove me around for some sight-seeing and then to the airport for home. What a weekend!

A few days later, Sunday, May 4, 1969, we took off for Amsterdam via KLM. Eunice had been to the vet and the various consulates to get the necessary papers to permit the poodles to run rampant over anyone and everybody and then some. She had made arrangements with KLM regarding the dogs and the required carrying cases. Our own gear, about a hundred pounds overweight, was checked in, and all four of us were ready. This sums it up rather succinctly but does not give much space to Eunice and the poodles, considering all the time and effort the three of them put into this operation. It is time for you to meet the pups, if not Eunice.

M. Pompidou and M. Jacques are perfect-sized toy poodles, each weighing about 5½ pounds. **Pompi is jet black, and Jacques is grayblack.** They are very intelligent, old hands at traveling, and strut around with full confidence in the belief that the world was made for them and that Eunice and I are on earth only to do their bidding. We have two small canvas tote bags each about the size of a knitting bag. When these come into view they know a trip is imminent and all hell breaks loose. They stand up on their hind legs and pirouette three or four times, all the while yipping with glee, and then Jacques will top it off with a back somersault while Pompi places himself in his bag. Once in these bags there is never a whimper or a sound. They know that they are being smuggled to some place good and that an itsy-bitsy mistake will cause them to be off-loaded. On a plane, a train, or a bus, all *verboten,* an occasional glimpse of their tufts sticking out, or their little red tongues, will bring smiles to fellow passengers who then become accessories to the fact. They make friends for us wherever we go. They dote on Eunice and are her bodyguards. If anyone approaches her they are immediately on guard. Trespassers, beware.

There was a lot of trivia that transpired, such as being called back from the runway at Idlewild Airport to unload because of a bomb scare; kudos for the personnel of KLM; the courteous treatment of all upon arrival in Schipol; the perplexed, but now friendly smile of the agent who was there to greet us.

After clearing customs, always pleasant at Schipol, we rented a brand-new Simca and loaded it and the agent's car and drove into town to the Mermaid, which was to be our home for a few days while we worked our way aboard *Hebe*.

The Mermaid is a barge boatel, operated by KLM, tied up in the harbor behind the new post office and across from the Naval Academy. It is a wonderful spot, has a cute bar at water level, and a rooftop dining room where only breakfast is served. Whenever a boat would go by, there was a gentle movement, which was betrayed by the swaying of the drapes. We could drive via the new tunnel to the yard in about eight minutes. It was ideal. Late in the evening after work, we would get cleaned up and go to a new restaurant each night. Of course, the poodles would go along, and only once were we apprehended. This was in the Victoria Grill as we were paying the check and one of them made a move that was detected by the maître d'.

After five days of scrubbing we moved aboard *Hebe*. It was raining as usual. We scrubbed some more, in fact, Eunice was still at it about seven when I moved into the galley and announced that we were going to have a celebration. I dug out a bottle of champagne, Eunice came forth with some wafers, and we had a great time in spite of the rain and cold. The butcher across the dike (the poodles' friend) had sold us some chopped beef—from what cut we will never know, but it looked good. I added the special spices he included and it turned out to be quite tasty. Bed was clammy—the heater would not work. Flannel sheets, three blankets, and two poodles notwithstanding, it was cold!

Life took on another dimension to which we adapted smoothly and readily. We were tied up bow to bow with *Andiamo* against the bank of the dike. Huge trees towered over us and the wind and the rain would shake some of the buds down upon our decks. No place for a paint job. The top of the dike was a narrow, brick-paved street bordered on both sides by charming, typical-Dutch brick houses. There was a large church, too, with a tall tower and clock. Climbing up its vintage walls were beautiful roses and off to the side was a tree in bloom, full of red flowers. I never did find out what kind of tree it was. In the immediate area of the church was all we needed to live . . . a butcher shop, where the dogs went every day on their own to get scraps; a baker shop that filled the air with delicious smells every morning about five o'clock; a good snack bar newly opened by a young Dutch couple, where we ate lunch; a hardware and paint shop that sold us our bottled gas; a tiny department store where Eunice got sheets and other odds and ends; and, down toward the entrance to the harbor, there was a charming little brick bank where we got money. The view from the dike was fascinating. The quaint street was filled with people—some with wooden shoes, cyclists both old and young—and small European cars. The street was just wide enough to let one car through with one car parked to the side. Glancing away from *Hebe* you would look down into the gardens and the countryside. You would marvel to yourself that the dike you were standing on was helping to hold back the sea, making it possible for all those lovely houses and gardens and people to be.

It was easy to adjust to life aboard *Hebe*, but the regimen was tough. The workers would come aboard at seven thirty in the morning which meant that we would have to have had breakfast before this. Lunch we would have ashore, and dinner usually would be aboard. Most of the time we were too tired to venture out, and the only place to go was Amsterdam.

Believe it or not, it took until May 15 to get *Hebe* cleaned up and in shape to waddle out of the yard. She had been laid up outdoors all winter with no cover, and the elements had taken their toll. The Perkins report to the contrary, the engines and other equipment had been sadly neglected. Each morning started with a litany of new things awry. For a while, it did not seem possible that anything ever could be set right.

Andiamo, directly ahead of us, was ready and looked beautiful. Dick Eames in Paris, had wired that everything was all right with our papers and that no triptyque was necessary for France. The latter news was confirmed by ANWB in Amsterdam and also by Dicky Bird (pardon our familiarity, sir), a member of RORC and an owner of a Fortuna 46 built at the yard. He had known *Hebe*'s previous owner, deceased, and was sure he would be pleased to see what we were doing to bring *Hebe* back to her original beauty. So saying, he bade us adieu and set off for Muiden. You'll never know, Dicky Bird, what you did for our morale, and we thank you.

On May 13, we took on a paid hand—a mistake. The idea of a paid hand was not a mistake—he was. The tall, handsome son of a seagoing Dutch captain and a French woman, Armand was not destined to be a yacht captain but could be a hit as such in the cinema. It became my task to awaken him every morning considerably after colors . . . that is, for a few days, until I blew my stack. He got the idea, but it took him a long time to put it into practice and we always were at odds. He thought I was crazy! I knew he was. Eunice and the poodles, however, overcame almost every problem, and this was no exception.

While we were living at the Mermaid, Eunice had scrubbed her fingers to the bone, literally, helping to get *Hebe* habitable. Now that we were aboard it was necessary for her to go into town for such things as new cooking utensils, cutlery, and linen. Hank's wife, Annie, had spent the winter here and knew all the right places to shop. While they were off, Armand and I did odd jobs that the yard was not looking after. The last chore was to get the spars aboard and properly stowed and secured. I prayed that I had allowed for sufficient vertical clearance for the bridges and tunnels we would meet along the way. I had figured that we could not exceed 11½ feet from the waterline. Mr. Kaiser, looking out from his balcony, said it looked pretty good to him. However, from the dock alongside it looked awful high to me. So we remeasured it. With a little bit of luck, we should get by—it was 11 feet, 3 inches.

One morning, a bit late, I was passing under the counter over the footbridge to the yard when I stumbled upon a sign painter working on the transom. He evidently had been quietly working since dawn. He had painted the name *Hebe* in the proper proportion, but the home port—"New York"—was so big that it dwarfed the name. I asked by whose good grace he had committed this travesty and his retort was "the big boss." I walked away in a funk. The paint had set and the job could not be changed without redoing the whole transom and we were almost ready to go. We are now known as "the little *Hebe* from NEW YORK."

We were making good progress, but there were still two very

important items on the agenda: insurance and signing the final papers, so that we could get an American Certificate of Ownership for *Hebe*. We asked our agent if he could get a reputable insurance outfit to see us. Also, would he please try to set up an appointment with the executor of the estate for 4:00 P.M. at the American consulate on May 14, the day and time having been cleared with the consulate.

On the morning of the fourteenth, in the midst of chaos, we were boarded by four representatives of D. Hudig & Co. of Rotterdam. They said pleasantly that they were prepared to issue an insurance policy to us on the spot if *Hebe* passed their inspection. They crawled all over *Hebe* and were satisfied. They also approved of our route and my credentials. I signed a check and we were insured. We recommend Hudig highly and we are still with them.

Next on the agenda was our trip to the consulate. We arrived at the appointed hour. There was much delay; the receptionist was busy talking with a boyfriend. At her leisure, she learned of our mission and we were told to walk up three floors, turn left, and we would be greeted. Our "party" had arrived earlier. An attractive Dutch woman, Mrs. Robinson, met us at the landing and ushered us into her office, where we met the executor and our agent. Mrs. Robinson told us it would be a few more moments; the Consul was tied up. Pretty soon a good-looking young fellow came in and started to speak in low tones to Mrs. Robinson. She spun around on her chair and informed us that the Consul was terribly sorry, but he had some people in his office and would not be able to perform the rituals there . . . would the outer office be okay? Certainly, we all said, have the Consul come out and join us. She said, "Mrs. Latham and gentlemen, may I present Mr. Jones, Consul General of the United States."

Well, we signed all the papers in quadruplicate or something, signed and paid checks to the executor and the agent, and then the Consul said that our certificate would be ready in a few days. I said, "A few *what?*" He repeated. Just one darn moment, I said, we are leaving Amsterdam on the sixteenth—certainly no later than the seventeenth—and we need that certificate no later than the sixteenth. He assured us there would be no problem, just call in sometime from where we happened to be, Bonn perhaps, and he would authorize the issuance of the certificate. No good, I said; that certificate must be in our hands no later than May 16. Tomorrow is a holiday, he advised. Just a moment, I retorted, tomorrow is a holy day in Amsterdam, but it has nothing to do with the U.S. and, as far as I was concerned, I was now on U.S. ground. Further, you have charged us for cables to and from Washington and I know damn well there is no holiday or holy day there, except that every politician thinks every day is a holiday at the taxpayer's expense. Mr. Jones, I went on, I would like to use your telephone. Certainly, local? No, Washington! I am a Republican, we now have a Republican administration and, by golly, someone there is going to see that I get that certificate no later than the sixteenth, and I'll pay for the call. Mr. Jones reflected and said, "Sir, your papers will be ready on the sixteenth." They were ready, but poor Eunice had to make two trips.

Stay away from government; go to the automobile club.

The next day was indeed a holy day and most places were closed, including the yard. Dick Eames had returned from Paris, *Andiamo* had had her sea trials, she had been carefully and copiously victualed and was all set to go. They were going to the Maas River and on up to the Rhine-Marne Canal over to Strasbourg. Dick figured he could meet us at Nancy where our routes crossed. He planned to leave tomorrow, the sixteenth, and was going to go only as far as the Nederlander Hotel, where he would base for a few days. He invited us to join him there for dinner that evening. Gian DeVries Lentsch was invited, too, and he offered to drive us in his car. This was an excellent idea since I could drop our Simca off at the Hertz place in Amsterdam and we would have that errand behind us. Of the greatest importance, by far, was that this was to be a combined going-away celebration. We had decided that we would set out the following day, May 17.

The rest of the day we puttered around doing odd chores, and after dinner we set off to visit with the executor at his home in Haarlem, a really lovely spot. His wife was charming and beautiful. Over coffee and brandy he asked if I knew the significance of the name *Hebe*. Yes, she was the daughter of Zeus and Hera and the goddess of youth, and also tended the wine cups for the gods until she lost her job to Ganymede. He told me that she was one of the

Getting Ready 23

reasons his father had named the boat *Hebe,* but also, by coincidence, his name was Henrick and his sister's Beatrice and the first two letters of each made the same name. We assured him that the name would remain.

In the morning, we decided to go over to the huge supermarket a couple of miles away and make our last big purchase before taking off. The market is part of a modern shopping center and almost as big as one I saw in New Orleans, which has forty-eight check-out counters. We roamed all through it and marveled. It carried everything you can imagine—clothing, drugs, beauty aids, hardware, household goods, and, of course, food. We loaded up on canned goods, but we could not get any canned hams, believe it or not. Perhaps they export their hams. Cream, butter, eggs, and chickens are really good buys. Don't buy the chickens except on Friday, though, because that is when they come to the market fresh. Knorr soups, which failed so miserably in the U.S., are a different product in the Netherlands, and we laid in a huge supply. They are easy to store, keep well, and are hearty and tasty. Spices are plentiful and easy to buy, but nowhere could I find Tabasco in Europe. Personally, I cannot cook without it, so if you're like me, I recommend taking your own. Paper goods were plentiful, including American-type toilet paper, and we bought a load of this. When we got through, we had over three large carts filled to the brim.

The Nederlander is situated on the Vecht River about a half-hour drive from Amsterdam. It is an interesting and scenic spot, and the hotel is a training school for young men who wish to become chefs or maître d's. It is supposed to be one of the outstanding spots in Europe for food, wine, and service. It was that night!

There was one sour note. When we got there, we were given a message from Armand that he could not start the generator. The impeller in the water pump, plus a few other parts, had let go. Gian said not to fuss, he would get into it in the morning and we could get away all right. Thanks to him we did forget about it and had a marvelous evening. Gian dropped us off about 2:00 A.M. at the gate to the yard.

Gian showed up while we were still having breakfast. He said we would have to go to Gouda where the Jabsco dealer was located. So, off we went. The dealer, who lives in a heavily wooded and beautifully landscaped part of town, had two sets of pump parts that would fit our Onan generator. We bought both.

Back at *Hebe,* Armand set to work making repairs and Gian and I went over the yard bill. As said, it was close to the original estimate and we were pleased with the quality of workmanship. So we paid up and Eunice, Gian, and I had a couple of drinks. Just as soon as Armand finished work on the generator, we would have lunch and then depart. So we thanked Gian for his help and said our goodbyes.

After lunch, we started up the diesels. They sounded good and were not smoking, or so it seemed. It was raining, but we had become used to this. I gave the order to slip our mooring lines and off we went with a long blast of our horn.

3

Under Way

The canal leading from the yard to the harbor of Amsterdam is very narrow. I had been through it once in *Andiamo* when she went out for sea trials. Since it was a Saturday afternoon, we did not expect too much traffic, but our way was made somewhat difficult because barges had tied up on both sides of the canal. We inched our way carefully, with Eunice and Armand on either side holding pneumatic fenders, just in case . . . we squeaked through.

Looking to our left we could see the baker waving to us from his kitchen porch, and we waved back. A little farther on we made a right turn. If you make a left turn here you can enter a lock and drop down into or onto the polder on which the shopping center had been built.

After a very short run, perhaps three hundred yards, we made a left turn and then shortly after that a right turn into the harbor. There was not much doing. The harbor waters were dirty but not any more so than in New York, the sky was leaden with occasional drops of rain; but it was exhilarating to be out and under way, and Eunice and I gave each other a big buss. The poodles were excited, too. They are accustomed to boats, but they had never had so much deck space to romp around on and they reveled in the luxury of it. As we would pass an occasional barge, one or both would let out a yip and receive a friendly wave or a deep bark in return. Almost every barge carries a dog.

It is not much of a run before you reach the entrance to the Amsterdam-Rhine Canal. As you enter you pass through an open lock used as a flood-control gate. Once in the canal you can look ahead for miles, on a clear day, that is. The canal is as straight as a string and about as interesting.

A mile or two into the canal we came upon our first supermarket. It was a very large barge, operated by Shell, offering everything from fuel to marine supplies to food. A handy convenience. We did not stop.

As we motored along, many thoughts flashed through our minds. Finally, we were under way . . . oh, Lord, where and how would we end up? Eunice's dear mother had died a year ago today and I knew that Eunice was having a private requiem with herself. Just how would we get along with Armand, and what about the poodles? We were somewhat behind schedule, and we worried about our friends who were to meet us along the way. The Arnspergers from Hamburg were driving over and thought they would join us along the Rhine somewhere near Bonn. Snorky and Phil were in Spain and expected to meet us in Koblenz. Lil was spending some time in Paris and hoped to meet us in Nancy. Sheila and Ivan in Geneva had actually made dinner reservations for us at La Pyramide in Vienne for June 11! Cynthia and Tom wanted to spend some time with us after they left Dick and *Andiamo,* probably around Lyon or Avignon. We had a date with Dave and his clan at Cannes, and Bill was planning to meet us in Livorno and hoped to go the rest of the way to Piraeus. Yes, good Lord, where, indeed, would it all end? We looked at each other with some concern, let out a big sigh, and said, "Let us pray."

When we had left Dick at the Nederlander the night before last and driven back to the yard, we had promised to stop by in *Hebe* and lay alongside *Andiamo* our first night out. The Amsterdam-Rhine Canal is not too interesting and both Dick and Gian deVries Lentsch recommended that we cut off into the Vecht at Nichtevecht, which would take us directly to the Nederlander.

What a difference. The Vecht is a must for anyone doing this trip. It is the original waterway to the Rhine and has been the main artery for barges, commerce, and war through the centuries. At this time of year, there was no problem with the water level, and the lock into the Vecht was open. In spite of the rain—and now it was pouring—we could not help but marvel at the change in scenery. Everything was lush with great big trees along the edge of the river. And the river itself twisted and turned with beautiful new sights at each bend. We were moving along slowly, soaking wet, but loving it.

There are many drawbridges on the way, as quaint and attractive as any you have ever seen in picture books as a kid. You give three toots and presently the bridge lifts with a tug of some strings like Bil Baird's marionettes. As you pass through the open bridge, the keeper swings out a small wooden shoe dangling from the end of a fishing pole. This is your cue to grab the shoe and drop in a few coins. We felt like Hansel and Gretel going through the woods and fairyland, only in a boat.

About an hour of this enchantment had gone by when suddenly we realized that we were approaching the Nederlander. We gave three toots on our horn as we came around a bend, and the bridge went up like a sword in salute. We slipped through, and there was *Andiamo* with Dick and Hank on deck waiting to catch our lines. Soon we were tied fast, happy to be together again. I checked the instrument panel, noticed that the engines were running cool, and, satisfied with that, turned them off, suggesting to Armand that he tidy up. The poodles hopped across to *Andiamo* and on to the shore where they also tidied up.

When you are happy, I guess you don't mind a little rain. We had completed our first run. It had taken one hour and forty-five minutes from the yard. The mileage?...we can tell you, but it is of little consequence.

Since his brother lives in this area, Armand asked if he could go off to visit him for the evening; permission granted. We changed our garb and cleaned up a bit and then stepped across to *Andiamo* where joy prevailed. Dick announced that our timing was perfect—Annie had just finished making hors d'oeuvres, the ice bucket was full, and what would we have? "We'll have bourbon," I said. Which reminded me that with all our careful planning and victualing we had forgotten booze. We bought two quarts of bourbon from Dick just in case of snakebite, a cold, or some other medicinal emergency.

The next morning, Sunday, Eunice got up before dawn and walked the poodles all around the village, though it was still drizzling and quite foggy. She met no people but did encounter many cats, geese, and roosters, all joining in the morning matins, with mooing and lowing in the background as the bass section of the opus.

It is always a joy to be awakened by my lovely, but this particular morning there was special news. It seemed as if our transom was black, and did I, darling, know why? Of course I could not answer and so went to look for myself. It was almost solid black and this buffaloed me because I could not remember any smoky exhaust the day before. Armand suggested that it was oil and dirt from the surface of the river. I could not buy this and decided that it probably came from our engines, which had not been used for many months and, undoubtedly, were blowing out a lot of carbon.

We had a hearty breakfast and then cranked up the engines (still no smoke), said our goodbyes and cast off at eight o'clock. There was a bridge immediately ahead, but the bridgekeeper last evening had said he would be ready and he was. We dropped a few pennies in his wooden shoe, gave a long blast on our horn, waved to Dick and everybody in general, and were off!

The enchantment of the river continued. There were lovely homes and beautiful gardens along the way. Once in a while we would pass a castle or pretentious home with interesting gazebos on the river bank. In spite of the rain, the birds were buzzing with song and flitting about us in a form of delight that was infectious. Armand had been through this river many times and was able to give us much information and local color as we moved slowly on.

Once in a while we would pass through a small village and create a little excitement among the few people who were up and around. Also, along the river banks, there was a surprising number of houseboats, which apparently serve as weekend hideaways or vacation homes. They were painted and clean, many had window boxes with new spring blooms, all had curtains in their windows.

Presently we came on to Breukelen, ("a little bridge" in Dutch), the home town of the folks who settled Brooklyn, N.Y. The town is situated on both sides of the river and for this reason, I suppose, made the river seem extraordinarily narrow, almost like a brook. The church bells were pealing and the people on their way to worship stopped to watch and to wave. It was good.

About three miles beyond, there is a town called Maarssen, and at this point there is a low bridge under which we had to pass in order to get back into the Amsterdam-Rhine Canal. This passage is also a lock, but because of the water level, the gates were open. When we approached, it did not seem possible that we could slide under without disaster. There was an attendant standing beneath the bridge and, sensing our queasiness, he beckoned us on with a great big grin. We slid in and under and, to our astonishment, we made it, although you could just about reach up and touch the bridge. We were advised to watch out for barge traffic and cautiously made our way out into the main canal. Eunice was below in the galley making hot soup (wonderful Knorr's) and sandwiches and so missed this.

The canal at this point makes a slight bend to the left and all of a sudden Utrecht springs up in front of you. Along the banks of the canal to the left, there was a large modern housing development something like the Al Smith project on the East River near the Brooklyn Bridge in New York. In spite of the drizzle, people were out in droves as if awaiting our arrival. There were cheers and frantic waving all along the way. We waved back and tooted our horn.

Utrecht slipped into the background. Now we were moving through the lowlands, all of which were in grass, with cows and sheep grazing everywhere. The gray landscape reminded us of Rembrandt etchings we had seen in galleries and books. The banks of the canal were lined with tall trees, probably poplars, that served as a windbreak. The low-hanging clouds made the sky one you have seen only in the old Dutch paintings.

Far up ahead there was a black spot. It got bigger and bigger and was right across our way. Presently it took shape: It was our first lock and would take us into the Neder Rijn.

It proved to be a large lock, capable of handling many barges. There were three barges already in and the lockkeeper was waiting for us. As we entered under the top part of the gate, he started everything in operation. Down came the top and from underneath came the bottom half of the gate. There was a bridge across and, as always, there were people watching. When they saw our flag they gave a cheer and a wave. We stayed as close to the entrance as possible where we would not get so much turbulence from the inrushing water at the front end of the lock. In a big lock, always do this. In Holland and Germany there is no charge for yachts in the locks if you are in company with commercial vessels, so we had just saved about five dollars. The standard fee for yachts without commercial consort is twenty marks or its equivalent, five dollars (1969).

The lift of this lock is twenty-eight feet. All of a sudden we began to realize that we had been tooling around the countryside for the past couple of weeks at about this much below sea level. Pretty smart, these Dutch!

The dogs had never been in a lock before and could not quite figure it out. It was a dark, sodden day, but down in the lock it was extra dark. As we started to rise they became very interested, and when we reached the top they leaped ashore and had a hearty piddle, a ritual they performed at every lock thenceforth. I suppose in dog language this is a warm welcome.

4
The Rhine

A heavy squall was roaring through when we came out of the lock. Ahead were three optional routes, all of which would take us to the Rhine. If we went straight ahead, which one barge did, we would go to the Waal or the Maas and then make for the Rhine; or we could make a right turn into the Lek, proceed on down to Rotterdam, cross over to the Maas, and come back up to the Rhine; or we could turn left into the Neder Rijn as originally planned, which is what we did.

Nowhere in our research had we learned about the true force of the currents in the Rhine, the Lorelei notwithstanding. Now we would find out. At this time of year the river is usually high, carrying the spring runoff from the Alps. This year it was exceptionally high. At 1850 rpm, we do an honest 9¾ knots and there were times when we barely breasted the river. This will give some idea of what you must be prepared to buck going upstream.

About every 200 yards, there are "groins" built out from either shore. These are stone breakwaters put in to protect the shore from erosion. Most of these were completely underwater but, at the outer ends of some, there were buoys that were being pulled under by the current. For almost half an hour, we watched a man in an outboard trying to make his way upstream. We were out in the current. But he would go along at a very good clip close to the shore between the groins and then come almost to a standstill as he attempted to round a groin. We were quite close together at times, and we waved back and forth chuckling at each other's problems against the current. Later in the year, the flood subsides and the current with it, to what degree we do not know.

The squall passed by, and with it the torrent of rain. The sun tried to come through but never really made it. It was tantalizing. The rain would come and go, too. It was cold — very cold for May.

We had not gone too many miles, when, believe it or not, we saw a water-skier right in the middle of the river. It would have been bad enough if he were wearing a "wet suit" but here he was with just a scant pair of shorts, and the air temperature was in the forties, the river temperature not much higher! Well, it takes all kinds. He did a couple of "fancies" for us, one hand holding on and the other waving at us in high glee as we went by.

Sunday was a good day to become acquainted with the river. Traffic usually is light or nonexistent, and today was no exception. One or two commercial boats came down the river, which gave us some practice with the *Rules of the Rhine.* On the Rhine, Mosel, and Danube, you should be rigged to run out a blue flag on a staff extending outboard to starboard when you wish to pass a vessel on the wrong side; i.e., to pass to the left, leaving the overtaken boat to your starboard. Remember, too, that the overtaking vessel at all times is the burdened boat, the same as in the United States. If you wish to pass on the wrong side, first run out the flag. If it is acknowledged, okay; if not, look out and hold your fire. If you see another vessel coming at you, look for the blue signal, but in *any* case get out of the way because no yacht has any rights over a commercial boat — and don't you ever forget it. At night, a blue light is substituted for the blue flag. Also, you must have on board a copy of the *Rules of the Rhine* even if you cannot read it.

Armand and I were cold and wet. I wanted him on deck because he had been up and down the river many times and could give me advice. Eunice made us some sandwiches and hot soup, which made us feel at least satisfied with our lot. Not long after our snack, I looked at our gauges and was alarmed to see that our port engine was running very hot. I threw it out of gear and asked Armand to go below to find out what was going on. Thank heavens for those walk-in engine rooms. He would get grease all over everything, but at least he could get at the problem, rain or no. The temperature slowly dropped, and I then turned off the engine. We seemed to be able to poke along reasonably well on just one engine, as those swift currents occurred only once in a while. The average current for this run worked out to be about four to six knots.

Armand came on deck to say he had found the trouble and would fix it when we got to Arnhem. I thought we could make Arnhem with no trouble and asked what was wrong. The drive shaft for the water pump was loose. We have fresh-water cooling and, consequently, have both a fresh-water circulator and also a pumping system for the sea or river water that cools the fresh water. I did not ask which was affected, but did some serious thinking about that Perkins report and what a damn fool I was to be conned by it or by our agent in Amsterdam. Well, haste makes waste and all that.

Patches of blue started to show. We were coming up on Arnhem. Maybe it would clear and I could get a dinner date with the purser and take her to a good restaurant that private research had uncovered—the Rijn Hotel. As we went by it, it looked attractive, but fate would not hear of it. It clouded over again, down came the rain in sheets, and we turned into the harbor to our left just above the bridge. Inside, off to the right, there is a yacht club for small daysailers. Over to the left against the town, alongside a wall, there were several barges tied up, sleeping lethal giants preparing for the fray tomorrow. I said to Armand, "Don't you think we should get permission before we tie up here?" He assured me that the custom was simply to tie up and be ready to move on request. After we were secured, Eunice and I walked across three barges to the wall, which went straight up for about twelve feet . . . she insisted it was fifty . . . she went ahead of me up a slippery steel ladder with one poodle in a tote bag and I followed with the other pooch in his tote bag. On top there was a large cobblestone area and railroad tracks, obviously the commercial part of the port. No taxis were in sight, no people, just cold rain coming down on all the world. There was one Volkswagen parked a few rods away and out of it came a brave soul to greet us. He said he had been driving along the river watching us for the past twelve miles. We were a very pretty American yacht, *nicht wahr?* Could he come aboard? So we had him join us for a couple of beers. He was no great conversationalist, but it was nice of him to greet us.

After he left, Eunice decided that she would not essay that ladder again, dinner or no. So I got out the hors d'oeuvres.

After dinner we went over the day's events and looked over plans for our next leg. We had covered about 70 miles today. Tomorrow, with a little bit of luck, we would make Dusseldorf, some 84 miles away.

And so to bed. The heater was still out of commission, and it was cold, really cold. At 32 degrees Fahrenheit, I looked across the cabin where the first mate was stretched out in comfort with her two pooches, and it occurred to me that it might be a mite warmer over there. It was a mistake. I got bit by one dog, growled at by the other, and I made a hasty retreat. That was the end of that ploy. Thank goodness for the extra blankets.

5
Kidnapped

Somewhere, off in the distance, I kept hearing "Jack, get up, someone is knocking at the back door." I stirred dreamily, and finally sat up, vaulted out of my bunk, and stood shivering in the cold. I sleep in the raw, a custom barbaric to some people. Anyway, I was about to ask Eunice what the dickens was going on when there was a loud, insistent rapping on the saloon companionway. Racing aft, I opened the hatch, and there before me was a stoic, unsympathetic Dutch face—we were under way, still secured to the barge of the night before! A woman was at the wheel of the barge, her expression just as unforgiving, just as stoic, as that of the man confronting me.

My watch read 0530, it was raining, and I was colder. Retreating below with an apologetic nod to our guest, I jumped into some shorts and pants, pulled on a sweater, returned to the bridge deck, and started the engines. Both responded immediately—Armand must have done a good job on that port one.

After bringing the helm to midships, I approached the starboard side and began collecting our lines, one by one, from the stoic Dutchman, and with a big, healthy bump they shoved *Hebe* aside as if to say the back of my hand to you, turned right, and went downstream.

Gad, suppose Eunice had not heard, we probably would have awakened in Rotterdam!

It was now 0545 — what a way to start May 19, I thought.

Putting both engines ahead slow, I started to make a big circle within the harbor. Eunice came on deck to inquire what she could do, and Armand poked his bewildered face out of the after hatch. We had a short conference. Eunice said she would start the coffee, Armand agreed to pull himself together as quickly as possible, and we decided that as long as we were up, we might as well proceed on our way out of the harbor and up the Rhine.

Eunice came up with the coffee, Armand took the wheel, and I went below to complete my toilet and to prepare breakfast for a cold and ravenous crew.

Once below, Eunice said, "Now, would you like to know the full story?" Fully awake and curious, I ventured a cautious *yes*.

It seems that at about four o'clock my charmer was awake in her bunk worrying about piddling the dogs. You will recall that it had been raining torrents the night before, and we did not scale the wall as planned, but ate aboard, and so the pups did not get their usual spree. While mulling this over she heard a discreet knock on the saloon hatch. She got up, donned some cover, and opened the companionway after first inquiring, "Who's there?" The visitor was a kindly Dutchman from next door to advise that the barge would cast off within the hour, her crew was enjoying breakfast now — and, "*Bitte,* would we be ready to catch our lines so that they could slip out?"

This seemed proper and most considerate, thought Eunice, especially in view of the fact that we had "latched" on to the barge uninvited.

So, she made every attempt to awaken her spouse, mate, me — receiving on each attempt a promise to arise forthwith.

Well, you know the rest. The unanswered question is did Armand drink too much or was the skipper too tired or both? For a clue, Armand does not drink. Very belatedly, my apologies to the crew of that barge and my sincere thanks for their forbearance of my languorous habits. Dogs. . . the poor dogs didn't see a tree until. . . .

Lest we do Arnhem an injustice by our abrupt departure we urge travelers visiting this part of the world to tarry a while. This city has much to offer. It played an important role in World War II though the scars have been covered and flowers bloom. There are good places to eat, there is a fascinating zoo, of all things, and there is much local lore to assimilate. Your guidebook will give you some leading clues. Better still, when in Holland, consult the ANWB.

6
Never a Dull Moment

Breakfast completed, we were in a pretty jolly mood, joking about our recent adventure and sopping up all the goings-on about us. It was still raining.

Though it was now 7 A.M., traffic was heavy in both directions, and we had to be rather artful dodgers. Presently, we arrived at the confluence with the Waal and traffic was, at least to two neophytes, unbelievable. Although we were apprehensive, there were no mishaps, every vessel confidently doing the proper thing. The din of the diesels beat a rhythm and cacophony we had never heard before and cannot even now describe, but you can really feel its importance, its urgency. We liked being a part of it and hoped that on some note we were adding harmony to a symphony.

Doornenburg was to starboard, Pannerden to port. Don't look them up—in all probability they do not appear on your map. They are small villages and blend into the low, almost flat countryside. The attractive scene reminded us of some of Rembrandt's etchings we had seen hanging in his home back in Amsterdam.

Not all traffic is comprised of barges. Presently, downstream came a handsome cruise boat, out of Switzerland. The many people aboard were startled to see a yacht in the crowd and waved at us excitedly. It was a thrill for us, too, because we had heard about the Rhine River cruise ships and until now had been surrounded only by barges.

Ahead we could see Lobith, the Dutch border town. We had been told that this was a free port where you could obtain certain items on your "want list," and, furthermore, we had to stop to claim a refund of taxes on parts aboard purchased in Holland.

To begin with, Lobith is not a free port, nor is it a point of clearance on the way south. This latter always stops me short since you go "up" the Rhine, but travel "down south"; i.e., you travel south up the Rhine because the Rhine flows north. Got it!

Traffic continued heavy, the current strong. We were on the right and had to get over to the left. With some careful maneuvering, we made it, but ended up above the customs and almost alongside a Shell supermarket. A barge had preempted us, so we swung around, the current taking us downstream at a terrific pace, and came about, this time to tie up alongside a huge barge that was moored to one of the Custom House docks. The current was so strong, however, that we snapped a wire-cored bowline in the process of making fast.

All of us—Eunice, me, Pompi, and Jacques—made for a first-hand and first-time visit to a floating supermarket. It was fun: a barge, housed-over, and inside, a veritable cash-and-carry department store.

Outside on the main deck, fuel, oil, and engine supplies were sold. Inside, on the same deck, was a self-service market purveying everything from canned goods, staples in package or bulk, frozen meats, ice cream, milk and cream, baked goods, crackers—you name it. Also available were household items such as mops, pails, swabs, sponges, scrub brushes, health and beauty aids, and paper goods. One deck below, down a grand stairway, a great assortment of power tools, hardware, paint, rope, and marine supplies greeted your eye. All like an old-fashioned general store.

Back aboard the *Hebe*, we cast off, snapping another line in the process, and joined the parade up the Rhine. A few miles ahead we could see three or four slick-looking cruisers about 40 feet overall, busily darting through the traffic and going alongside every vessel traveling in either direction. It was the German Customs at work.

They came alongside us, maintained our speed, asked for all passports and papers, fell off a bit, came back, returned passports and papers, saluted, and with a big smile bade us *"Gute Fahrt!"* Eunice, who speaks German fluently, explained to them before they could pull away that we would like to claim a refund on taxes paid in Holland, etc. They told her we should put in at Emmerich, the German border town just ahead. Once again, a salute and a bow this time, ending with a bigger smile and another *"Gute Fahrt!"*

What a pleasant way to handle customs, I thought.

We broke out the German courtesy flag. For this purpose, I had rigged a staff to starboard athwart the main tabernacle. We were also flying the New York Yacht Club burgee from the bow. While in Holland we had flown the Dutch flag and the Cruising Club burgee. Why, I don't know, except that Armand liked it that way. We noticed that the commercial boats carried their colors twenty-four hours a day, under way or no, while we followed the American custom of making colors every morning at eight, and taking them in at sundown. Armand thought I was absolutely balmy. Also, contrary to the advice of some, we flew the U.S. yacht ensign. At no time, ever, did anyone ask what it was. It was recognized everywhere.

As we approached Emmerich, we sidled our way over to port, passed under a large bridge, and pulled up to the Bundesgrenzschutz dock at the entrance to the harbor. Large signs boldly proclaimed Anlegen Verboten (docking forbidden). The wind was howling from the north, and the rain was coming at us sideways. To determine where we should go, Armand went ashore, up a steep bank, and through the park that covered this area of the waterfront. He returned with little information. The current was very strong here, and we decided to move inside where we found a fairly large harbor, quiet water, and a most attractive setting. To the right, there was a good-sized marina or yacht club, but no room for us; at the head of the harbor there was a commercial installation, gravel hoppers, and all the like; over to port against the park were three well-kept floats all displaying "Anlegen Verboten." We tied up there. These floats were for the use of the customs boats we had encountered earlier. One had come in and invited us to tie up here. You couldn't ask for better treatment.

It was now about eleven and Eunice allowed as how she could do with brushing her teeth, a shower and a shave, and all that, while Armand and I attended to formalities ashore.

The Customs House was on the other side of the park, which, incidentally, was in bloom and beautifully kept. In fact, in spite of the rain, there were men weeding and raking as if they really enjoyed it.

Once inside, we soon learned that there is no free port in Emmerich. Further, no additional formality was required in connection with our visit. We pointed out that our passports had not been stamped. This merely drew a smile with the remark that, if we really wanted a souvenir, they would be happy to oblige.

There were tax forms, however, for me to complete for the tax refund. These were processed and sent to Holland where the refund was effected. Simple.

Eunice and the dogs met us in front of Customs and from here we went on a tour of the town in the rain (will it ever stop!), did some window-shopping and made a few purchases.

The town is fairly high up and the view from the road along the river affords an interesting sweep scene of the countryside. There was a department store with a good selection of merchandise where we bought Armand some needed clothing. One street back from the river we discovered food shops, a wonderful-smelling bakery, banks, churches, and many other good sights and smells. In front of most food shops, there were tether posts just for dogs, which are not permitted inside. Whenever we emerged from a store our pooches were surrounded by the local gentry—a great introduction for us to happy and friendly people. Perhaps it was because of the weather or the early season, but we did not see any tourists. We hope this is not always so, for Emmerich deserves to be on the itinerary of the traveler.

Almost all of the butchers here and everywhere in Germany where we shopped were women. The prices were interesting, too. For example, six big pork chops, ten slices of thick bacon, and a large chunk of beef cost $3.39—not bad. On the way back to the boat we picked up a bottle of wine and a huge bunch of garden fresh carrots for another seventy cents.

At the floats where we were moored, Pompi, a perennial show-off, jumped in front to lead the way. There was a space of about a foot and a half between the first and second float to which we were tied up. Our Hero mistook the dark water between for terra firma and dropped in. He was taken aback, but we fished him out with no trouble. I am not sure, but I think that Jacques gave him the doggy-world "hee-haw."

Eunice fixed lunch—ten large sandwiches. She had started making only five, but Armand needed filling out, and I was quite hungry, too. The beer consumption was on the high side, also. Eunice said she was now fixing four meals a day and would be glad when I could take over for all meals.

We decided to spend the rest of the day here. It was late, cold, and raining. So we set to work fixing the curtains in the saloon; putting teak oil on the saloon deck; checking the batteries, the engines, and port water pump; and fixing the heater.

While I prepared dinner, Eunice and the pups braved the rain and went for a stroll in the park where she found a crucifix, an omen of good luck.

We had a magnificent dinner of pork chops, cauliflower with cheese sauce, stringbeans, and wine.

The next morning, greatly refreshed after a tasty breakfast, we took off. Outside, it was very cold for May, and misting, which by now was par for the course. Inside, it was mighty cozy with the heater on.

We put out into the Rhine, making a careful turn upstream and giving long blasts on our horn. After settling into the cadence of the river and all its burden, we looked astern at a beautiful collage of rose, gray, red, and green—Emmerich, we shall see you again.

It was not long before we began to see a common sight along the banks of the river—in fact, along all the waterways of our route. Every few miles we saw camp sites or trailer camps, which lend considerable color to the local scene—literally. Evidently the government sets these up with many of the essential services available for the happy traveler, whether he arrives on foot, in an automobile, or in a boat. These are tidy installations, generally, and from our vantage point, very gay to look at with varicolored tents, shade umbrellas, and flags. A veritable ray of sunshine on a rainy day.

Looking ahead we couldn't believe our eyes. Coming down the river, with a bone in her teeth and her blue flag run out was a huge ship. She seemed to fill the river—it was like the *Queen Mary*. I yelled below so that Eunice, who was doing the dishes, could catch a glimpse from the saloon windows. It was the *Britannia*, a German four-decker cruise ship, beautifully kept, and—judging from the people on her decks and the many faces in cabin windows and the dining saloon, where several were having breakfast—the cruise business was flourishing.

When the passengers observed our flag there was a great cheer and much friendly waving, to which *Hebe* responded with merry toots on her horn and waves from us all. These cruise boats make regular round trips between Rotterdam and Basel, with stops at places like Cologne and Koblenz. The rates are reasonable, the food is good, we are told, and it must be an exciting way to see the Rhine country.

The scenery along the Rhine is not much until you get to Bonn. I am referring to trees, hills, craggy rocks, castles, and everything you associate with this legendary river. The countryside is mostly flat like the Dutch lowlands, with cows grazing everywhere, in some areas right down to the river's edge. There is a slight swelling on the horizon when you approach Arnhem, but farther on this subsides and disappears into the flat world around you. However, if you have forgotten your ancient history, you will get a dramatic recall of those old Romans. Their viaducts are still in use today. At one point, a mile or so away, a village distinguished by a tower loomed against the sky, and I wondered what it was doing over there all by itself, so to speak. Eunice looked it up in *Der Rhein von Mainz bis Emmerich*, or "pony" to me. What we were looking at was the small town of Xanten, population 6,500, historically the home of Siegfried the dragon slayer, the hero of the Nibelungen legend. Archeological discoveries indicate that this area was already settled in the Stone Age and it has been continuously populated ever since. At one point, it was the strongest Roman garrison outpost in this northernmost Roman province. A well-preserved amphitheater has been uncovered, as well as the Roman legion barracks (Castra Vetera). The tower that had caught my attention was St. Victor's Cathedral. This church grew out of a fourth-century burial chapel that has been enlarged through the centuries. Partially destroyed in World War II, it has been rebuilt. The other large building we could see was the five-sided basilica, which is the most important Gothic structure in the Rhine area. Years ago, the river used to flow by this settlement. Just like the Mississippi and other rivers we know, the Rhine has changed course here and there, leaving landmarks and other areas more or less isolated by its meandering.

These Roman hand-me-downs gave me religion. I started to muse. Compared to our civilization, how fabulous they were. What will we leave to posterity? If we erect something like Penn Station or Grand Central, some mercenary slob comes along and desecrates it, tears it down, and builds a glass tower that leaks from its opening day until the next developer comes along. It takes an Act of Congress to hold and preserve some of our outstanding landmarks.

Is the river dirty? Yes, unbelievably foul. Every barge, every town and city, every factory dumps all of its refuse into the drink. All of the countries involved, however, are rightfully alarmed and are beginning to do something about it. There is little physical evidence of it as yet, but it will come, probably sooner than in the United States. Europe is older and wiser than we are in many respects. One obvious thing it has done is to clean up and cultivate the shores of the river. In Germany, for example, we saw many flocks of sheep grazing on the banks, which are government owned and flourishing under this regimen.

The industrial development of the Rhine is something to behold. From Emmerich to Dusseldorf the river passes through the largest and most modern industrialized area we have ever seen. Essen, the Ruhr, and Duisburg were only names to us until now. During World Way II the entire area was bombed relentlessly, but now the steel mills, power plants, and chemical works look like a planner's dream. We traveled along 18-20 miles of unbroken manufacturing activity.

Remember we told you that charts of the Rhine would not be needed? That proved to be correct. Few highways are as well marked as the Rhine and, for that matter, the Mosel. Every kilometer is marked by a sign on shore; distance in kilometers from Basel, Switzerland, appears on signs every ten kilometers. You know where you are at all times. Clearances for the bridges and overhead wires are also posted for both normal and flood conditions.

At several points along the Rhine, there are ferry crossings. These are listed in *Wesca,* which, incidentally, should be read intently as you travel. They are self-propelled but use different means of bucking the current. Some use an overhead wire or cable with a sheeve traveler, a kind of large pulley. Some are hooked onto an underwater cable. There seems to be a special kind of rhythm between the ferry pilots and the barge men. How they miss each other is a wonder, at least the first few times you witness it. But then, they have been at it for years.

During the week, traffic on the Rhine is like the Long Island Expressway. Barges all over the place, going upstream, downstream, or across stream, and you just look out! Some are behemoths that run well over six thousand tons. All day long, the steady thrump, thrump of their diesels fills the air. They carry automobiles, coke, chemicals, cement, junk, lumber, steel, grain—everything you can imagine. Many of the barges are company owned, but there are also many that are owned by syndicates and individuals either on time or outright. The latter are the boys to watch out for. They fight like crazy for a cargo, and don't you get in their way. They want to get where they are going in a hurry and then pick up another load before the next guy beats them to it. Usually they are manned by man and wife, with possibly an extra hand who may be on shares or on wages. The after end of the barge contains the wheelhouse and the living quarters for the family below. The hand has quarters forward. In most cases, the living quarters are spotlessly clean, with fresh curtains in the windows, flower boxes in some, and invariably a dog for companionship as well as for protection. It is surprising to see the number of babies. I guess with no television, the people have nothing else to do. Some barges have playpens on the sun deck atop the house, some have swings for the kids, and most carry a small car astride a hatch. This is used to tour in when tied up.

From our observation, Holland seems to operate the most tonnage on the waterways, the Germans next, then the French and the Belgians and the Swiss. The Dutch are stolid but friendly; the Germans very methodical, also friendly; the French friendly, but their barges are not so well kept; and the Swiss are all spit and polish. We guess that these latter are government owned. Do not get in the way of these fellows either—they're a pretty arrogant bunch.

But let's get back to our voyage. We were just above Wesel, and some of you might be interested to know that we were doing 8½ knots through the water but only 4 knots over the bottom. We did not tarry at Wesel, though there are facilities for yachts. As a matter of fact, this is the finishing point for the annual long-distance sailboat race from Mannheim, a distance of 241 miles. Would you believe it!

Plodding upstream, we passed under many bridges, mostly new, the old ones having been destroyed in the war. The ruins remain as a poignant reminder of that fierce struggle.

About this time, a distraught Eunice came on deck and declared that Pompi was gone. She had searched everywhere below, what's to be done, could we please turn around? Without a word, Armand, sensing the crisis, swung *Hebe* around and headed back at slow speed. All the while I was thinking that finding a black toy poodle in a dirty, choppy river filled with barges on a rainy day was not going to be a picnic. I took over at the wheel so that Armand, who had about a three-foot reach over me, could, just in case, grab him in with a boat hook. Eunice went up in the bows. We had been at this for about ten minutes, looking every which way at every black shadow or ripple, when Eunice, cold and wet, dashed below to get her foul-weather gear. Soon she returned on deck, resplendent in her outfit, wearing in addition a very sheepish expression and holding Pompi close to her bosom. It seems that there had been a loud clap of thunder, a noise of which Pompi is deathly afraid, and he had burrowed his way in and under Eunice's storm gear. With a huge sigh of relief and a suppressed "I swan," we came around and resumed our way upstream. Another crisis passed.

Duisburg is a city of 500,000. It claims to be the largest inland harbor in the world and produces some thirty-two percent of Germany's steel. Huge mountains of iron ore line the river, and tractors crawled over them looking like small ants. The heavy overcast was polluted with orange-colored gas, the whole effect looking for all the world like a Monet. It was difficult to breathe, our eyes smarted and teared; this was air pollution like we'd never seen before.

A few miles further on we passed Krefeld, the home of Bayer Aspirin.

Late in the afternoon the rain stopped, and a gorgeous pink and blue started to assert itself in the West. Everybody was on deck, and Armand and I celebrated with a beer. Up ahead, sparkling in the late light was Düsseldorf—a pretty sight from this approach.

Over to the left, on the east bank fairly well into the city is a concrete breakwater, and, behind it, up on a knoll a couple of interesting clubhouses stand guard. As we entered the harbor and came alongside the slips of the first club, we were told by a dockman that this was the rowing club but if we could not find a place at the yacht club, immediately ahead, to come back and he would try to take care of us. The Dusseldorf Yacht Club did have a slip and Armand did a superb job of backing in, to the applause of club members peering out from the clubhouse. The basin is very crowded, with a minimum of turning room even for craft smaller than *Hebe*. Before we were tied up, the club had the American flag flying at the starboard yardarm of their tall mast. This was the kind of treatment and service we got during our short stay here—and everywhere we stopped.

All secure, we hopped ashore, thanked the dockmaster, an attractive young blond, who, we learned, was a furniture maker by trade and who hoped someday to get to the States. We signed the guest book. There was no charge for the first day, and water—good water—was free. Our transom was quite black from the exhaust, and Armand started to scrub it down immediately. There is a Perkins distributor here, but Armand did not think it was necessary to call him—our port engine had acted up a couple of times during the day, but he insisted that he could cope.

A couple of older club members came down to greet us and to look us over. They asked our route and destination. One of them insisted that we would never make it under the French bridges, and so they got some long poles and measured our vertical clearance from the waterline. As high as it looked from that floating dock, even to me, it still measured the same as in Holland, and I decided to make no change in the way we were rigged. One of our new friends assured us he was only trying to help, and he still thought we would not make it. On one thing the two of them did agree most heartily—our route was without exception the most beautiful way to travel through Europe. We had a drink all around. *Prosit!*

The clubhouse has very good accommodations, showers, etc., and was run at that time by a pleasant married couple. The wife did the cooking, and she was no amateur. We had a tasty repast washed down with steins of draft beer—all this with a magnificent view of the river and its omnipresent traffic.

The next morning was truly glorious. If you did not know the words to "Oh, What a Beautiful Morning," you would have made them up; hell, you would have written the song! It was the first time we had seen the sun in the morning since we left Amsterdam five days ago.

Eunice, Armand, and the nice-looking former cabinetmaker took off for the marts while I puttered around and more or less got ready to move on up the river, hopefully to Oberwinter. We had been informed that there was no place for a yacht to stop between here and there. Steph had confirmed this on the phone last night.

Steph, incidentally, I have known ever since she was a gleam in her mother's eye. She had married her brother's roommate at West Point and was stationed with him and their three boys at Bad Godesburg. He was now a full colonel, assigned as military adviser to Bonn.

The gang came back with bundles of goodies—one and a half pounds of asparagus for only $1.25—plus cleaning supplies, a couple of steaks, and a half-kilo of chopped beef for $3.25 more! Women butchers here, too. Eunice also got some white paint and varnish, which Armand allowed was not as good as Dutch but would do. I never saw him use either voluntarily so I guess any brand would have been all right.

It was close to noon when we set out, and, as we did, down came the American flag from the club's yardarm—right on their toes, that bunch. We waved good-bye and exchanged *"Gute Fahrts."*

From here on up the river, the scenery becomes more and more beautiful. The hills get bigger and steeper until finally you are in the old castle-on-the-Rhine country.

By late afternoon it was drizzling again, but this time we did not mind because we were coming up on Cologne: the park on the west bank, the bridges with many trains scurrying back and forth, and finally, right before us, standing beautifully in a gray mist, the renowned cathedral. This had been bombed in round-the-clock raids by the British, but by some miracle the twin spires remained standing. From our riparian point of view, the reconstruction looked complete.

There is a yacht club here on floats right out in the river, parallel to the shore. With such a strong current running, it did not seem a good idea to tie up.

About eight miles up the river in Godorf is a Schutzhafen (storm harbor) that can accommodate about sixty commercial boats up to 2,500 tons each. It is a modern installation, and we poked our nose in to look around and immediately got the "bum's rush." The loudspeakers squawked an authoritative *Achtung!* and in plain German told us to get the hell out of there. No matter, we were only looking.

Four miles further on, we were about to pass an island on the west bank when I noticed that our port engine was acting up again (damn, why hadn't we called Perkins?), and so I cut it, came about, and then turned in behind the island where we had seen a few boats. Anchored out was a large Dutch botter and we were invited to come alongside. What a break—no anchor, I thought. The botter was owned by a German of about thirty-five or so, who had lived and worked in San Francisco. He had come back, bought this old hooker, and was fitting it out to go around the world. He and a friend aboard were doing all the work themselves. There was an older man in a rowboat who agreed to row Eunice ashore with the pups and wait while they did their thing. Ashore, Eunice called Steph again to let her know our plight. This was in Uedorf, a cozy little village on the west bank. It also is a comfortable and safe anchorage behind the island. When Eunice returned, we all had a few beers, and, after a tour through the botter, the two men bade us *"Gute Abend"* and they were rowed ashore by the old gentleman.

We passed Bonn early the next morning. It is a bustling, up-to-date city. The government buildings seem modest in size, a mere nothing compared to the U.S. embassy "spread" in Bad Godesburg we were to see later. Our taxes at work! This is probably one of the many reasons the Germans are doing so well.

The current here runs fairly strong, about four knots, but we were able to cope even though we had only one engine. Sure enough, there was no place for pleasure craft to tie up in Bonn, which seems strange for the capital of West Germany.

Proceeding, we passed many hotels, one of which was the famous

Dressen where Chamberlain gave away his umbrella, and then some, to Hitler. This is in Bad Godesburg, a beautiful setting—at least one of them had good taste. Over on the east bank we could see the seven dwarfs' "Siebengebirge," the seven hills or mountains where Snow White and her little men are supposed to have held sway. A gorgeous trip, this.

Oberwinter is only about nine miles further on and with only one engine we made it easily in not too long a time. The harbor is as advertised. At the head of it is a yacht yard and docks, but no space was available for us. Along the shore there were some smaller docks, all posted "Anlegen Verboten." We tied up to one about halfway in.

The town is enchanting in a typically German storybook sort of way. Eunice climbed the steps up the bank to telephone Steph, and, when she returned, like the Pied Piper of Hamelin, she had a swarm of children behind. Two young lads were all over *Hebe* every day while we were there. They said they wanted to help with work, but after one swipe with some sandpaper, well, they were just like kids anywhere and played Mark Twain, or his German counterpart, on the Mississippi.

This time I had Armand call Perkins in Koblenz to make a date. In spite of a long Holy Weekend—Friday through Monday—the distributor agreed to have a man meet us Saturday afternoon when we hoped to arrive. "Where?" I asked. "Oh, somewhere just inside the Mosel, I think," was all Armand could offer. Such a thorough lad.

Steph drove over that afternoon to pick us up for a steak cookout at their house in Bad Godesburg. Once there, Bill gave me a tour around the estate—the U.S. embassy and adjoining units, that is. What you and we are paying for is *something!* "Our" people were tripping all over themselves on the way to the tennis courts.

Next day, Steph took Eunice shopping for a load of staples, meat, and whatnot. This accomplished and delivered to *Hebe*, the girls took off for some sight-seeing, and, from the look of the pictures Eunice took, you had better believe that this is indeed a beautiful part of the world. Way back up in the hills, they visited the Maria Laach Abbey, parts of which date back to the ninth-century Romans. While they were away, Armand and I got the engine patched up and scrubbed our transom, which was black again.

That evening we drove across the river to the Schulz Hotel in Unkel, upstream, and had a superb dinner with a really good Rhine wine.

When we returned around midnight there was a note pasted on the companionway hatch announcing that our friends the Arnspergers from Hamburg had arrived. *"Hebe* is beautiful, will see you in the morning. We will spend night in Remagen." Much of their gear was aboard, which caused Armand to remark that we now looked like a barge. Eunice had phoned them the night before to tell them where we would be. It is only about 200 miles, so they made it easily.

Sure enough, about seven next morning, Gisela, Hans, and Jost, their young son, came pouring down the companionway singing, "What's for breakfast?" in German, of course. The plan was that Jost would stay aboard for the trip to Koblenz while Gisela and Hans would drive up, visit some friends on the way, and meet us when we got there.

The Jewells—Steph, Bill, and young Billy—also came aboard for the trip to Koblenz, the other two sons having gone to Berlin for a Boy Scout convention. The Jewells would take the train back to Oberwinter to pick up their car. Altogether, it was a happy little group. According to the log, we took off at 8:30 A.M.

We had two very good helmsmen aboard in Billy and Jost, though each of them thought the other was not so hot. Regardless, we let them steer—under close supervision—and they were pleased. The crucifix must have been working, too, for it was a lovely day, and no barge had barged us.

As we came abreast of Remagen, Gisela and Hans were on the steamer dock waving gaily. Remagen has recovered somewhat from the rigors of the war, but I could not help but stare at the gaunt remains of the "bridge" and think back—one of my brothers lost a leg there serving under Patton.

Looking ahead I could not believe my eyes. Sure, I'd had some Rhine wine last night, but certainly not that much. Eunice assured me that I really was seeing aright and that up ahead the river *was* blanketed from east to west bank by spinnakers! Soon we began to hear cannon, and presently we were in the midst of the long-distance race from Mannheim to Wesel. Apparently, we were witnessing the start of the second leg, from Brühl to Wesel. The fleet was comprised of what looked to be Luders 16's at the low end and on up to cruising boats of around 50 feet. The cannon we heard was from the race committee boat starting the various classes. For me, it was like a busman's holiday. If you think you have seen everything, wait until you watch umpteen sailboats starting a downwind race under spinnakers and at least four knots under their bottoms coming your way. The barges were catching hell today for a change!

Brühl, for the benefit of yachtsmen, is an excellent harbor with all facilities available, and we can assure other travelers that the countryside and the mountains are worth a look. We did not stop and so cannot pass on any clues in the way of hotels or restaurants. As a harbor it seemed to be equal to, if not better than, Oberwinter.

We worked our way carefully upstream through the fleet, past the committee boat, and they were some taken with us, too. Once clear of all starters we turned the con back to our two quartermasters who would alternate under the supervision of Armand, who had been up and down the Rhine a few times. I went below to prepare lunch — salad (my, what fresh greens), sandwiches, cheese, soft drinks, Rhine wine, and beer.

During this time many nice little scenes came into view suddenly and as quickly disappeared downriver, but remain indelibly in our memories — Burg Rheineck, a beautiful castle, poised high on a hill; a barge plodding along with the womenfolk painting the "house"; or, at Andernach, another floating supermarket and a new harbor under construction (yachtsmen, check your *Weska*, it might be in operation now); a very tidy barge with a fenced playground atop the house with swings and a seesaw and three happy blond tots; and then a group of racing canoes, their crews with raised paddles, cheering us loudly, *"Heil, heil, heil!"*

At precisely 12:15 P.M., a great moment occurred — Eunice took off a sweater for the first time since we left Amsterdam. It was a warm, gorgeous, yummy day.

Not too much later, the port engine hotted up again and we had to proceed the rest of the way, not too far, on one engine. Every day the same thing, fix the blasted pump at night only to have it conk out after a short run next day.

The head-on approach to Koblenz is spectacular. To the right, on

Never a Dull Moment 53

the west bank, there is a park, and obliquely ahead, on the same side and to the immediate south of the meeting with the Mosel, is a huge plaza once surmounted by a monument commemorating the unification of Germany under Bismarck—The Deutsche Eck. On the left, on the east bank, it is impossible to see what really goes on because the river narrows and the land, all of a sudden, assumes a vertical attitude—very high up. After the turn into the Mosel, you look up and aft and there is the famous Ehrenbreitstein, a very large and impressive fortress that has guarded the Rhine for many centuries.

We were out of the rushing current of the Rhine, the water almost still, and ahead of us were two barges waiting for the lock to open. All three of us rested with an occasional "slow ahead" to straighten out and breast the slight current. We were joined by a couple of "hot-rodder" pleasure crafts, which added noise and some nuisance to the scene. From the plaza of The Deutsche Eck, the holiday throngs hallooed and waved excitedly at the action and, we believe, at the presence of an American yacht.

In Germany there is no charge for the locks if you accompany a commercial craft. If you are a lone pleasure boat, the charge is five dollars, unless you can use the smaller do-it-yourself companion locks into which we could not fit. These other locks will accommodate boats up to about 35 feet.

The lock opened and disgorged two barges coming downstream. Our fleet, now two barges and three pleasure boats, entered the lock at 2:10 P.M. and we were up and out by 2:42, a lift of about 14.5 feet. No fuss, no charge.

About half a mile up the river on the west bank we could see a yacht club with lots of boats and people. Armand said the Perkins men would not be there, but over on the east bank. So we went over and tied up to a barge, the M.S. *Recklinghausen*. There was no one to greet us. Nothing now except to wait. There was another barge ahead, and ahead of this was a public camping area and a small beach.

Presently, we were boarded by Gisela and Hans who had been at the club and had seen us come out of the lock. They were followed by Ernie and Leonard of Perkins in Aschaffenburg and they, too, had been at the club. Why not?

Ernie spoke with an unmistakable cockney accent, which threw us for a loss. Per'aps Perkins 'ad sent a man over? No, Ernie had been a British prisoner of war for most of the conflict and had taken to the language of Soho like a duck to water. He evidently came along for the ride; Leonard did all the work.

At about this same time we were bumped rather sharply by a powerboat coming alongside with a load of Saturday-afternoon Coast Guard auxiliaries who claimed that we were illegally parked and demanded a ransom in marks. Eunice rose to the occasion, and while I could not understand a damn word of this confrontation, she apparently was letting them have "what for" in her best Hamburgian accent much to the amusement of our guests. As a matter of fact it was very funny, they demanding fines and Eunice claiming damages. Finally a "compromise" was reached—they apologized for their rather unseemly language to the Fräulein, promised to learn to operate their boat with better expertise, and collected two marks—fifty cents. Eunice felt she had lost the war, but Hans thought it was darn cheap entertainment and quickly anted up.

Ernie and Leonard made an appearance loaded with parts, ours; water-pump shaft, valve assembly, and all injectors, etc. They opined that the engine had been neglected for a long time. Ha! They would return on Tuesday after the Holy Days and would meet us at the yacht club to complete the job. Their charge was fourteen marks per hour plus travel time, and this would be put on our bill. They had been aboard two-and-a-half hours. Aschaffenburg is 75-80 miles from Koblenz.

Gisela and Hans drove the Jewells to the depot, and we took off for the yacht club where we received a most cordial welcome by the president, Mr. Walter, and members, who helped us tie up. The Mosel-Rhine Yacht Club has excellent facilities, good water, a launching ramp, a good bar, and snacks—but no regular meals. These can be obtained at a hotel immediately upstream, on a terrace by the river or indoors if it is too cool.

The events of the day were too much, really, and I was too bushed to prepare dinner. Hans knew this and invited us to one of his favorite spots a short distance up the river in Winnengen. The meal was scrumptious and the setting beyond belief. As I look back on it now, it seems that we were momentarily on a lily pad floating somewhere in wonderland.

The next day was something else! Jost woke us up and said there was no water, no light. Gad, every day a surprise. Obviously the batteries were down, so Armand started the generator but it registered no charge. After checking out the whole system we discovered the main fuse had blown. Fortunately, we had a spare and got everything under control for the nonce. Fortunately, too, we were still tied up to the yacht club and all hands were able to go ashore to brush their teeth and all, while we grappled with the problem.

After breakfast, Hans suggested a drive up the meandering Mosel in the direction of Trier, a nice idea. First we stopped at a boating and camping site in Winnengen where we purchased very good charts of the Mosel. We had never received the ones ordered by mail. Then on to Kern, where Hans's stepmother had come as a girl to study art with her tutor before World War I! Behind this village back in the hills is the **Burg Elz**, a marvelous fairy-tale castle well worth visiting. It is about an hour's walk from a *Gasthaus* some three miles behind Kern. The path follows a lovely babbling stream for about the first half-hour and then climbs up through a forest mostly of pines that scent the air to perfection, and the needles underfoot make a lush carpet. Soon you arrive at a clearing where, rearing straight up, is the unbelievable castle—a jumble of turrets and towers. I had never seen one like this since I had pored through the pages of my *Book of Knowledge* as a kid. It's a tourist spot to be sure, but it is real—don't miss it.

At Pommern, we noticed lots of bunting and flags flapping a merry welcome to a local wine tasting—could this be May wine? Stop we did, and fun it was. The air rang with song, accordion accompaniment, and the sound of clogs dancing on the cobblestones. Under a big tent, wine was dispensed with abandon.

On to Cochem, a delightful little city situated at the top of a meander of the Mosel, with steep hills rising on both sides. Happy people everywhere, talking, singing, sitting, no one rushing; it was all too good to be true. The architecture here is old-world and unspoiled. We crossed over to the east bank and drove to a *Kaffeehaus*—high up overlooking all below and both sides of the meander. Steam-powered toy trains chugged along the shores and in the river little toy people were water-skiing and swimming. To help us contemplate all this, we sipped iced coffee and spooned ice cream *mit schlag*.

This three-day holiday we were caught up in was Whitsuntide. Whitsunday is the seventh Sunday, the fiftieth day after Easter. In most Catholic countries, this time of year is observed as a festival in commemoration of the descent of the Holy Ghost on Pentecost Day. In Germany, it is known as Pfingsten. It occurred to us that the Holy Ghost had indeed descended and blessed this land, for everywhere we had been these past few days, the earth had acknowledged His presence and had joined the celebration with a riotous burst of breathtaking colors of red and white thorn, lilacs, wisteria, buttercups, mustard, chestnuts, broom, peonies, geranium, and iris.

Back at the yacht club, Gisela and Hans stopped to phone friends who had invited them for the evening. We went aboard to start dinner. A few minutes later, they climbed aboard with the great news that our friends the Davises had arrived in Koblenz and were on their way out to join us. At least something was working, I mused.

Before we had left the States we had set up a control center with our chum, Ivan, in Geneva. We would call him every day or two with a report on our whereabouts, and everyone who was to join us along the way could get a fix on us by calling him. Also, Eunice and Hans had stopped at the Hotel Pfalzerhof in Koblenz to leave a message for our pals should they arrive. In spite of our problems, we had arrived in Koblenz on time, albeit broken-down. The Davises had phoned Ivan upon their arrival at Frankfort Airport. He told them that, by the grace of God, we were somewhere in Koblenz and to try the Pfalzerhof. So, "Eunice, my love, add two settings for dinner and let's get two more bunks ready."

It was good to see our friends, and they hit it off splendidly with the Arnspergers, an eventuality you cannot always forecast. It was drinks all around and then dinner; veal roast, kidneys, carrots (scraped and cut by Gisela), roast potatoes, salad, cheese, apples, crackers, and grapes. The Arnspergers had to leave prior to the salad course, alas.

We gabbed until midnight, swapping experiences since we had left home. Finally, I could not hold my eyes open any longer in spite of the good company, and sneaked off to my bunk. As I was drifting off to dreamland I thought I heard Phil expostulating "I did it, godammit, I did it, I broke the head!" Phil is a large man and the picture he conjured up sounded very funny to me as I dropped off into slumberland — after all we had two other heads and only one Phil.

7

The Mosel

Of all the rivers we have seen or traversed, the Mosel stands out as unique. From Koblenz to Apach at the French border, the river twists and turns, perhaps writhes would be a better word for it, for a total of 242.2 km. or 150.16 statute miles. Believe it or not, the straight-line distance is just a little over 81 miles.

The meanders pass through toyland villages, castles in the air, and between mountains carefully manicured wherever the sun might hit so that the vineyards can produce in abundance and quality. The vines are planted with Germanic precision looking like infantry on inspection on hills so steep cultivators must be lowered and held at each working level by cable. And the work seems to be done with devotion. For example, on a slope that gets the bare minimum of sun (facing northwest, let's say), reflectors of shiny metal or glass or slate are placed beneath the developing grapes to maximize the benefits of the sun, and all this is done by hand. These vineyards are everywhere and you wonder how in the world the amount of wine generated by all this could be consumed—ever.

It is not necessary to own a boat to enjoy all the pleasures that this river and its valley offer. Germans love to hike it or bike it. There are many camp sites with excellent facilities along the banks, and, too, there are many interesting inns or small hotels with good food available. Don't you believe that the Germans eat just bratwurst, home-fried potatoes, and cole slaw. Also, it is possible to go by train, steam(!) or diesel. Service is frequent and excellent. Stops can be made at will almost wherever the scenery grabs you. Finally there are sight-seeing cruise boats that make stops at most major villages and towns.

The current in the Mosel is slight, less than a knot usually, but nowhere in our experience was it more than 1½ knots. The markings are clear, explicit, and in good repair. There are thirteen locks, all of them modern, which have been built or rebuilt since the end of World War II. If your boat is 35 feet or under, there are smaller companion locks that you can operate manually. Locks are in operation only during the daytime to one half hour after sunset. A hydroelectric facility is an integral part at almost every lock site.

For those of you who wish to do this sort of thing by boat, charts may be obtained at the riverside dock at Winnengen just above the Koblenz Yacht Club, or from the Automobile Club. The charts are available for a nominal charge. They are in color, with signs and legends interpreted in three languages. You may purchase the usual marina or fishing gear here also. When you are through with your purchases, go up the bank, across the road, and through the town wall. Try it after dark for the best effect. This will be your reintroduction to your old-time children's storybook memories of Hansel and Gretel. At least to us it was sensational. And the food, and the wine, *Ach!*

Now a few words about the Mosel locks and working your vessel into them. Please, we are not talking down to anyone, nor are we wagging our finger at those who feel they have been through this before. The Mosel locks are activated from the front (your bow) gate when going south, and the water powers its way through the ports when opened. Never, never allow yourself to be number one entering, even if the tower or control orders otherwise. The turmoil, eddies, and pressures will pop you around like a cork and snap your lines or pull your bitts, believe us. Going north is not quite so bad, but, even in this situation, it is better to be last in.

Let's get back to where Phil broke the pot, or, perhaps we should say, the morning after. Well, our pattern did not change, for on awakening I discovered that we had no water, no electricity, and only one working toilet. It was a beautiful day though. No matter, all of us went ashore to use the club's facilities—showers, hot water, everything.

Inasmuch as we cook with gas, breakfast was no problem. After a sumptuous repast, it was decided that all would go touring with the Arnspergers, except Armand, Phil, and me.

With the tourists gone, the three of us went to work on repairs. The generator had some minor defect that we quickly corrected, and presently we had electricity and water pressure. The broken head was beyond repair, so we just swept up all the shattered pieces and dumped them overboard. Next we tackled a wash job on the topsides, and then went ashore to mosey about and look at all the boats in the water and at those hauled out in the small yard. A couple of natural-finish mahogany hulls caught my eye, and I queried a man who was doing a little sanding on one of them. He informed us that he was in the yacht race we had witnessed on the Rhine, that he was the class champion, that the race is an annual event starting at Mannheim, and that, at the end at Wesel, all boats must return under power, be towed, or hauled by trailer. I wondered if we would go to such trouble back home for a bit of fun.

Sometime in the early afternoon, Mr. Walter, president of the yacht club, came to us to announce that the Mosel was going to be closed down Tuesday for the annual inspection, so that all locks could be repaired if need be. He assured us that we were welcome to stay and have our engine repairs made, but advised that we move on to Trier inasmuch as the locks would be "down" for a week. The Trier basin is above the last German lock and we could make it easily in a couple of days. I thanked Mr. Walter for all his kindness and then asked Armand to get on the horn to Perkins at Aschaffenburg and have their men meet us at Trier. Soon after, our gang returned from their tour, and from where?—Trier. They told us that the locks were going to be closed and Hans had made a reservation for us in the government harbor there. Smart friends! Just how lucky can you get. We decided to leave in the morning.

We left after an early breakfast and it was not too long before we entered our first lock. Armand said that the lock "super" wanted us up forward because a cruise boat was coming up behind us. I told him that we would move out and wait for the cruiser to enter. Armand relayed this and lost. Madder than hell, I went ahead. We put out four wire-cored lines (admittedly old) and waited. The cruise boat entered and the Captain knew he had a show . . . all passengers were summoned forward to witness an execution. And by golly he almost had one. We popped every line we had out and bounced around like a cork. It was like riding a bronc. With strenuous fending off, and power from our limp engine we survived—barely—battered, scraped, and dented, but afloat. The skipper of the cruise ship gave us a couple of friendly blasts of congratulation on his horn and as his vessel passed us after we were clear of the lock all hands gave us a cheer. Remember what we said about being first in a lock!

From here on, everything was roses. The hills and vineyards were all as advertised. Workers stopped to wave, cars along the shore beeped, and all aboard were merry and gay. At Cochem, we stopped alongside the steamer dock so the Arnspergers could go ashore for they were going to drive to Hamburg. Farewells were made, toasted with that wonderful Mosel wine. We slipped our lines and waved and waved until we made the next bend. Our friends stood on the dock waving madly until we disappeared. We had had a great time together, in spite of some mishaps.

That afternoon it started to rain hard. When we reached Enkirch, I noticed a barge entering the lock about a half mile ahead and, looking at my watch, I decided that we couldn't make it in time and so we tied up at a broken-down boatyard. This proved to be a big mistake on my part. Enkirch is a dreary town with hardly anything to offer. The girls came back from market with a poor selection only because they had little choice. They did enjoy the gardens, however, and they did get hot bread.

The next morning, as we came out of the lock and saw what we missed the night before, everybody wanted to give me the deep six and rightly so. Just ahead to starboard was an attractive dock to an inn with cocktail bar and lounge, and a little further ahead were the twin towns of Traben-Trarbach, a really charming site. Shops, hotels, and scenery. What a *Dummkopf*, I!

The next place of interest is Bernkastel-Kues, noted for its wine, castles, and scenery. The tourists and natives waved cheerfully as we passed. We should have stopped, but we had to make Trier that evening.

Piesport is a well-known wine town a bit further on, but we made no stops except for the locks, and these were negotiated in stride — no fuss.

Entering Trier is very interesting. It is a much larger city than any we had seen since leaving Koblenz. High on the hills to the west are monuments and churches silhouetted against the sky. A gondola lift rises from the city on the left and goes to the top of these hills and to a restaurant. The view from up there must be magnificent. Passing through we noticed strange looking buildings along the river bank. They looked like short silos topped by large conical hats most of which were askew. These are granaries that were used in the days of old.

We passed under a heavily traveled bridge that seemed to be the main link between the two sides of the city. It was built by the Romans, and the many air raids of World War II did not knock it out.

Into the lock and up. There the lockkeeper told us that France, with no warning, had decided to close the waterway for a week, but would hold the lock at Apach open for us until ten that evening. It was now about seven. Pondering this, I decided against it. We would have to reach the Perkins people again, it would be added mileage for them at more cost to us, and there would be another border involved. We thanked everybody and moved into the government harbor, where, thanks to Hans, we were warmly received.

That night, we celebrated. We got a taxi, drove into town, gave Armand the night off, and then plunged underground into the restaurant that is several feet under the city and that used to be at the riverside in the Roman days. The food is not great, but the experience is a must. While there, I got a phone call through to our "dear" friend in Holland and chewed him out roundly. My language was not choice and should have been censored I was told, but I was madder than a boil. He was the type who records every conversation and he did this one. If I were back in his country then, he probably would have sued me. Anyway, he got the message that we wanted a new head pronto pronto and that the engines were not as represented. He promised to be over within a week with a new Simpson Lawrence head, our new awning, and maybe some help on the engine.

The rest of the evening was spent drowning my memory of him.

8
Trier

Morning came bright and clear—clear, that is, except for my head. With a pounding headache and my eyes looking for all the world like a couple of Indian navels, I started making breakfast to the accompaniment of wags and hearty twits from all aboard.

The head brass from the Bauhof hailed us during the meal, and we piped them aboard. The Oberinspektor was Herr Ernst Hermann Ehrke, a balding, 28-year-old engineer who had the responsibility for the six locks from Zeltingen to Palzem. His companion, Herr Michael Streit, was *"Werkmeister im Bauhof,"* superintendent of works, really. He had been in the Luftwaffe when Ehrke was born. They were "super" guys from first appearance, and, as it turned out, to our fond *"auf Wiedersehn."* They told us that the locks would be down for a week in the German sector, but that the timetable for the French would be unpredictable. To our utter astonishment, Ehrke and Streit informed us further that Apach had closed down at seven the night before. Thank God we had not gone on.

The government basin here is very modern (all new) with four railways and a complete machine shop. The supervisory personnel live in five gaily painted stucco houses in a fenced compound. Adjoining it is a large garden where vegetables and flowers are grown by the wives; a very attractive setup indeed, where we were made to feel at home.

Eunice and Snork Davis went into town to shop and mosey about while Phil and I waited around for the Perkins people to show up. We did not have long to wait. The man arrived about mid-morning in a well-equipped Volkswagen van, along with our parts. His name was Baldur Frank. He seemed to know his stuff and was quite personable. Wasting no time, he donned his coveralls and, with Armand, disappeared into the port engine room. Phil and I could not fit into that act, so we puttered about on deck doing the usual sanding and varnishing.

Suffice it to say that Herr Frank and Armand worked all day installing the injectors, valves, etc., that had been removed at Koblenz. At the end of the day, they tried to start up the engine, but it was no go. Our German friend said he would put up at a motel and be back in the morning. We shrugged "what else," said "see you *'Morgen fruh'*, and gave Armand the night off with no restrictions.

The gals had returned in the afternoon with victuals and stories and excitement galore. After the usual happy hour and dinner, we agreed on a schedule for the next day. Inasmuch as we could not contribute any helpful work in the engine room, and we had nothing else to do for a week, we would go sight-seeing.

In the morning, we took a cab into town to see Herr Streit's friend who ran a gas station and rented cars. We felt it was essential to have a car for the week. The proprietor turned out to be a former U.S. prisoner of war somewhere in the Miami area for most of the duration. We gathered that he had been a crew member of a German submarine that had been apprehended off the Florida coast. He rented us a Taunus, a German-made Ford. Off we went to Longuich to see the mayor about some wine (Eunice and Snork had met him while touring with the Arnspergers the day before we left the Koblenz Yacht Club). As we reached the edge of town, we came upon a three-way stoplight that changed to red. I jammed my foot to the floor and almost hit the road—nothing happened! I pulled the emergency brake, and we started to stop, but from the right came a Volkswagen from the local VW service department and the driver knew and I knew what was going to happen—it did—we went smack-dab into him broadside! The owner and driver was resigned to his fate, got out, looked into our jalopy, and said he could see it was not our fault, and wasn't it lucky he was so near the VW people. Naturally, there was a lot of excitement around us but no panic or finger-pointing except from the gas-station guy who was there almost when it happened. He must have known something was loose or not functioning. We waited for the police to arrive. They did—in a VW van in which a hearing was held. I pleaded guilty, paid a fine of $5, and a tax of $1.25. According to the law, we had to pay for damages to our car, the insurance company paid for damages to the car we hit. It was all added to the bill. A more unlikely experience could not happen in the United States, at least in the New York area.

With considerable argument we got another car and proceeded to Longuich to buy some more of Rudi Schmitt's good wine. He was not in, but would be back for a songfest that evening. We were urged to return for the fest.

Why did we go to Longuich?—because Eunice and Snork had had such a warm reception from Rudi Schmitt, *Bürgermeister* and vintner par excellence, when the Arnspergers drove them over to Trier from Koblenz on Whitsun Monday. They had gone to his wine cellar and had a private *Weinprobe,* wine tasting. They tasted five wines and brought back samples for the boat. They were:

1. A '67 Spätlese, strong and fresh to serve
2. A '66 Longuich Herrenberg Spätlese, light and delightful
3. An elegant '67 Beerenspätlese that had won a bronze prize
4. A '67 Auslese, very light and fruity
5. A '64 gold-medal winner—a Beerenauslese made from golden grapes, a special treat for Whitsun Monday.

Rudi explained that this was not for sale—he had only forty to fifty bottles left and he was keeping them for home consumption. This was the kind of wine you drink, he said, only when the cow calves or a woman lies in childbirth. Rudi enjoyed every drop of the visit and every drop of the wine as he expounded on its virtues. Eunice asked him how he felt after a *Weinprobe. "Lustig und gesund"* (happy and healthy) was his answer. He was a large, round-faced, round-bellied fellow with laughing eyes. Eunice told him she wanted to buy some cases for the *Hebe* but that they couldn't carry it back because their car was too full of people and dogs. He volunteered to pick us up at his pier, if we stopped on our way to Trier, and drive us by car to his cave for another *Weinprobe* and to deliver the wine to the boat. This was why we wanted to go to Longuich!

Back aboard *Hebe* we were told by Baldur Frank that there was a crack in the cylinder head and that no more work could be done until a new head could be flown in from England. You can't fight fate, so we had some schnapps all around and bade our mechanic friend "so long, but hurry back, hear?"

After dinner the Davises announced that they were tuckered out and suggested that we go on to the songfest without them. We did; it was memorable.

Longuich is a very small town situated about nine miles north of Trier on the east bank of the Mosel. There are about 300-400 residents, if that. When we arrived, the town was ablaze with light and reverberating with excitement. A big circus tent had been put up, as well as a couple of smaller ones. There was a carnival-style midway with pinwheels, dodge-ems, and a small dance floor. People from miles around were milling about, talking, laughing, and drinking wine. Remember, as we were coming up the Mosel we asked ourselves how so much wine could be consumed by the world? Here at Longuich was a pile of empty bottles so high you wouldn't believe it. The Germans at a songfest don't sniff and sip wine, they guzzle it, and we joined them! This wonderful nectar was going for ten, fifteen, twenty, and twenty-five cents a glass, priced according to quality. In the process of joining this fest, we were momentarily unmindful of our two poodles. Pompi had made a friend of a tall, good-looking, young German, who introduced himself as Heinz Etteldorf. He worked for the Bissel Carpet Sweeper Company in Trier and was engaged to Annemarie Schmitt, who was competing in the songfest. He had a catching personality. His English was fair so that I could converse. He bought us wine, we bought him wine. He told us that Annemarie was a little put out with him because he was not singing, but getting a bit *carousel,* in German, a wee tight. What a nice way of putting it! Why not get a little "carousel" together?

Annemarie, finished with her singing, which we did not hear, finally espied her betrothed fondling Pompi, and also drinking while conversing with a couple of strangers. After being introduced to us, she slowly warmed up, forgave Heinz, and became eager to know us better. I congratulated Heinz on his taste in women. This warmed her up even more.

Annemarie was a bookkeeper for a group of doctors in Trier. Both of them wanted to come see *Hebe,* could they come on Sunday? It was a date. Two attractive young people! We bade them *"Gute Nacht,"* then went in search of his honor the mayor, Rudi Schmitt, who was still giving speeches, so we gave up and returned to our nest at 3:40 A.M.!

Before going off on more side trips, let's talk about Trier. It was founded by Caesar Augustus at about the time of Christ, and, according to Will Durant, "rose to prominence as the headquarters of the army defending the Rhine." Two hundred years later, under Diocletian, Trier or Treves (Augusta Trevirorum) replaced Lyon as the capital city of Gaul, and in the fifth century A.D. it was the greatest city north of the Alps.

When the Romans built, they built to last. Their works defy time and are still serving the people. For example, the Roman bridge, mentioned earlier, withstood a tremendous amount of bombing in World War II and is, even now, the main link between the two sides of the city and is a part of the main auto route north and south.

In the center of town, there is a large open square where the daily farmers' market holds sway. The vegetables and fruit offered are scrumptious. Facing the square from the south is a large Roman Catholic church with little historical importance, but, nevertheless, impressive. To the north is the famed Porta Negra, one of the original city gates in the original Roman wall. Past the gate is a Hilton Hotel. What a contrast! On either side of the square are many interesting shops — a great butcher shop, with a good selection of meat (but still no lamb). Confectioners and bakers seem to abound, and these took all of Phil's spare time. Every night, for example, it was, "What is our little surprise this evening, good friend?" whereupon he would sheepishly produce from nowhere a magnificent piece sculptured in fresh whipped cream! This latter, of course, has nothing to do with the Romans.

In another sector of town is the Basilica. It was built by the Romans out of brick and has served the city in many ways. At times it was used as a covered or enclosed public market. It is remarkable in that there are no supporting columns inside. The open area within is huge—wide, high, and long. It is as large as—if not larger than—the old Madison Square Garden.

Within a few blocks of the Basilica stands the cathedral. Its seven floors represent seven different styles of architecture inasmuch as it was built and rebuilt and expanded through the ages. The earliest Roman building dates back to the fourth century, and is followed in succession by Merovingian, Frankish, two different Norman styles, an early Romanesque, and finally a late Romanesque. The last dates back to the thirteenth century.

Within walking distance of the cathedral, we noticed a large area where construction work had been halted. This was going to be a fancy new apartment complex, but the excavators came upon some unusual foundations and artifacts. The city fathers called a halt to further construction and brought in expert archeologists. Another part of the original Roman city had been uncovered. This is now an open "landmark" and part of the scene for all tourists now and in the future.

Further on toward the river are the remains of the elaborate old Roman baths built by the Emperor Constantius in 305 A.D. Some of these are still in operation. Fascinating! And there were hot, cold, and lukewarm baths in those days, too.

Herr Streit told us that he was indebted to the Romans, for as an escaped prisoner of war, he managed to get back home to Trier by offering Roman coins to his captors. The Romans had a custom of tossing coins into the river as they crossed the bridge over the Mosel, and when the locks were installed at Trier thousands of them were washed up. As a 17-year-old recruit in the Luftwaffe in 1941, he had taken some coins with him to war as good luck charms. They worked—he got home safely. Not so lucky was his brother-in-law who also came to visit the *Hebe*. He had been released from a Russian prisoner-of-war camp on Christmas Day in 1949, 4½ years after the end of the war, but was sent home to Silesia, a part of prewar Germany that ended up as Poland after the war. The Poles kept him working in the coal mines until 1969, the year of our visit and twenty-four years after the end of the war!

Since we had nothing to do other than to eat, drink, and rest, we decided to go touring. We drove southwest across the border into Luxembourg at Wasserbillig and then to the city itself along the route on which General George Patton was killed.

We drove through German Customs without stopping. At the Luxembourg Customs at Wasserbillig, all they wanted to see was the car's registration. On the way back, no one stopped us. The whole trip from Trier to Luxembourg took less than an hour.

The old walled city of Luxembourg is enchanting, to put it mildly, perched as it is on a craggy rock. The view from the cathedral is spectacular, not just of the surrounding countryside, but of the city itself. Eunice wanted to return to An der Stoop, a cafe-restaurant she remembered from her UNRA days, but was told, *"il n'est plus là."* A shop lady near the cathedral recommended the Cafe de Commerce near the station. It is located on an attractive square with a bandstand a few rods away. We entered for a late lunch. The atmosphere was warm and friendly; the tables were neatly set with clean linen. French and German were spoken fluently, and currency was no problem. They would accept francs, marks, Swiss francs, or U.S. dollars. The clientele was middle class, native. Our food was excellent, not rated by Michelin, but tasty and well-served. The wine, it goes without saying, was very satisfactory—local table wine, not vintage. We all had potage, pâté, and good French bread. The Davises opted for *omelettes,* Eunice chose *veau avec champignons,* and I tried the *steak au poivre.* Dessert of *fraises Chantilly* was the *pièce de résistance.* With three *café filtres,* the whole check came to DM 63, or less than $16.00. The two pups behaved beautifully in their little zipper bags hanging on the back of Eunice's chair. No one noticed until they were rewarded for their silence with the last morsels from Snorky's *omelette.* As we dined, we noticed that the place was filling up and becoming rather crowded. Presently, the *proprietaire* turned on the TV, and a buzz of excitement started to fill the room. Looking out front, we noticed a lot of adults and children pressing for space to peer in the window. We looked at each other and queried, "What's up?" Almost immediately we got our answer—a rerun of the American TV show "Daktari" was on!

Back aboard *Hebe,* Armand told us that Herr Frank would be in from Aschaffenburg with a new head (ha! ha!)—not his, but our port engine head. What a lousy pun, but Armand was catching on.

Trier

The next day, Sunday, was a good day. Minding me own peas and potatoes below in the galley, I heard excitement on deck. Annemarie and Heinz had arrived, and Herr Streit turned out to be Annemarie's uncle. Further, it was a holiday (first Sunday after Whitsunday), and the local children were dressed to the nines.

Annemarie wanted us to drive over to Kesten to see another one of her uncles, a successful vintner there. We told her dinner was in the oven and asked them to join us. They had eaten and they would go over the hills to uncle's and would see us after dinner. Heinz gave us a merry wink and off they went. We were just finishing dinner when they returned with two cases of Mosel ('64 Spätlese) for which we had advanced some dough, plus a bottle of pure nectar—a '59er, according to the Germans, *ein goldenes Weinjahr* and a Trockenbeerenauslese, to boot! Annemarie's uncle had seen us go by last Wednesday, had waved, we had waved back, and he wished to express a feeling of friendship to the Americans. How good of him! It occurred to me that they had been gone (over and back) only about an hour and a half while it had taken us several hours to go one way by boat. Those meanders are something.

Monday, I decided to stay aboard with Armand to be on hand when the mechanic arrived. The others went into town.

Herr Frank arrived from Aschaffenburg at about ten with the new parts and an air of confidence. He and Armand disappeared below and, from the sound of things, worked furiously. I made sandwiches for lunch and served them with beer, good German Beck. Baldur thought everything was going well and with luck the engine would be running smoothly by mid-afternoon. The time came, and with crossed fingers I watched him start it up. After a few balky coughs and much exhaust smoke it took off and started to hum "like a good diesel should." But, alas, in a short time he shook his head with some concern. It seemed that a bronze oil line leading from the bow end back to the gear box and filters was leaking badly and had to be removed. This was done; but now what? Armand suggested the machine shop here at the basin and arrangements were made. Armand came up with some good ideas once in a while, but never did learn how to take a compliment. It developed that the line was perforated and would have to be brazed in several spots. This would be done first thing in the morning.

The gang returned and Eunice gave me a letter from Eames who had crossed into France at Kehl-Strasbourg. We used Poste Restante all along the way, which is a good idea for anyone touring without a set schedule doing this kind of thing. Dick said, "You darn well *do* need a *triptyque*" and advised us to write our friend in Bonn. We reacted fast to this. I wrote a letter to Bill asking him to inquire through the French Embassy and to advise by phone or letter pronto if we had to do anything, and if we did not hear from him, we would assume we were clear. Eunice and I then drove into Trier, mailed the letter, and called on the French Consul. *Triptyque? Mais non, monsieur,* this is no longer necessary. Could I have a letter from him to this effect? No, said he, it would not be needed, and, if there was any question, just tell the border *douane* he had so ordered. We returned to the boat. Phil had dinner going on the charcoal grill on the afterdeck and Snork had the canapés and drinks ready. We never did hear from Bill.

The next day the oil line was installed and, insofar as we could tell, everything was okay. I asked Herr Frank to inspect the starboard engine, but he said it was not included in his orders! With a little coaxing, he agreed to check it out. He tested it at various rpm, tried the gear box ahead and reverse, and checked the injectors and valves. All okay, eureka!

Now came the bad news. He had instructions to collect in cash, no charge, no checks. This just about cleaned me out and so Eunice took my picture with my pockets turned inside out. Fortunately, Eunice, always the provident, wise one, had some cash stashed away for emergencies. Some twelve hundred dollars lighter, we were now ready to go. We bade our friend, Baldur Frank, good-bye and wished him well on his drive back to Aschaffenburg.

We were indeed indebted to our friends in the Bauhof, and Eunice had invited them all to a party that afternoon. It was a great success. They brought wine and we served more wine. We had assorted hors d'oeuvres, beer, and whisky as well. They signed our guest book and Herr Streit did a magnificent color sketch in our log of the local ancient round crane towers with cocked hats. We had a grand time.

Tomorrow we will return the car and call Ivan to tell him that we are on our way. Letters explaining our delay had been sent to Lil in Paris and to Dave in Detroit. All is well — we hope.

We did not get away as early as planned. Our chores took a little longer, and even more exasperating, the oil line needed additional work in the shop — Baldur must have been in a hurry. As a matter of fact, it took the entire morning to find and fix the tiny holes that showed up when the line was put under air pressure. It would have been simpler to have bought a new line except that nobody had anything like it in stock. To have ordered it would have added three more days of waiting.

At lunch we bemoaned the fact that our new head had not arrived. Who should arrive as we were cleaning up in the galley but van den Akker with our new plumbing, as well as our new awning. He apologized for being so tardy, offering many weak alibis. His wife and daughter had driven over with him, it was his twenty-eighth wedding anniversary. We suggested that he take his family sight-seeing for the afternoon; we would meet them at the town dock in Wasserbillig late in the day. It took Armand with some help until about five o'clock to get the pipeline connected and tested, plus the head fully installed.

Ehrke and his fine large boxer, Baldur, fresh from football practice came down to see us off. We took in our lines at 5:47 P.M. With a long blast on our horn we left Bauhof Trier and moved into the river as we waved *auf Wiedersehn* to him and to all in the area.

It is not too many miles to Wasserbillig — a forty-minute run — and as we approached the dock van den Akker was there waiting. He took our bowline as we came alongside. We invited him and his family aboard, got out some of our fine Kesten wine and drank a toast to the celebrants. Both his wife and daughter wanted to see what improvements had been made to the *Hebe* so Eunice showed them about. Van den Akker seized upon this opportunity to present a couple of bills that were settled immediately. I asked about some dough for the engines that had been grossly misrepresented. He could not explain why we had had so much trouble, but would take it up with the insurance company. I knew that this was a crock of nonsense, but just in case, I gave him a copy of our engine repair bills. Naturally, we never heard a word about this.

After their departure we decided to stay where we were for the night. It is a fairly interesting spot with the Sauer River entering the Mosel just astern of us and a small village, Oberwillig, immediately across stream. The Sauer is not navigable except for canoes and rowing shells.

It was the end of the day and we started to draw crowds. Any boat that ties up and particularly a foreign yacht, especially an American one, usually pulls a pretty good audience. Husbands and wives and lovers paraded slowly along the dock looking us over carefully, some stopping to talk and asking if they could come aboard. This continued for some time past dinner. We invited a few aboard — very pleasant. After dinner we hopped ashore to do a little exploring. The waterfront here is a small parklike area. At the northern end near the Sauer we noticed a sign pointing to a comfort station. It seemed pretty fancy, so we peered into the *"Hommes"* and the girls looked into the *"Dames"* — most unusual to have the sexes divided, we thought. But, holy mackerel, inside was a showplace — the walls were done in beautiful tile mosaic! Now, if you ever get to Wasserbillig, be sure to check us up on this.

Before leaving Germany, I want to put something on the record. As a provincial American with vague memories of World War I and clear memories of World War II, I had been anti-German all my life. My experience in Germany changed all that. Eunice and I and our friends could not have been treated more graciously anywhere. The people had been fun, friendly, and more than helpful. The food, the sights, the progress they have made — everything had been a delight. At no time anywhere did we hear anything anti-American and never once were we treated discourteously. Maybe these people discovered something, too, from their travails and tribulations and horrors of World War II. Let's hope that both of us have learned a little.

9
Triptyque

Ever since our departure from Amsterdam, it had rained every day, some days all day, some just off and on, and some hardly at all. In the morning it was dismal—chilly, gray, raining. But this was not all the bad news—our number-one battery bank that starts the port engine was dead. Obviously, we had not charged it sufficiently after testing the engine. Fortunately, we had acquired a set of "jumpers" from Herr Frank before he took off. Using these to tap in on bank number two, the port engine jumped to life. The starboard engine started with no fuss. We let both engines warm up and charge while Armand scurried about town to get our empty Butagaz tank filled or to make an exchange. Here is a thing to remember! Dutch couplings will not fit the German or Luxembourg tanks. We still had one full tank, so off we went.

Between Wasserbillig and Grevenmacher, a couple of miles ahead at Mertert, there is a very interesting set of caves high up on the east bank of the river that indicates that at one time, before the advent of man to these parts, the river was at that level. When the river cut lower, these caves became exposed and primitive man moved in. Later, industrial man mined gravel and dolomite from the caves, the latter a substance used in refining steel.

Just beyond Grevenmacher, at a place called Wellen, there is a lock that we took in our stride; lift, twenty-two feet; cost, $2.50 (there was no commerical craft with us). Out into the Mosel again we moved into a big meander to port, then a turn to starboard and coming out of this, there was a straight run past Wincheringer to Wormeldingen (don't you love these names!). We went under a bridge here and then into a couple of tight meanders leading to Palzem, the last lock before the French border. The distance from Wasserbillig to Palzem is about ten miles. The lift here is twelve feet, cost $2.50.

From Grevenmacher to Palzem, there are many vineyards on both sides of the river. In spite of the rain, there were several people tending the vines. In some areas, the vineyards rise so steeply it is necessary to lower the power tiller at the end of a cable with a man on foot guiding it back up between the rows as it is reeled in by a power winch on a jeep. The workers were not so devoted as to let us pass unnoticed — they waved and cheered us on.

After leaving the lock at Palzem and our cheering section, all of us began to get a little excited with Germany on the left bank, Luxembourg on the right bank, and only seven miles ahead, the customs at Apach, the entry into France.

At Apach there is a long stretch of dock that boats tie up to while getting cleared. Armand made everything secure as Eunice and I got all the papers and passports together, and strode gaily to the *douane*.

We went up a few steps and into the office, which was in the charge of a young, round-headed, black-haired Frenchman in his mid-twenties. His face was stoic, a pungent Gaulloise was hanging from his lips, the smoke was burning his eyes as he ruffled through our passports, Permis de Circulation, inoculation papers for the dogs. Finally, he handed all the papers to Eunice and said in French, *"Mais où est votre Triptyque! Il faut quon l'aura"* (you must have one). Eunice tried to explain that we had been assured that a *triptyque* was passé, no longer necessary. "Who assured you such a thing?" The French Consulate in Trier, the French Ambassador in Amsterdam, the French Military Attaché in Bonn. We tried everything, but nothing worked. His sneering reply was *"Mais, madame, vous êtes mal resignée."* You *must* have a *triptyque*. He was adamant.

Now Eunice rose to the occasion, using all the guile and Gallic sense of drama she had learned so well *à l'école* as a child. She prated on in rapid French, stomped her feet as an enraged Frenchwoman should, and finally spilled a few tears. He gave her a pitiful look and ushered us out, demanding that we get a *triptyque*.

By this time, I was madder than a hornet and I blew my stack, raging at him and all the French in general, and concluded that the U.S. was nuts to have helped the French through the years with men, money, and arms. He didn't understand a damn word, but asked what I had said. Eunice told him. He looked at us coldly, haughtily snuffed out his cigarette (his third or fourth), shrugged his shoulders and replied, "We gave you Lafayette!"

A pleasant German Customs agent, Herr Bendzko from Perl, came across to us and suggested that we join him in the German Customs Office. He was very helpful and explained that this happens all the time. He would call a taxi that would take us back to the border on the German side of Wasserbillig where we could obtain a *triptyque*.

The taxi arrived driven by a man, Herr Muller from Perl, who had undergone a laryngectomy, probably for cancer of the throat. With him was his wife who was pleasant enough, but who had little to say. Maybe she was getting tired of the act. However, off we went and soon we were back in Wasserbillig. Before we left we noticed six huge motor transports being detained by the French at the border.

As we crossed the Sauer into Germany, an officer straight out of Graustark stopped us. He was a sight to behold! He wore a typical German outfit: military cap with high front crown, formfitting tunic, riding breeches, beautifully polished black boots with shining spurs, and a flowing cape snapped over his shoulders. Topping off all this, he carried a riding crop under his left arm and in his right hand was a long cigarette holder with lighted cigarette — Colonel Klink without the monocle!

He poked his head into the front window and with a huge grin asked, *"Triptyque?"* Ja! Ja!, I thought. Only about a stone's throw away we saw a sign hanging from a small building advertising *triptyques*. I could have sworn it was not there when we drove to Luxembourg.

We entered and learned that Herr Kreck was ill, but that Frau Kreck understood the technique. First we must join the German

Automobile Club, and this would be $3.50. We anted up and presently we had a certificate of membership and a *triptyque* good for a three-month stay in France! "Frau Kreck," I asked, "is there anything else?" *"Nein, mein Herr, nein, danke."* We thanked her effusively and stepped out into the open, sunny, real world. It had stopped raining.

"Jeez," I said, "can this be real?" Eunice said yes, but only we would believe it. Putting my arms around her I gave her a big buss.

We stepped into our waiting limousine and without as much as a "Home, James" we were under way. Our German film star waved as we crossed the border. What a well-rehearsed act!

Back at the German Customs the six huge trucks were still being held by the French. We paid off the taxi and went inside to confer with our advisor. He had some forms that we were supposed to fill out in detail covering inventory of such things as fuel, cigarettes aboard, wine, liquor, etc. He did it for us and walked with us to the *douane*, where a new man was on duty. We thanked our guide and helper and bade him good-bye. He would accept no tip, but he did take some cigarettes.

The new Frenchman on duty stamped us through, stamped the *triptyque* and said we were free to go. I asked who the other guy was, but he would give no answer, just a *"Je ne vous comprends pas."*

Back on board we ordered beer and song for all. We cast off, entered the lock and started to relate the saga to the Davises and Armand. We yakked about it all day and then some.

It was late, 3:40 P.M.; everybody was starving. The gate opened, we shoved out into the Moselle (the German Mosel) with a long blast on our horn and hoisted the tricolor on our mini starboard yardarm.

Looking back on it all, this was much more fun than buying a *triptyque* in New York for $2500. Our total cost for the excursion back to Germany was only DM 59 ($15.00), but how many were in on the "racket" and how do they divvy it up!

10
France

Our goal for the day was Metz, a city much battered in the various European wars from the days of Joan of Arc to General George Patton. We figured we could make the thirty-one miles easily before the locks closed down at 7:30 P.M.

It started to rain again—an almost daily occurrence, it seemed. Armand and I took turns at the wheel, while the others stayed warm and dry below in the saloon. The scenery was dull—quite a change from what we had become accustomed to in Germany. Gone now were the tidy banks and the carefully manicured vineyards. Instead we gazed upon wild brush and weeds. The terraced vineyards had not only fallen into disrepair, they had fallen down the hillsides!

Traffic started to pick up, with barges going both ways, most of which were coming down river. Remember, the locks in France had been down for over a week and, of course, this backed-up traffic was now anxious to move.

The locks in France may be used by yachts without charge, though it is advisable to tip the lockkeeper a couple of cigarettes. I was a bit generous at first, but soon learned better ways, thanks to Eunice and a dwindling supply of American brands.

The speed limit in the river offers no problems. You can go pretty much at full cruising speed, that is, if you are a barge, an auxiliary sailboat, or a motor-sailer. We cruised at about eight knots until we approached a barge and then would drop down to five or six.

At a place called Thionville, we entered l'Écluse Robert Schuman, the first lock of the Canal des Mines de Fer, which is really a canalized section of the Moselle leading to Metz. It was 6:07, Armand and I were drenched and cold, Metz was still eighteen and a half miles away. There are four locks to be negotiated in this canal. There is a fee for each lock, but we were not required to pay it. These locks are not so large nor so modern as those in the Mosel. They leak a bit and the force of the inrushing water is not so strong or violent. With Phil, the girls, and Armand on the lines, we managed quite well.

Two locks later, at Talange, the lockkeeper came out in the rain to tell us that the locks at Metz were probably closed by now—they usually close at 7:30 P.M.—it was now 7:31 P.M. However, we were lucky, Eunice had gone to walk the pups and had spoken to the two barges ahead of us. They had already phoned ahead to the lockkeeper at Metz and they graciously offered to let us pass them so we'd be sure to get there first and wouldn't be locked out, but please tell the lockkeeper that the barges were, indeed, on their way! Eunice thanked them with well-chosen French words and American cigarettes. When the lock opened and we were clear, the barges pulled over to let us pass in the cold, wet drizzle.

Finally, we arrived at Metz, passing under a new bridge built on top of a bombed-out bridge, then by a high-rise apartment house and into the lock l'Écluse de Metz at 8:46 P.M. The lockkeeper had waited. We told him the two barges were coming. Once through the lock, we tooled around the crowded, filthy harbor but found no place to tie up except to some high-sided barge—very difficult for dogs to get ashore and tough for the gals! So we moved out and back to a long concrete pier dividing the large and small locks, where we lay for the night. It was still raining, all of us were damp, chilly, and pooped. A good dinner of leftovers (veal roast, spaghetti, green vegetables) plus beer tasted mighty good even though it was 10:30. No one had trouble sleeping that night.

Wonderful smells awakened me early in the morning. Phil was cooking breakfast, a blend of bacon and coffee was in the air, plus something else — Eunice had gone ashore before daylight in the cold drizzle to walk the dogs and had come back with several loaves of hot French bread and freshly baked croissants! What an eye-opener! Up in a jiffy and into a great breakfast. Armand went into that bread as if he would never eat again, and we knocked off the croissants like kids in a candy store. Our first morning in France was a *succès fou.*

After that meal, in spite of the drizzle, it was understandable that all of us had a very rosy attitude toward life as we cast off at eight, a wee bit late.

Our goal today was Nancy to free Lil, the sleeping beauty, from her frightening, lonesome vigil. It is only 31 miles away, but there are eleven locks to manage, and we are now in the canal-river system, which means slower speed, no more than four knots legally. Both the river and canal are considerably narrower and shallower than what we had been through. Also, we are in the Vosges, which accounts for the increase in number of locks — we will continue to climb to a summit of a little over 1200 feet until well past Nancy. The scenery varies from drab to industrial drab to neglect to bombed relics to spectacular.

Perhaps we should talk a little here about the weather, not that we don't mention it from time to time. It had been raining, at least part of every day since we left Amsterdam. Our heater conked out at Koblenz and we had been unable to fix it. Yesterday it was miserably cold, today was to be even worse — 40°F, the highest. Snork stayed in her berth, Phil would leave his only to help with lines in a lock. Frau Kreck in Wasserbillig told us about a big snowstorm in Switzerland, and yesterday a lockkeeper looking us over wanted to know if we had our skis because it was snowing down south where we were headed! Such fun.

Before we explore further, maybe this is the time for more information. For example, the French inland waterway system was planned, dredged, built, and planted along about 1830–1840 A.D. Most of the same locks function today, even though they leak. The banks of the canals and rivers were landscaped and planted with trees, which today tower over the waterways making a lovely shady passage. (Our earlier comments with respect to scenery, aura, etc., will be amended as we progress.) The locks for the most part are a maximum of 18 feet in width, an important factor, which leads to some more advice on handling your vessel when entering or leaving a lock. As in the previous instance, we apologize if we seem to be presumptuous. Friends have told us that in approaching a lock, the wind would knock them off just as they were about to enter. Could be, but remember, your boat displaces water, and you are also pushing water ahead. At the same time, the water in the lock has to get out, so you get pushed to one side or the other. The solution is to approach with enough "steam" to put steering pressure on your rudder (not full ahead) and maintain this until you are in the lock; then you put her in reverse — easy. Have plenty of fenders out on both sides, hand a line or two ashore, and you have it made. You can do it alone if you follow the basics just mentioned. With a width of 18 feet within the lock, you almost can reach either slimy side without a line. You can overdo this. For example, I am a sailboat man, so when approaching a lock I would hand the wheel to Armand, who is a powerboat man. He knew what to do, but sometimes he overdid it. At one lock he crashed in "full ahead" and then put her "full astern." After looking over both graven sides of the *Hebe* I exclaimed to him, "Even I could do that." From then on, for some time, I handled the wheel at all locks.

The lockkeepers are mostly old vets or wives of vets, or just wives whose husbands have other jobs. It is a good idea and fun to help crank the gates closed, and then to crank them open again. At many of the locks it is possible to get eggs, live chickens and rabbits, and sometimes fresh vegetables. Often you will see a sign "Eau Potable" on the side of the house. Don't be afraid, it usually is excellent drinking water.

But we are on the way to Nancy, and, at this moment, we experience our first thrill in spite of the rain and cold. In a place called Arnaville, we entered the Pont Canal, which took us over a roaring, bubbling brook cascading down a beautiful, lush hillside. This was our first time in a water bridge — a canal over another piece of water. We had read about it and seen pictures of it, but this was real! We would pass through two more before reaching Nancy — at Vandieres and at Dieulouard.

Curiously, all of us seemed to be more aware of the new surroundings, and ultimately we became enchanted with the charm of rural France; it isn't regimented, it's just there and it grabs you. I do believe that the Pont Canal is what really awakened us to the beauty of our new environment.

A couple of miles farther on we came to an overhead footbridge. A sign in French read "Extreme caution, construction ahead." Thank God for Eunice! The canal was very narrow at this point, barely enough for two barges to pass. On the east bank was a house somewhat like a lockkeeper's, but no one was about. Ahead, a half mile or so, we could see some activity that looked like dredging. What to do? Well, with a long blast on the horn we moved on, and about 300 yards ahead out of nowhere came a huge pusher tug blowing at us and all the world. There was nothing to do except crowd over to starboard and hope to the good Lord that all would be all right. It wasn't. The tug banged against our fenders, scraped our sides, and the skipper yelled something unintelligible that could not be heard nor understood over the roar of its diesels. Undoubtedly it was something derogatory. This occurred at a place called Pagny-sur-Moselle. If you pass this way, your passage will be easier because this short section of canal, including several locks, was being eliminated so that all traffic would be directed into a newly dredged stretch of the Moselle. We fervently hoped the elimination process did not include that lovely Pont Canal.

The rain had let up and all hands were on deck. French workers on the embankment, startled to see a large white yacht, watched helplessly as we got creamed. We waved at them sort of resignedly. They responded with a vociferous, friendly cheer. After all, we had survived.

As we enjoyed a bite of lunch *avec de la bière* (Becks!) at about 1:00 P.M., we passed through a lovely town with a beautiful church and interesting old buildings on either side of the waterway. To our right was a turn with a lock, but, to our astonishment, there was a broad piece of water straight ahead and evidently quite navigable. This was at Pont-a-Mousson. Consulting the *Inland Waterways* we could find no comment, and so proceeded slowly ahead. Very soon we came upon huge dredges and work boats. We got frantic signals to stop and go back, which we did. When this new section of canal is completed, barge traffic will benefit greatly and visiting yachts will have less work to do, but they will miss some pretty scenery. On the other hand, the

French will probably plant these new sections as they did the old. In a few years, trees will be joining hands overhead and the new will be as beautiful as the old.

A little old lady was working the lock we should have entered in the first place. She was somewhat startled to see Pompi make a perfect leap ashore before we were fully secured. He was doing what he and Jacques had become so expert at — a quick leap to the top of a lock, a hasty piddle on the grass, the trees, the rose bushes, or anything else in sight, then a sniff or two of the lockkeeper's dog. Funny thing, the dogs never got into any fights — probably a Franco-American agreement of some kind. As soon as they saw the *Hebe* start to drop down or vice versa, they would leap back aboard.

Not having any charts for the area, we set up a system with Eunice reading from the *Inland Waterways*. She would identify each bridge or lock number, the village and kilometers to the next point of reference. This seemed to work pretty well except at Frouard — Eunice was in the galley. We came upon this industrial town late in the afternoon. There were many bombed-out buildings with people living in some of them. To our right, there was a railroad bridge over a "hole in the wall" that was an entrance to a lock, and I blandly remarked how fortunate we were not to have to go through that. In a few minutes we found ourselves at a dead end. Looking up, we saw a couple leaning out of their windows, chuckling and gesturing that we turn around. I said, "Damn it, Eunice, why in hell didn't you warn me about this," at which the others guffawed and coined a phrase "It's all Eunice's fault." Whenever I would start to make some equally intelligent observation in the future, the chorus would start. Ultimately, they tamed their old curmudgeon skipper.

We spun *Hebe* around nicely (with two engines this is no trick) and slowly headed for the "hole in the wall." There was a sign overhead that read *"DANGER electriques nus sous tension"* (DANGER, live electric wires). Ha! Who was under tension? Under the railroad bridge we went with not too much to spare and, as we did, a train went roaring by overhead. Gravel from the roadbed, tons of it, it seemed, rattled down on us, and the noise was deafening. We inched ahead and out from under to find the gaping gates to the lock. It was big — not in width especially, but in the height or lift, which was about 28 feet. No lockkeeper, no one to catch a line, but there were bollards set into the sides to which we made fast once in the lock. Without a word from anyone, the gates closed and we started to rise. Armand was at the bollards and did an excellent job of moving up the lines as we rose. The dank stink was like that of a whale when it blows. In just a few minutes, we were up and still no lockkeeper—I wondered where he hides—the gates opened for us to proceed.

Looking about and aft the view was spectacular. We had come across a valley that now was plainly visible and quite pretty with the late latent sun slanting down on it. About 75 yards ahead we dead ended into a canal that crossed us like a T. What to do?—no markers. We turned left, which the sun position directed me to do—we were in the Canal de la Marne au Rhin that would take us to and through Nancy, where the Canal de L'Est resumes. As I looked about, it was recorded that I remarked, "So far everything in France is broken down; the equipment is old, shabby, rusting, and badly taken care of; the countryside is gorgeous, but it ends there." Funny, I don't remember that.

As we proceeded on our new course we could do nothing but expostulate over what we saw below to our left. The canal hugged the west side of the valley, and we wondered how it stayed up there with us in it. As we neared the heavily settled areas, streets, houses, and cars were all below us. What a sight!

Lights started to come on below in the valley, twinkling like stars, then as it got darker, lights came on all around us—we were in the middle of a metropolis with cars darting by on both sides of the canal, horns tooting, all unbelievable. We were in Maxeville, just outside of Nancy. Ahead to starboard was an Esso station, a perfect place to stop. We made fast alongside; it was 7:15 P.M. The friendly proprietor noticed our ensign and reminded us that today, June 6, was the anniversary of D-Day—a day of sorrow for all the Americans who had lost their lives in defense of France, a day of rejoicing for the freedom of France. He was happy to welcome Americans. It turned out that he and his son were going into Nancy for the TV commemoration of D-Day and would be happy to drive us to the Hotel Europe. But first, we must fall back and tie *Hebe* to the bank. He would fuel us in the morning after he serviced a barge due in at 6:30. His nine-year-old son got some stakes that we drove into the ground and we tied to these. While we were getting cleaned up, he called the hotel for us and learned that Lil was out to dinner. Good, we had time.

All prettied up, we presented ourselves to our host for deliverance. We piled into his sedan. The drive to the hotel was delightful—wide streets, big trees, a pleasant aura, plus an animated Frenchman and his boy. At the hotel we thanked them, promised to be ready for fuel in the morning, and bade them *"Bonne Nuit."*

Inside the hotel, the hôtelier was terribly excited when we made our indentities known. *"Ah, oui, les gens du bateau. . . ."* He would get mademoiselle *tout de suite, mon Dieu,* how wonderful, she's been waiting so long, *mais oui.* After darting in and out, reassuring us on each appearance, many minutes later, he made a triumphal entrance with Mme. Clarin on his arm, and with a broad grin of victory. Lil looked at us in wonderment for a moment, and then erupted with, "Eunice, I've been waiting so long, I've almost forgotten what you look like."

With the greetings and introductions completed, Lil suggested dinner at a perfectly wonderful restaurant she discovered, to which we repaired immediately. It was indeed good, no Michelin star, but good. We had a marvelous dinner plus $65.00 worth of champagne to celebrate our arrival, a super preparation for getting up early to fuel.

With some difficulty we did get up on time. It was misting, and the barge had not arrived. So to breakfast, in the middle of which the barge made its appearance. But there was no hurry, for the skipper and our host were inclined to chat. Incidentally, this barge took on only forty quarts of diesel and filled one can of kerosene.

After the barge moved out, Armand and I walked *Hebe* into position. The dishes had been washed and stashed away, and the girls watched from the saloon as we started to fuel. Our Esso friend was sure we would be off immediately until I told him to pump 250 gallons, which startled him a mite. When the meter hit the mark I yelled down to Armand who was watching the fuel gauge in the hold to ask how it looked. He suggested we try another 125 gallons. M.

Esso thought I was nuts, but happily started his pump again. His eyes bugged as he exclaimed *"Quelle bateau!"* We also bought 5 gallons of lube and settled our bill—$80. His son gave Eunice a gift, a French flag with a key ring, and we said our good-byes.

Moving along the canal we had to go under many bridges with very little clearance. We were sure we should be writing our friends back in Düsseldorf that they were correct, but thanks in part to our heavy load of fuel, we made it to the so-called yacht basin and tied up at about 10:00 A.M. There were no facilities here, except water. Across the street was a chandlers where I bought a coil of ¾" international orange floating line. Leaving this with Armand, we took off for the hotel to fetch Lillian. It was a delightful walk uptown through a magnificent square past the Hotel de Ville.

Lillian had a head almost as big as mine, only it didn't show. She was agog with anticipation for her next adventure and, after her detainment, was wild to go. However, there were many things to do. To Post Restante, for example, where we found a letter from Dave advising that, due to our delay, we should meet him and his gang at Nice instead of Cannes. We answered him, and also sent word to Ivan in Geneva of our whereabouts and an estimated arrival time in Lyon.

Lil had told us about the wonderful Farmer's Market here. It was truly exciting—fresh fruit, vegetables, meat, poultry, pâté, marvelous cheeses! We had been unable to buy lamb up to now, but I had vowed that, once in France, this was what we would start with. When I saw the price, I rebelled—$3.75 per pound for a leg. Never!! So we settled for baby turkey and loaded up with other goodies such as mushrooms, baby carrots, lettuce, pâté, cheese, and fruit. We took a taxi back to *Hebe*.

Armand had been busy, too, while we were gone. He had scrubbed *Hebe* beautifully clean and had touched up some of her wounds. In addition, he had made up four new mooring lines with the bights all spliced, and, heaven knows, we could use them. I complimented him for a thoroughly fine job.

Eunice and I had an anniversary coming up on June 9. Since time was running out, and we were unable to visit many stores (this was a Saturday), Phil and I went across the street to the chandlers to find something special. Can you transform a local Nancy waterfront chandlery into a glamorous repository of precious objects for giving? Well, we did, and came away with a "museum piece," a copper and crystal chandelier for presentation at the proper time.

11

To the Summit

At about 6:45 A.M., Armand and I arose to get things going. We put the coffee water on and, after warming the engines, cast off. Our "yacht" basin was now occupied by three rather large barges, and being a Sunday, these three were lying "dormant." We bumped two or three times before we got straightened away. Not another soul from below ventured forth. That really was a helluva dinner last night!

We poked our nose out into the waterway and made a right turn. It was a truly beautiful morning, rare for us—the air was sweet and clean, even in downtown Nancy. Ahead was what looked like our nemesis, an awfully low, ominous-looking bridge. We moved ahead slowly, ever so slowly—we cleared by one-quarter of an inch! It was a good thing we were loaded with fuel. This was our last close squeak—on bridge clearance, that is—so we made a note in the log to write our friends in Düsseldorf that they damn near won their bet.

We moved along at about 4-5 knots, passing under many bridges at first, then fewer, as we reached out beyond the city. The three of us had coffee on deck as we made our way. In about forty-five minutes we passed under a railroad bridge and came upon our first lock of the day, #26 and #26bis (a double chamber) at a place called

Laneuville de Nancy. We entered easily and, five minutes later, moved out just as easily, with Armand fending off.

But now we were in a dilemma—straight ahead was a lock and off to the right was another canal and lock. The book has no charts, nor any directions on this matter. By instinct, intuition, and super deduction (ha!), we determined to go right, else proceed on the Canal de la Marne au Rhin to Strasbourg. This would have been a great detour had we not been so behind in our schedule. We tied up alongside the bank for breakfast.

Our friends below had gotten up and had things going pretty well. The table was set with servings of sliced oranges and peaches, fresh from the Farmer's Market at Nancy. Coffee was ready, the French bread was warm, and there was butter galore. As we enjoyed this, the barge *Albatross* passed us, and as she did, the French bread disappeared. Where? Armand had found a new love, an inherited taste from his French mother, no doubt. Oh, well, we'd get some more along the way, maybe.

Everyone on deck, and off we went into lock #13 at 9:10. This was the beginning of a climb comprising fourteen locks, rather close together. At 9:17 we were out and going for #12, which we cleared at 9:31.

Into #11, out, and into #10, a double lock, which we cleared at 10:30. The woman lockkeeper used a long hook to take our bowline from Armand—a good idea—then asked if we didn't want to put out a sternline, too. I was at the wheel; Eunice ran aft and handed up the line. Then she started turning gears to operate the lock. Snorky had gone below to take a shower, Phil was in the galley watching to make sure the pilot light didn't go out on our gas hot-water heater. Lil was in a deck chair, Pompi and Jacques were on the bridge—all enjoying the warm sun.

As we came out of #9, we could see #8, #7, and #6 straight ahead, looking almost like huge steps. At lock #7, the girls decided to get out and walk ahead to meet us at #3. It was a shame we did not have our cameras ready, because the girls marching along with Pompi and Jacques running free, made a beautiful picture—a veritable fashion show on a Sunday in pastoral France. The lockkeeper at #8 was a very attractive young woman, and, much to our surprise as we cleared, she ran ahead to operate locks #7 and #6 as well. Our girls helped at each lock and got back aboard at #3, having bid our lovely lockkeeper *adieu* back at #6. Incidentally, as we were climbing this series of locks, I went below for something or other and happened to notice our saloon compass was as wacky as a court jester. And why not? Someone, with an eye for beauty and a bent for home decoration, had arranged a bouquet of poppies and other wild flowers in a Maxwell House Coffee tin smack-dab against the compass! We were not steering by compass, but this kind of thing could not be tolerated. The skipper took corrective measures, which did not help his popularity for several hours.

Locks #5 to #1 at Fleville provided a variety of colors and lovely settings. Up to this point all the lockkeepers' houses were identical; yellow stucco houses with two chimneys, red tiled roofs, red shutters with white trim around the windows, and red-and-white trim around the doors. There was one exception; at lock #3 the lockkeeper's house had green shutters—obviously, the keeper was an individualist!

Here at Fleville, we were high up, about 600 feet. Mistletoe was abundant in all the trees. In our climb to the summit of the arete from lock #13 to #1 we had traversed but one-half mile, ahead, that is.

We now were in a small *bief,* backing and filling, waiting to enter the series of locks going down. We were slightly apprehensive, fearing that going down was more difficult than going up. To add to our concern, the name of the first lock was L'Écluse de Mauvais Lieu (lock of the bad place). From our vantage point, it looked like a rather sharp descent. We worked our way down a couple of locks and into a *bief* at #5, which was loaded with currents, countercurrents, and, as a result, we had a bad time getting into L'Écluse Richardménil. In addition, the wind picked up, making steering more difficult. It was a big drop compared to the others. Altogether, the leaks, back eddies, and wind conspired to give us a thrill. At 2:05 P.M. we were out, but where to go? No signs, just beautiful, lush countryside—so we turned left along the Moselle. We had completed the "Branche de Nancy," and now we were back in the Canal de L'Est going south. A few minutes later we moved over to let a barge pass from the other direction. We were in a pretty little town called Messein.

At 2:45 we came upon lock #45 at Flavigny, starting another climb. There were many spectators, and the lockkeeper, I guess just to demonstrate authority, asked for our papers. The poor guy is there all week with no audience and then comes Sunday—he has to do something important—so we presented our papers for boat, people, and dogs. All in order—everybody was happy.

On through lock #44 with many Sunday watchers in the cheering section, but then we came to gate #43, still in Flavigny, which let us into the spectacular Pont Canal that carried us over the Moselle. What a sight! Men fishing below, three islands washed by the swift river—shallow here; our situation was almost unbelievable, suspended high in the air, so to speak. The entrance was elegant with huge lamps wrought magnificently in iron on both sides of the canal, and a beautiful handwrought railing all the way across, ending with another set of lamps. Surely, you have seen this kind of thing in pictures; when it happens to you, it is something else.

At mid-afternoon—4:00—we passed *Albatross*. The day continued pleasant, comfortable. We noticed an old couple fishing, a very picturesque and touching vignette.

At about six o'clock, things started to happen. We were coming on to Neuviller-Chateau. Ahead we saw a modern miracle—a car going across the canal. We had not been drinking, everybody saw it, so it was a fact—a car riding on water. As we came closer, the miracle was solved; a swinging, but floating, bridge reached across the canal. The car went across to do some milking, the bridge was hauled back to let us pass. Pretty nifty, we thought. Instead of having the cows come in to the barn to be milked, the farmers go out into the field to milk the cows, without washing them first. Not as hygienic as our system, but the cows are contented.

Approaching lock #39 we could read a roadside sign that blazoned "Epinal Ahead." Cars were speeding along the highway, but in no sense was it cluttered like the Long Island Expressway.

At lock #38 it was announced that two of our three heads were overflowing. Ah well, there is always something, isn't there? Repairs could wait—they would have to wait!

At 7:35 we arrived at a turning basin in Bainville-aux-Miroirs, lock #36. We tied up to two trees and a stake that Armand hammered in. We had negotiated a total of twenty-nine locks; one at Laneuville, thirteen up and five down in the Branche de Nancy and ten to here—all this through slow, primitive, difficult, hand-operated locks designed and built for nineteenth-century traffic.

But, there are more important things. Dinner, for example. We had roast turkey, French-bread stuffing, rice, zucchini (Armand couldn't take this—it tastes funny), topped off with meringue and macaroons, compliments of Phil Davis, and coffee, of course. For those who were up to it, cheese and fruit.

Eunice walked the dogs. It was a two-sweater night; all the stars were out, including a satellite.

The next day, June 9, was our anniversary. Armand checked the oil, water, and engines, while I put on the coffee water—we used Nescafe, the big tin—it has a better flavor. Everything was okay, and so we cast off from the trees, pulled in our gangplank, and went for L'Écluse de Gripport #35. The same lockkeeper at #38 was working this one. Where locks are close together, one man or woman will work a group of them. He bade us a cheery *bonjour*.

At du Moulin #34, the lockkeeper reported big storms in Paris. It was beautiful here.

Everyone below was getting up and Phil was squeezing orange juice, which was passed up to the deck crew.

At lock #32, the lockkeeper's house was a picture. The garden in front was filled with blue phlox and there were flowered arbors over the doors. The name of this place was singularly apt—Écluse de la Plaine des Charmes!

At 8:07, a little late, we made colors, fed the dogs, and then repaired to Phil's magnificent breakfast.

Speaking of colors, the practice in Europe is to wear them at all times. Armand thought we were nuts making colors at eight and taking them in at sunset. We taught him how to fold the flag, and, ultimately, he was pretty proud of his skill at this. He and Lillian did flag duty every evening at sunset.

I had been looking over our schedule and perusing the *Inland Waterways* to determine how we were doing in the way of catching up. We had planned to go up to Épinal just to look around, but the branch canal seemed to me to be too time-consuming. I suggested that the girls go ashore at Portieux, get a cab to Épinal, and we would go ahead. At first, this frightened them—how would they get back, where would we be, etc. I assured them they would have no trouble, just get a cab when they were ready to leave and follow the canal until they found us. Sold!

Lock #30 was before us, and a woman was working all four gates alone, so we had to wait. We could see the Moselle below to our left with some really beautiful beaches (Les Plages). The French do a good job of keeping these clean and attractive. Not so the canal or canalized parts of the river!

We came upon Portieux at ten-thirty, and the girls took off full of excitement over their adventure.

For the past few days, everyone had suffered some discomfort—yesterday it was Armand's turn, today it hit me; chills, fever, the miseries. I hit the sack at about eleven and did not awaken until about 5:30. In the meantime, Armand and Phil handled *Hebe* through fourteen locks with no call for help. When I went up on deck, they said I should go back to bed, "No need for you up here." This really was braggadocio, but they had indeed proved what we said earlier—with care and judgment, you can pretty much go through the locks single-handedly. Of course, more hands make it easier.

Ahead of us was a large Belgian barge steering drunkenly. He made a pass at a lock, hit one side, and was forced to back off and try again. We, perforce, had to sit and await developments. Finally, the barge entered and, after lifting out, we approached only to find that the Belgian skipper was not the only one a bit tipsy—two lock hands had had a good start and wanted a handsome tip, i.e., more than a cigarette or two. They were disappointed, but have lived to survive, certainly.

Since the crew on watch had done such a magnificent job all day, I did not interfere, still feeling on the rough side. We entered lock #14 de la Montée de Golbey, the first of a series of fourteen steps up to the summit. Looking ahead you could see almost all of them—very exciting. It was a little less than two miles' progress, to go up fourteen steps!

Traffic was fairly heavy and we had to wait for a barge to come down. At a bit after seven we moved out of #11 and tied up to the bank since lock #10 had closed for the night. The barge out of #10 incidentally entered #11 where she tied up for the night. It's a game of give and take.

The girls returned by cab at 7:30, hair done, manicured, cathedral and other points of interest covered, all agog, and ready to go. I was pretty much in the same state, only ready to go to the loo! However, I pulled myself together long enough to make a presentation of the beautiful copper lamp purchased in Nancy. After a toast to the occasion, I rushed to the head and oblivion for the night. The others went to the Café de l'Étang at Golby, a marvelous farmers' saloon where all the locals had their own napkins in their own rings in their own boxes. Dinner included a tasty potage, two entrees, salad, two local wines, fruit, cheese, and coffee — cost for everything for the five of them 45 francs, or about $9.00, including tip! In addition to the complete dinner, with seconds, Armand consumed three loaves of French bread. A growing boy of 25!

In the morning, I felt somewhat better and was up and about feebly. Starboard engine took a quart of oil, port none. Eunice and the dogs went ashore and walked ahead to lock #9. Starboard engine was running hot, so Armand went below to check. At lock #7 the port engine went hot. Our filters evidently were getting clogged in this dirty canal water. But there were compensations. The lockkeeper was a pretty young woman in a pink blouse, blue apron over a blue skirt, and wearing carpet slippers over dainty feet. In the background was her house with spring flowers peeking out of every window and a TV antenna mounted on the chimney. In the yard, two dogs chased the clucking chickens, pigeons cooed from their cote, and the rabbits unperturbedly munched lettuce in their hutch. Somewhere in the background a radio was emitting hot jazz.

Out of #7 into #6, where the same lovely creature in blue was in attendance. She warned, *"Vous croissez et puis vous attendez* (You cross and then wait),'' which we did. Thank God for Eunice. I thought madame was telling me to mind my manners.

Well, anyhow, we came out of the lock and turned left into a *bief* to await the huge barge coming down. Most barges have their business astern, i.e., the family cabin, engine, et al., are aft. What emerged from the lock was unique, to say the least, and you would not believe it unless you saw it. "Eunice, *attendez,* grab your camera." The foredeck of the barge was panoplied with a very colorful awning, beneath which were hung flowerpots, and against the forward gunwales was an array of potted flowers. In the midst of all this, was a buxom blonde swinging in a hammock. This had to be Cleo and her barge.

Espying Eunice with her camera, she posed in many postures, completely unaware of anything except her own immediate prominence in a contained world of admirers. Her mate, aft at the wheel, must have been distracted, or else lost in his own world of dreams. Suddenly, there was an awakening, a crash into reality—the barge had missed the entrance and darn near knocked one of the gates loose. The awning came down, completely enveloping Cleo; the flowerpots and potted flowers were strewn everywhere; and an angry goddess fumbled and crawled her way out from under the debris. The ensuing dialogue shouted from one end of the barge to the other unfortunately was not taped, but we'll wager that every four-letter epithet available in French was used fluently and abundantly. It made you want to cry in a way, to see this simple tableau of sham elegance and dreams dashed to bits. Using the cacophony of the moment as a shield, we quietly slipped into lock #5. Lifting into view and looking aft, everything was still in shambles.

As we climbed, the scenery became more and more reminiscent of Maine—tall pines, with that heady, clean-air aroma. At lock #1 we broke into the clear; we had reached the summit, an altitude of a mere 1,200 feet, but it seemed astronomical to us! With four gates to every lock, and every gate turned by hand, we felt we had literally lifted our forty-one ton boat up every inch of the way. In two hours and fifteen minutes, we had passed through ten locks, with but one mishap—a broken lifeline stanchion—and that due to carelessness.

By now it was getting warm with a clear sky above. The canal banks here were protected with a crude, but effective, arrangement of driven stakes interwoven with reeds.

Ahead of us was that same Belgian barge moving along at about 3 knots maximum. No matter how many times we blew for him to move over, the skipper adamantly stayed mid-channel and on one instance left the wheel and stomped furiously on his small poop deck, signaling with his finger that the speed limit was 6 kilometers—or about 3½ knots—no news to us.

It was all for the best, probably, because our gauges now showed both engines running dangerously hot. I cut them both and steered over to starboard alongside the bank where we made fast.

Hebe's route, from Amsterdam to Athens.

Hebe under sail in the Aegean Sea, off the island of Aegina.

(Above) Jacques and Pompi ignoring the sights of Bonn; lying at anchor on the Rhine. (Below) Üdorf—Heinrich Lüdsdorf, retired after 42 years on the water, rowed Eunice and the dogs ashore.

(Above) Looking ahead toward Burg, 61½ miles past Koblenz, on the Mosel. (Below) Looking back at Burg, 62 miles out of Koblenz.

(Above) Enkirch, 54 miles north of Trier on the Mosel. (Below) The Roman baths at Trier, built about 305 A.D. by the Emperor Constantius, now protected as a national historical site.

(Above) Entering the lock at Palzem on the Mosel, about eight miles before Apach at the French border; Eunice at the wheel. (Below) Remich and Caves St. Remy, 2½ miles south of Palzem on the Mosel.

(Above) Nancy, the Quai Ste. Catherine—the "Yacht Basin" where **Hebe** tied up. (Below) Heading out of Lock No. 6 near Fléville on the Branch Canal to Nancy and the Canal de l'Est; Lillian watches the starboard side.

Armand opens the gate in Lock No. 4 at Richardménil, at the junction with the Canal de l'Est; **Hebe**, going south, is descending.

(Above) The Bridge at Avignon, from upstream. (Below) Port St. Louis, the last lock to the Mediterranean.

(Above) Stepping the sticks—raising the masts—in Marseilles. (Below) Waterborne jousting, a regular weekend sport in Marseilles, beneath the Abbaye St. Victor, built about the second century A.D. on the ruins of an ancient church.

(Above) Marseilles from the plaza of Notre Dame de la Garde. (Below) The harbor at St. Tropez, Bastille Day.

(Above) La Darse and the Institut Oceanographique, a division of the Sorbonne, founded by the Russians in the days of the czars. (Below) **Hebe** in harbor at Elba.

(Above) Mooring in the ancient harbor at Civitavecchia, built by Trajan on the site of an ancient Greek harbor; Port of Rome. (Below) Naples harbor.

(Above) The market in Naples.

(Below) Embarking from Naples.

(Above) Armand and Pompi, on the way to Greece. (Below) The ruins of the Temple of Apollo, about 69 A.D., at Corinth. (Overleaf) The author entering Patras, Greece.

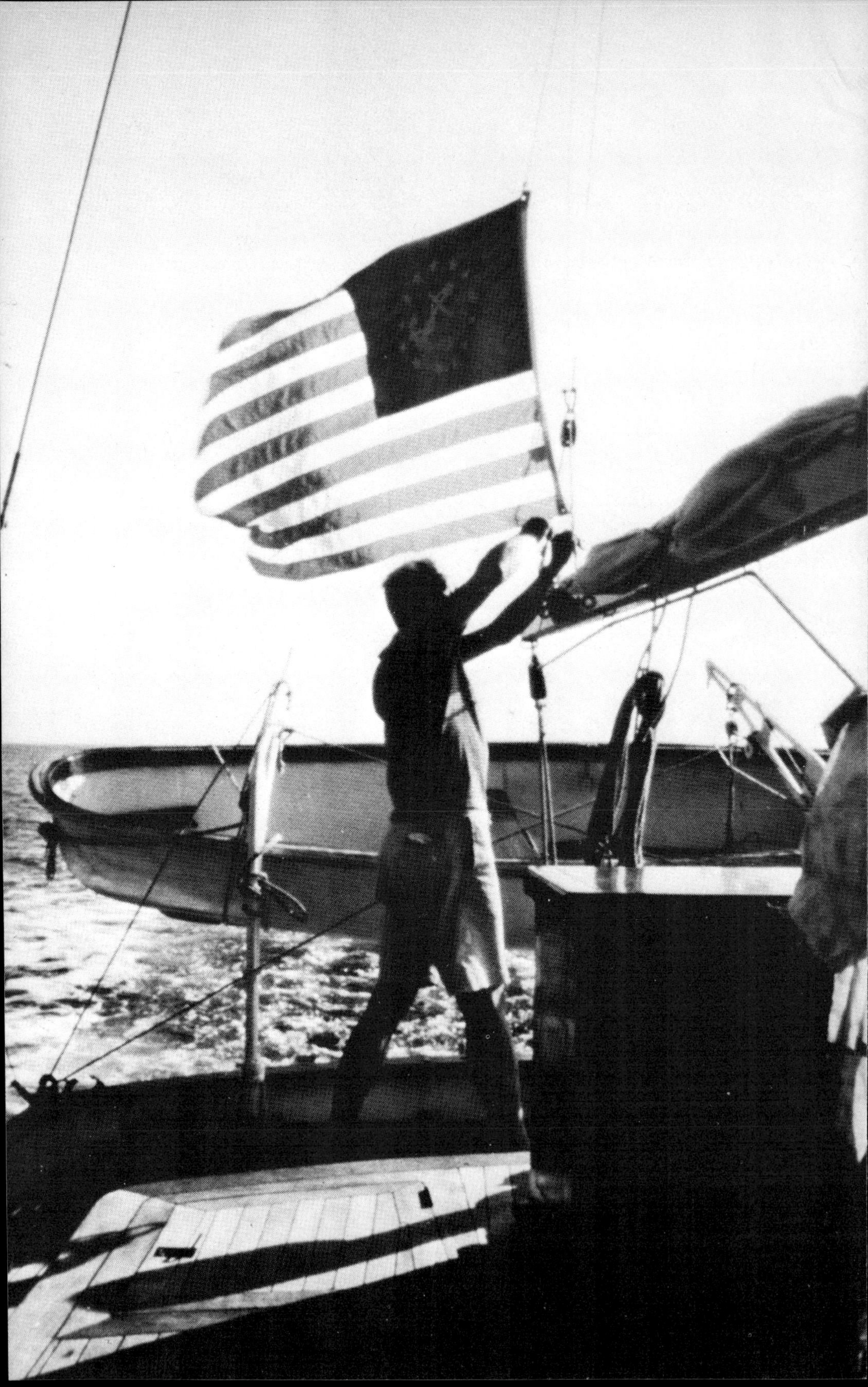

To our right, the bank dropped off into a broad valley, and there was a roadway passing beneath us to Chamousey, a small village situated on a plain to our left.

Armand and I went below to discover that both intake valves for our engines were clogged but good! So we suggested to the girls that they go for a walk. They accepted the idea with alacrity and, with both dogs, scrambled down the bank and disappeared through the tunnel beneath us into town. It was ten A.M.

Frankly, I did not know what to do. If we removed the intake valves, obviously we would admit a considerable amount of water. Armand had an idea that we might be able to push or blow whatever it was against us with our hose. I doubted that we had sufficient pressure, but nothing ventured, nothing gained. We asked Phil to stand guard on deck while we did what we could below, either to sink us or save us. Armand got out a section of hose and hooked it up to our pressure system, which operated at about fifteen pounds. When everything was hooked up, we looked at each other with some trepidation, and then I turned it on while Armand directed the nozzle. In a few minutes, we had water gushing through the first intake. We turned off our hose and feverishly closed the valve. We repeated this operation on the other intake with the same effect. We looked at each other querulously, then sat back and rested a bit. We thought we had won, but we would have to test.

A lot of things go through your mind when working below in a steel boat. In spite of insulation, it is possible to hear other boats coming and going, and also to know whether they are single or double screw. As we labored we could hear the barges come and go, and unable to do anything about it, we could feel the thud when we were hit or grazed. It was aggravating, in fact, maddening, that we could not respond effectively. When we felt sure that our problem was corrected, we tidied up as best we could and went up on deck. Phil greeted us with hope and despair—hope that all was well, and despair over the manners of the passing barge fleet. (We later learned that the fleet was blaming us for the slow passage, not the real culprit from Belgium.) Looking over the port side we saw streaks of black and mud and weeds, but nothing really serious. But why? This is sometimes the way of the bargee, that's why. They "own" the canals the way the New York cabbies "own" the streets.

We tried the engines. Everything was okay, and water was pouring out of both exhausts at a better rate than we had experienced ever. Salute to Armand! The trouble was simple—we had sucked up, coincidentally, two pliofilm sheets smack dab against both intakes.

It was about beer time (rule of thumb, anytime after eleven), and after one or two, we got tidied up and waited for our brides, who returned about 12:30 full of stories about their foray, plus a few pictures in Eunice's camera. Evidently, Chamousey is a delightful French village in the true tradition—small country store, large church. The girls, always on the alert to inspect a church, got a bonus—a wedding was in progress. They interloped in the back of the church and cried, as all women do at weddings. Why, I'll never know, for this is what they have in mind from birth, isn't it? Why not rejoice and smile?

Whatever, they repaired to the village bakery and stocked up with hot bread and other goodies. On the way back they encountered an old woman hauling wood—a most poignant shot on film, I might add. I regret I was not there to assist.

About 1:00 P.M. we approached lock #1 du Bois de Trusey, which marks the end of the summit level and the beginning of our descent. At lock #2, Girancourt, Snork and Eunice went ashore and got four bottles of local wine and six hampers of French beer, just to be prepared.

We tied up to the left bank for drinks and lunch. It was cool and pleasant beneath the arch formed by giant plane trees on both banks of the canal. As we sipped and chatted, a woman on her bike with a basket full of eggs for the market pedaled along the towpath toward us. She stopped and chatted a while and we bought one dozen for 2.8 francs (seventy cents).

As we sat there enjoying the respite, I mused to myself that we had reached the summit successfully without serious damage, with everybody in good spirits. From here on, it would be mostly down. I wondered what lay ahead.

12

Sojourn in the Vosges

Relaxed and at peace with the world after wine, salad, and cheese, I broke the spell and we moved on into lock #3, down, out, and into lock #4, which was being worked by two old women with an old coal miner watching, the inevitable cigarette hanging from the corner of his mouth.

The locks in this series are very close together. For example, from #3 to #10 it is only 4 kilometers (about 2.4 miles). All of these locks leak and piddle, but they work and are enjoyable experiences.

At lock #7, Eunice went ashore with the dogs and camera. She marched on ahead and took pictures of *Hebe* coming out of #8 *"de la descente du Void"* at Ilzemain.

When we were secure in #9, a pleasant, middle-aged lockkeeper told us that a barge had sunk in lock #25 at Harsault about eight and a half miles ahead. He thought that *les Americaines* would be more happy tied up to the trees on the west bank of the *bief* below, rather than to be in the parade of barges. No, he did not know how long it would be, maybe two, maybe three days. So we thanked him and did just as he suggested — we could not have been "more happy" as it turned out.

This, however, changed things a bit. The Davises had firm

reservations for a plane back to the States from Paris. Ivan, our listening post in Geneva, had to be apprised of this latest delay.

It was only about 250 to 300 feet at the most to the next lock, and the yard in front of the house was bustling with children all agog over the developments and the arrival of an American boat.

Eunice walked over, crossed the lock, and introduced herself to Madame Robert Janvier, a pleasant, intelligent soul, with two front teeth missing. She told Eunice that she and her husband had been bargees, but with so many children, ten, she was like the little old lady who lived in a shoe and didn't know what to do. So they got the job of lockkeeper here at #10, with the house and its garden and whatever embellishments go with the job. Robert drove a taxi while she and the children tended the locks and looked after the house and gardens.

Neither she nor we could have wished for a more ideal and lovely spot. The *bief* was like a round pool, surrounded by many tall pines. The water was cleaner than much we had been through, and we learned to our great surprise that there was a magnificent spring a few yards from the boat. Madame emptied her two twenty-liter jerry cans (about five gallons), pouring the water into every available canister or pot in the house and sent them over to *Hebe*. Armand lugged this delicious water until our tanks were full (twenty trips—twenty quarts a trip).

Eunice and Madame reached an immediate and warm understanding of each other. She quite evidently ruled her brood with an iron fist, but nevertheless with loving pride. Gérard, fifteen, had been "placed" with a pâtissier; Colette, twelve, was mother's chief helper; the twins Christianna and Joseline, ten, were "placed" with a family in Maxeville; Jean Claude, nine, an angry and unhappy lad was still at home and still going to school; Mireille, an eager and attractive button-eyed young miss of eight, was entranced by Eunice; Phillipe, seven, was a mischievous imp; Chantal, six, was a pretty thing; Pauline, five, was the youngest, spoiled, enchanting, and known as La Pupice. Now, let's see if we've got them all. No, by gosh, I missed Michele, fourteen, who went to l'ecole fourteen miles away, every day by bus. Mireille informed us that papa had a beard, and Gérard's voice had changed.

Eunice told Madame about us and our immediate need for a

téléphone and learned that the *cabine de téléphone* was at lock #13 and was *ferme* at six. There still was time. Mireille asked if she could lead the way, and could she please put on her red blouse, to which she received a loving and knowing *oui*. And off they went, two new friends with Mireille leading Eunice by the hand and calling her *tu*.

If you have ever used the French telephone you will appreciate the frustration of the exercise. Eunice was able finally to get the Gare at Epinal and the train schedule to Lyon and then to Paris, but only after three stabs. Geneva, naturally, was impossible! Mireille and Eunice trundled back and bade each other *"bonne nuit."*

Back aboard, Eunice brought us up to date. The Davises would have to leave in the morning, the eleventh. There was a train to Lyon with time for a layover before proceeding to Paris. So let us proceed with more important things such as cocktails, dinner, and the enjoyment of our idyllic rendezvous.

With dinner cooking below, canapés and cocktails were served on deck. Eunice regaled us with the saga of her sally to lock #13 and our new neighbors. As if to punctuate her excitement and pleasure, each sentence was accented by the whippoorwills in the brush, and each laugh was echoed by our cuckoo birds somewhere in the trees. Between sips I would duck below to check on things. Snork and Lil had taken care of the salad. Phil, of course, was our sommelier and pastry chef!

It was still light as we came up from dinner and Eunice suggested we walk down to #13 to see if we could do something about the telephone. The two of us took off, the others saying they would take care of the debris and cleanup.

The walk was interesting and fun. We crossed the lock and talked a bit with the ménage at #10 and then dropped down the hill on a nubbled dirt road that skirts the east bank. Looking out into the canal, we could appreciate the wisdom and hospitality of our lockkeepers at #9 and #10. Indeed, there were barges lined up above and below the three locks we encountered. The bargees waved to us to which we responded with a friendly *bonsoir*, for, after all, we were now members of a fleet sharing the vagaries of a common route, and we had come to know each other as we passed or fell back.

Darkness comes late in June up here, and so we had pretty good light walking down. Just below #12 across the canal was a beautiful sight, a lockkeeper's house painted white with blue trim and a garden profuse with what looked to be lupine, delphinium, and phlox — really a gorgeous sight in the fading light. We might add that in broad daylight this spot lived up to its promise. Madame Janvier told us that all this was the work of a lonely old widow lockkeeper, who was looked up to by the local lock people.

Arriving at #13, darkness had come upon us. Below the lock, I espied that Belgian slob who would not let us pass. He and his wife either had gone to bed or off to visit. His little car carried on top of a cargo hatch was still there. I would have loved to poke a few words at him.

We went across a bridge and up a lane about a hundred yards to where we came upon a village. Eunice took the road to the left, stopped at a farmhouse, and said, "This is it." To our right was a barn full of cows that gave us a friendly moo or two. By now, the stars were pretty bright, and the combination of everything was very satisfying. To our left across the road was the farmhouse with the *cabine de téléphone* in the front hall. Eunice walked up to a terrace and knocked — no answer — knocked again and cried, *"holla"* — all of a sudden the shutters of an upstairs window were flung open, and the farmer, wearing a nightcap with tassel and a nightdress, poked his body out the window and berated us both. He was impervious to appeal, deaf to our plea. No telephone until 8 A.M. tomorrow. It was only about 10 P.M., if that, so what was his beef? He must have been banging the operator, but why did he have to wear that absurd costume, and no wonder we could not get Geneva!

Well, back to *Hebe*. It was simply gorgeous — a starry night, the village dark, the barges dark, a frog croak now and then, the air smelling of newly mown hay and of pine, and, looking up, we saw a satellite tumbling by. I grabbed my bride in my arms and gave her a buss with profound apologies that I did not have my nightcap with me.

The next morning, June 11, we awoke to a brilliant sunny day in our secluded cove far from civilization. No people, no boats, no cars, no telephones. In fact, the only contact with civilization the length of this series of locks was the phone at locks #1, #13, and #25.

Since this was the Davises' last day with us, we had a leisurely breakfast together—our first breakfast together since they had joined us in Koblenz—as we were always up early and off to the next stop. By 9:30 all the chores were done, and we were squared away for departure to lock #13 near Thielouze, where we thought the Davises could get a taxi or car to take them to the railroad station in Épinal. Eunice had gotten the train schedules and figured out the connections to Lyon via Dijon and had confirmed the hotel reservations in Lyon for that night.

We thought we had it all planned, but things don't always move in the Canal de L'Est. In fact, nothing was moving that day. When she heard our engines start up, the lockkeeper's wife from lock #9 came by to tell us to stay put. M. Vautier, the chief at lock #1, was due to come by in an hour or so to tell us what's what. We thought we'd ask him to drive the Davises to Épinal, but, of course, he never did arrive. Eunice asked the lockkeeper's wife if she knew anyone with a car who could take the Davises to Épinal. She offered to go and hunt up a car for us. An hour or so later, she returned with the news that she couldn't find anyone with a car. We'd have to walk to lock #13 and telephone the station at Épinal for a taxi to pick up our friends. There was no urgency about her suggestion. Time, it seemed, didn't play much of a role in the lives of the people up here in the Vosges.

However, as the only train left Épinal at 1:00 P.M. and it was now 10:55, Eunice had to dogtrot all the way to the telephone at Mme. Daubié's house in Thielouze and then hope she could make contact with a willing taxi driver who would come out into this wilderness to fetch a fare.

By 11:20 Eunice arrived breathless at the Daubié's farmhouse and asked madame to please phone the railroad station at Épinal for a taxi—and hurry! There followed a comedy routine of husband and wife, sharing one pair of spectacles, trying to find the telephone number. They looked in the telephone book, in the newspaper, in a notebook, on the wall by the phone where a lot of unidentified numbers were scribbled on the wall. Finally, in desperation, Eunice took the Épinal phone book, found the classified section, placed the call, and explained to a fairly intelligent woman at the other end exactly where the taxi driver would find the *Hebe*. "Take the main road from Épinal to Thielouze, but, before crossing the canal bridge, turn right and follow the towpath along the canal to lock #13. What town? No town! *Compris? Compris!* How long before the taxi would be here? It was anyone's guess.

That mission accomplished, Eunice tried to place a call to Geneva—the one that didn't get placed the night before. Madame would help. They got the operator in Geneva, but she couldn't understand Mme. Daubié's French. Eunice got on the phone, but by this time the connection was so bad neither party could hear the other. It's a wonder the Hasslockers didn't hear the whole conversation without benefit of telephone. Finally, the operator said all lines were busy, wait, and they would call back. When? They didn't know when. Eunice shouted down to Geneva to cancel the call if they didn't get through in ten minutes, and spent the next ten minutes explaining to Mme. Daubié not to accept the call from Geneva. Eunice said she would return later or the next day to try again.

Eunice took off to walk back to the boat and, as she came down the hill toward the canal, spotted a white Citroën approaching the canal from the opposite direction. This couldn't be the taxi already! On the chance that it was—or that it was a vehicle with wheels that might be commandeered for taxi duty, she tore down the cobbled hillside shouting, *"Hê, Monsieur le taxi"* waving a white hankie and scattering children, chickens, and geese. Wish I'd had the movie camera to record that one!

Well, she caught up with the taxi a few hundred yards along the towpath, got in, and rode back to the boat in style—and in time for the Davises to make their train at Épinal.

Meanwhile, back at the boat, Armand and I had walked *Hebe* into lock #10 to give her a thorough wash. The lock served as excellent staging. We were able to do an especially good job—saloon top, bright work, and topsides right down to the waterline. She gleamed.

Below, the Davises were getting packed and gussied up for their day's adventure, while Lil did household chores.

Prior to departure, Phil presented his fishing rod to an incredulous Michèle Janvier; we took pictures, and said a sad adieu to Snork and Phil.

June 12 is a big day in our lives, but today proved exceptional.

First, it was the forty-ninth anniversary of Eunice's parents' wedding, and, second, it was our son Jay's thirtieth birthday. What a shame we were not together.

We were up early, and at seven Michèle came rushing aboard to tell us to get in line, the locks were going to open. We started the engines and were in the lock at 7:32—Michèle, Colette, and Madame working the lock. This was so sudden, we were not prepared to leave our new friends so abruptly. As a matter of fact, there were a few tears on both sides for we had become accustomed to each other. Philippe brought us *fraises des bois,* and the other children gave us flowers. Mireille said, "You must come again, I will never forget you." *Au revoir, amies,* we will not forget this day, ever. Indeed, we have not.

Down we went, and out into the clear, with the children traipsing along the bank waving, prolonging the agony of our farewell.

As we emerged from #11, that lovely house we saw last night was to starboard—pink and blue surrounded by a garden of pink lupine, phlox, begonias, and daisies—more beautiful than ever. At #12, Armand worked the lock.

13

Hebe Is Winged

There was a TV antenna on top of the house and colored streamers at the door to keep the flies away.

Next, Écluse de Thielouze #13, *cabine de téléphone*. And so, on we went in the day's parade waiting our turn into a lock or sometimes waiting for a barge to come out going north. The day was brilliant, not too warm.

We reached #18 about 10:25, and Eunice went ashore to buy wine or whatever. The store here at Uzemain was almost like Old Mother Hubbard's cupboard—no wine, no meat, but she did get 2 pâtés, bread, and eighteen eggs for eighty-four cents.

Traffic was heavy both ways and we had to wait in the *bief* at L'Écluse de Chamois-l'Orgueilleux. There was *eau potable* and a telephone here, but not time for the latter. As we poked out of #19, the barge *Bostoc* emerged from #20. We slowly passed very close.

Coming out of #20, there is a bend to port and, as we cleared, we noticed a large Belgian barge coming up the middle, full ahead, and pushing a bow wave that, at the moment, looked like a small mountain. I blew at the bastard and went into neutral. My theory was to wait for perfect aim, then to gun our way through the wave and charge alongside the barge. Instead, we got lifted and pushed up, coming down with a tremendous and sickening thud, careening off to port and completely out of control. The Belgian skipper waved merrily and did not reduce speed—he must have had a hell of a time at the lock. Eunice, always on the ball, got the name, *Malverne* out of Brugges, #BR6719B. We later learned that he was heading for Brugges from Lyon.

We could not steer ahead with any control. There was a terrific clatter and vibration coming from our starboard wheel. However, accidentally I discovered that we had a modicum of control proceeding in reverse on our port engine alone. The imperturable French fishing along the banks did not change stance or otherwise act aware of anything out of the ordinary. So, we limped along slowly toward lock #21, little more than a half-mile away, aptly named Pont Tremblant. The canal widened here and afforded us an opportunity to tie up along the west bank. I remarked that it would be necessary to go over the side. This drew an immediate response from Armand, "That's something I won't do!" I assured him I did not have that in mind, got into my shorts, and went over the side and under with my diving mask. The water was too dirty—even with direct sunlight I could not see a thing. Surfacing, I climbed up on the bank and suggested we turn *Hebe* around so that I could stand in shallow water and determine the damage by feel. Shortly, we had everything arranged and I went in again to dive and feel around.

There is a fairing piece against the hull that meets the top of the rudder when it is amidships. Groping around, I found that the rudderpost evidently had been bent astern at the collar. Consequently, the rudder could not pass the fairing piece and we could not steer ahead except in a wide circle to starboard. Astern, it was obvious now, we could steer somewhat because the port engine would tend to counteract the starboard rudder effect to the opposite. As for the prop, it felt somewhat twisted, which might explain the chatter and vibration.

Back on deck, I sat down and had a beer to think things over. It was almost 1:00 P.M., Eunice was in the field picking daisies, with the pooches frolicking in their momentary freedom. Lil was pretending to read unconcernedly, but listening and watching like a hawk. Armand was glowering. Finally, I asked Armand if he could uncouple the rudders down in his quarters. There was a heavy tie rod connecting the two rudders near the forward bulkhead of his cabin. He went below and reported that he thought he could do it. But, lunch first; we had had enough. We ate on deck and had a cheese omelet, wonderful French bread, and salad. Barges passing south waved with wonderment, those going north waved at *les Americains* having lunch.

Lunch over, everyone was in better spirits. Eunice did the dishes, Lil pored over maps, Armand repaired to his quarters for work, while I rested and wondered what next. There wasn't room enough below for me to help anyway. However, I did draft a detailed report of the incident for our insurance people in Rotterdam and for the French canal authorities.

Armand did a remarkably fast job and said we were ready to go on one rudder. Eunice walked to the lock to hand in a report of the accident and to advise that we would be ready to move in ten minutes. It took us a little longer, actually, but at 4:32 we did get into lock #21 L'Écluse du Tremblant. The lockkeeper had told Eunice that he could not accept the report. We would have to submit it to the "super" of this series of locks at Fontenoy le Château. We moved out in very fast time, eight minutes to be exact, and were confronted by a French barge, *L'Etoile,* who tooted at us to move over. At lock #22, we had to wait for two barges to move out before we could proceed. After leaving this lock, we passed the *Rêne* going north. We were so close, Armand leaped aboard and fended us off. At lock #23, Eunice hopped off to go to market. She rejoined us at a swing bridge that we cleared with no difficulty. Lock #24 was manned by a very pretty blonde, unimportant, but worthy of note. *Résolu,* a barge loaded with logs, passed going north, and we gave her four toots. Some moments later a big, immaculate, Swiss barge, *Thielande,* passed, and we arrived at Harsault lock #25 where it was necessary to wait for traffic. Finally, at 6:44 we entered. It was a big drop, the area was a mess; a baby, together with two or three tiny tots, was in a wire enclosure with chickens as toys. The lockkeeper was distraught, to say the least. It seemed that, a few days ago, some clumsy barge had pulled a large stone making a big hole in the lock, and then sank—our culprit! "Today the barge had gone and *mon Dieu,* the traffic! no time to tidy up, *pardonne.*" We negotiated #25,

#26, and #27 quickly and with no difficulty. At 7:55 that evening we tied up just north of the lockkeeper's house at lock #28 in a lovely *bief* surrounded by high craggy rocks. Around the house there were white flowers, yellow iris, lupine, and daisies—a riot of color. Eunice said it was a Cézanne scene. I had to take her word for it, but it was beautiful. We were at de la Basse Jean-Melin in Hautmougey, which is the beginning of the Saône watershed. For the day, we had made eighteen locks with time out for repairs. Armand washed two shirts, while I prepared dinner—turkey, potatoes, carrots, no wine. I fell asleep at the table; Armand helped Eunice ashore with the dogs. There was a considerable amount of lightning and thunder but no rain that night, at least so I was told.

14

Marchons vers Lyon

Bridey was up at 5:30. She was probably nervous and couldn't sleep wondering what would happen to us today. Well, heaven knows, we had had a few anxious moments.

The day broke clear, but overcast developed early. We were ready for the lock when it opened. On the other side, we passed the barge *Incredule III* going north and exchanged pleasantries. The trees and fields were alive with a variety of birds that were extremely talkative.

The Saône country offers an interesting change in real estate from that which we had traversed — all of it interesting, pleasing with wild flowers everywhere.

At Montroche, we entered lock #30 with the river making a beautiful, natural waterfall to our left. There was an old couple in charge who were evidently quite pleased with their lot. Their house and garden sparkled from the careful attention they had been given. In answer to the old man's query, we told him there were no boats behind us insofar as we could see. A little further on, we came upon a man sharpening his scythe and cutting the grass between the locusts and oaks along the banks of the river. It was necessary for us to wait for the lock and in doing so we went aground on the left bank just as the lock opened. We heard a loud crack emanating from below—it was Armand's lavatory—the rudder quadrant had smacked it. Ah, well! So we threw a line to our man with the scythe, who made it fast to a tree, and with the port engine in reverse and winching in the line we were soon free. With a *ta-ta* to our friend we gathered in the line, entered the lock, and disappeared as we dropped two meters, a little over six feet.

We emerged into double S-curves with stone walls on either side—rather spectacular, but hardly a place to pass or meet another barge. The sun reappeared and burned off the haze. Lock #32 presented the neatest house we had seen yet, crisp lace curtains in the windows with the gardens ablaze with white lupine, pale lavender rhododendrons, and red and pink poppies. As we moved out of the lock, a car was passing to our left. The driver stopped, rolled down his window and shouted, "United States, God bless you!" We won't forget that.

Along about ten we arrived at #35 in Fonteney-le-Château, where we showed our papers (*permis de circulation*), and Eunice presented the report of our accident. The lockkeeper was courteous and recalled the Belgian barge and was not too complimentary about her. He promised to pass on the information in French and English to the proper authorities, cleared us through, and wished us a *bon voyage a Marseille*. Eunice went into town to phone a M. Dumont of Chantier Naval at Chalon-sur-Saône, while we tied up at the bridge below.

Fonteney-le-Château is a darling, sleepy town and worth a stop if not a sojourn. It has an excellent *boulangerie* (bakery) and good markets where Eunice stocked up on veal roast, bacon, bones for the dogs, potatoes, and carrots. She reported that the Chantier Naval looked forward to our arrival.

At Montmotier, lock #36, the river to our left meets a dam and makes a lovely waterfall. The lock was tended by a neat, pretty girl, sporting the best looking legs I had seen in France. Eunice said to her, *"Tres beau,"* at which she smiled proudly.

We came upon a barge tied up to the banks just before the entrance to lock #37. A woman was washing the dinghy. She told us that they had a broken rudder and her husband was phoning the "insurance." Help was coming from Nancy. I looked at Eunice as if to say even the pros have problems.

As the Angelus pealed throughout the countryside, we came out of lock #38 at Pont-au-Bois. An enormous estate was perched on a hill behind attractive fencing ahead on a bend of the waterway. This scene with its reflection on the water was a magnificent sight. What a weekend retreat!

It was getting hot, which reminded us for some reason to check our water. We took on 150 gallons at lock #39 for one dollar.

Armand began to complain about the heat. I got into some shorts and Lil made another of her daily changes of attire. She was always smartly arrayed, a refreshing sight, a good morale builder. We teased her about it, but encouraged her to keep it up, for, who knows, we might encounter Aramis in all his finery coming around a bend on his white steed and ready for romance.

At Selles, there was a cafe that looked very inviting in the *bois* to our right. We did not stop; perhaps you will be more fortunate.

At 3:25 in the afternoon we arrived at Corre, TV antennae everywhere. Open laundries, old and new, line the banks of the canal. There are stone slabs slanted into the water where the women meet to scrub and flail their wash — an interesting sight. The town itself is suburbia.

This is the last lock of the Canal de L'Est and now we will enter the Saône. The lockkeeper asked for our *permis* and then offered us charts of the Rhône at $7.80 and of the Saône at $8.00. We had the Rhône, so I purchased those of the Saône. These are excellent, four-color charts with easy-to-read type and legends. We were advised that traffic to the north was heavy, with two barges now approaching — "*Attendez,* pass to the right."

The valley at this point is wide, and visibility today was excellent — we could see for miles. The farms looked prosperous though the buildings were not always in good repair. Eunice said not to worry about them, the farmers all undoubtedly had gold coins or bricks buried in the ground or under the manure heap.

After about an hour's run, we approached a red light, the first signal or marine direction we had encountered in the French waterways. This was the entrance to #1 d'Ormoy, a modern, electric lock. There was a barge ahead and both of us had to wait a few minutes. This lock and others that follow are long and will accommodate more than one vessel. We entered and left in tandem.

The banks on either side were covered with Queen Anne's lace, and the trees were clustered with mistletoe. The river was well marked, the air cooler, water deeper, and we could move along at five to six knots.

At 7:40, too late for any more locks, we pulled alongside the west bank at Montureux-les-Baylay behind four barges; *St. Antonius* out of Strasbourg immediately ahead, then another Frenchman, and two Dutch barges. Prior to our "incident," we had been in the van of this armada. A young lad from *St. Antonius* came to inquire if we were all right. They had seen us tied up near L'Écluse #21. We explained our troubles. He said that he would talk this over with his *père* and return.

The father had a friend at Trave, eight miles downriver, who ran a big gravel business and had his own dry dock. The boy came back with the telephone number, and he and Eunice left for a nearby farmhouse. Papa had said that Chalon was very expensive. Also, he advised that we get a pilot at St. Jean de Lux below Chalon; failing this, we *must* have one from Lyon south. Perhaps in the morning we should follow him, but, with his speed of better than eight knots, this was impossible. And so was the answer from Trave. The patron said he would not attempt to haul us. We thanked our young friend for his concern and help, and invited him to dine with us. He had eaten; he would see us tomorrow.

Dinner was beef bourguignon, spaghetti, carrots and wine. The skipper fell asleep.

The morning was very foggy, but it started to lift at about 7:30. *St. Antonius* departed a little later and we left at 8:30 passing *Ariadne* and *Oscar,* the two Dutch barges out of Maastricht who decided to wait for the sun.

Colors were made at 0850, late, by gosh.

We passed St. Valere, the nicest town on the Saône so far. The Café de Marie was jumping (at 10:00 A.M.!), hordes of people waving, and girls, girls everywhere. Armand was agog. We stopped at the gravel works in Trave where Eunice went to see M.C. Robin, the patron. It was a very up-to-date operation, but no, he would not haul us, he was not covered by insurance. No amount of pleading would change his mind. So off to Scey-sur-Saône, at the head of lock #7, where we had to tie up and wait our turn to descend and proceed to the tunnel ahead. There was a small restaurant with a sun deck, the F.C. Cornnet. A pusher tug from the gravel works was busy darting back and forth doing errands, and finally it got in line, too. Eunice did a little campaigning to allow us to pass the fleet, and, to our surprise, she was successful. Traffic to and from this lock is one way all the way to Port St. Albin at the other end of the tunnel at Ovanches. The direction is determined only after a vessel or group of vessels is cleared through. Those in charge were now setting up communications for all of us to proceed south. We waited for about an hour and a half during which a cool beer or two helped ease the pain and allay the heat of the day.

With Eunice back aboard we were given the signal to enter the lock, and, after leaving the lock, we slowly crawled past barge after barge until we were at the head of the procession from which point we could see the signal tower. Presently the light turned green and we put *Hebe* ahead slow to be followed at intervals by the string of barges. Having read Irving Johnson's account of tunnels, frankly, we were quite apprehensive, but with all due apologies to him, the experience was not bad at all. Perhaps he had prepared us for the ordeal. This tunnel is 2,200 feet long and about 18 feet wide, and there is a chain running the entire length of one side on which you can pull yourself through in case of breakdown. The pinpoint of light at the other end made an excellent target, and I found steering to be relatively easy. Permissible speed is 3 knots, which makes sense. Eunice was stationed on one side with Lil on the other. Each had a flashlight that they were directed to point ahead or down, never at the helmsman. Our voices reverberated eerily. Armand stationed himself amidships and was acting like a windmill, the purpose of which was never clear to me. He did manage to knock some of the stalactites loose, so that our decks became covered with considerable debris. There are some exposed live wires overhead, but miraculously Armand missed them. We emerged into the sunlight unscathed and pleased with ourselves. We could see the first barge trailing about fifty yards behind us. Altogether, it had taken us eight minutes to pass through.

At lock #8, there was one barge waiting for our group to get by.

In this section of the Saône, almost every lock is preceded by a "guard gate," the openings of which look terribly small as you

Marchons vers Lyon 115

approach. These gates are an essential part of the flood-control system and are used usually during the spring floods, when the mountains let loose their winter accumulations.

Later on in the afternoon, thunderheads started to build up and, as we came on to Savoyeu and our second tunnel, the heavens opened up with a violent storm. The tunnel here is about 2,100 feet in length and is fully lighted throughout. Frankly, I preferred the unlighted tunnel; the light was too distracting. When we came out, it was still raining but the violence had passed. Ahead we could see our friend *St. Antonius;* to starboard, there was a priest fishing in solitude.

About an hour later, we arrived at lock #14 in Beaujeu. There were two barges ahead; it was 7:28. The lockkeeper let the first barge through, but *St. Antonius* and *Hebe* had to tie up for the night. Armand jumped ashore as I threw a line to him. We made fast to a large pine on our starboard quarter and to some locusts ahead. The rain had stopped, the air smelled wonderful, and the sheep nibbled contentedly in the pastures. Lil and Armand took in the flag and folded it in their ceremonious fashion.

We ate late— 9:30 —and well; veal roast, roast potatoes, salad, and wine, with soft music from Luxembourg in the background. To no one's surprise, the skipper fell asleep. The still of the night was interrupted only by his snores, the hooting of owls, and the call of a cuckoo.

Early Sunday morning, it was very misty and foggy. The barge ahead was barely visible. We waited until eight before entering the lock, and when we cleared through we saw three barges going our way, but still tied up to the bank waiting for the fog to lift. As we passed *Lucitania,* she expressed concern for us and our *gouvernail.* A little past nine a lovely breeze came along and swept away the fog. This brought Lil on deck in all her morning glory. What a wonderful fellow traveler!

At lock #15, Pompi jumped ashore and chased the chickens and baby geese and, believe it or not, they made friends! I asked the lockkeeper if he had any chickens for sale. He disappeared to ask his wife, returning quickly to let us down in the lock. As we started down his wife appeared with a big, friendly smile and a large, live rooster weighing six pounds. I did not relish the thought of letting blood on our teak deck, and Eunice tactfully told her that he was too beautiful to kill. The rooster was released and scampered away in fright, but the woman obviously did not share Eunice's opinion and looked hurt.

In a few moments, the city of Gray loomed ahead. On both sides of the river, there were signs reading *"Zone reservé aux sports nautiques."* The French do a very good job with this kind of thing. Certain areas are reserved for water-skiing, and pleasant sandy beaches are maintained in others. The water in these spots usually is moving and quite clean.

At Gray we tied up alongside a *quai*. This is an attractive town and in spite of its being Sunday, everything was open — *pharmacie, boulangerie, pâtisserie, épicerie, charcuterie* — and we made the most of it. There was a big restaurant "Au Martin Pêcheur" with attractive terraces and colorful umbrellas, plus a dock for yachts that we did not try. The town enchanted us, however, and all of us would gladly return to try its charms.

It was a very special day — the runoff election between Pompidou and Poher. Circulars and posters were everywhere.

We went through the lock and had to show our papers and then entered a large *bief* or pond where we encountered a green punt with red trim and a man fishing from beneath a huge Cinzano umbrella. The umbrella, at least, reminded us of the first Storm Trysail Block Island Week, a biannual event.

We turned into a long, straight canalized section of the river to find the banks crowded with people picnicking, waving to us, fishing, or just plain old-fashioned sitting in the sunshine. At Heuilley-sur-Saône, a little further on, a little old woman called out in English, "I love you." Eunice asked why there were so many people not voting, to which everyone shouted back that they had voted early in the morning. Eunice chuckled and held Pompi aloft asking in French, "Did you vote for M. Pompidou?" and then went on to say that she had Pompidou in her hand. This provoked a happy roar of approval and many, many laughs. Some retorted that they knew M. Pompidou was a dog, but did not know that he was black, which produced more laughter. Eunice now stepped on our gas box astern holding our two little black toys overhead, wishing everyone well, and may your candidate be the winner. Yea!

At three that afternoon, we arrived at the lock at the junction with the Canal de la Marne a la Saône. It was closed. Armand jumped ashore and walked ahead to get permission to pass, but no, it was election day and everybody was off at three—so we tied up—it was fun. People from Dijon, Nancy, everywhere were having an outing—we joined the party and had an extended cocktail hour. A man named Wassen gave Bridey the name and address of a good pilot in Lyon—Robert Frouard. It showered off and on. We did some laundry in between the showers and our sips. At dinner, we had a magnificent Piesporter Reisling.

Eunice arose early in the morning to find it very misty, and so she took off for a stroll with the pooches and let us sleep away our sins, at least for a while. I got up around 6:00 and woke up Armand. We checked the engines—everything was in good order and no oil was needed.

Listening to the radio we got the official news of the election; Pompidou fifty-seven percent, Poher forty-two percent—a pretty good win. A barge, *Ste. Rita,* loomed out of the mist, going north. The sun broke through and started to work on the mist. We got the green light. I felt that this was going to be a great day. Eunice raised a mild complaint that she had had the "con" only twice since we had left Amsterdam. I said, "Baby, she's yours!" So into the lock and away we went. In a few moments, we passed a neat town, Pontailler, where we saw a sign *"Hostel des Maronniers"* announcing a newly stuccoed inn. There were small boats tied to a dock, but we glided by and did not stop. A mile or two ahead, we passed under the bridge at Lamarche, where there was a church with twin towers. The river here is wide, the air was warm, the water so clean you could swim in it, and there was a gentle breeze from the south. There was no traffic. Presently we came upon a canalized section of the river at Flammerans. Eunice put us through the narrow gate handsomely. At Poncey-les-Athee, there was a sign to our right indicating "do not enter," which was a square with red on top, white in the middle, and red on the bottom; so she put *Hebe* in neutral and laid off, waiting. We could see a barge coming up in the lock ahead. When we got our signal to move, Eunice took her in square in the middle of the lock. The water action in these locks was so smooth we did not tie up to either side, but Armand and I were alert to fend off if need be. Coming out of this lock we passed an empty barge, *Diane*. Ahead in the distance we could see Auxonne. Lil, having finished the breakfast dishes, came on deck in costume number one for the day as we passed the French barge *Le Bleu*. At Auxonne, there is a water-sports area, a yacht club, a very modern beach club, and a place for both swimming and diving — a very lively place. We passed under a railroad bridge as a train rolled overhead making a tremendous roar. Lillian was reading intently about Burgundy. A terrific blast broke the idyllic scene — a jet had gone through the sound barrier.

Shortly we noticed a huge dredge lying at an angle, flying signals for us to leave it to starboard. As we approached, the dredge lowered her anchor cable permitting us to pass. Eunice was doing wonders. There was mistletoe in the trees that reminded her of the Druids. Beef cattle were lowing in the fields to our right.

At beer time, we passed the junction with the Canal du Rhône at St. Symphorien, which is where we had hoped to be last night. Again, ahead, we saw a large dredge and two big barges. This time the signals directed us to leave them to port. Around the bend we could see St. Jean-de-Losne where the Canal de Borgogne joins the Saône. All this was mighty exciting. Burgundy country — many cuckoos and crows, campers on the banks, very bucolic, but no sign of wine.

Lock #1 at St. Jean-de-Losne was hand operated, much to our surprise, and was tended by a man in shorts, sandals, and sunglasses. Armand helped with the lock.

Below the lock, we noticed many campers in scanty attire seated at a rustic table — Eunice called it a modern *déjeuner champêtre*.

We arrived at lock #2 in Châtelet at about two in the afternoon. When we got through, Armand took over on the wheel, and we went below for lunch. Through the windows we could see *châteaux* in the hills to the west. They looked inhabited — a beautiful sight. Eunice was proud of herself as a helmsman, and properly so, but anxious to get back on the wheel. She gobbled up her lunch and raced back up on deck to resume command.

Later in the afternoon, we went by Charnay, a cosy little farm town featuring a church with an interesting steeple. Further on, we passed a magnificent country estate on the right bank and on the left a farmer in shorts was haying with modern equipment —

tractors, rakes, etc. — a nice contrast. Everywhere there was beauty, tranquility. At one point we espied a blasé swan sitting on her nest. She watched us go by and then stuck her head back under a wing, probably thinking "foolish people."

At Verdun des le Doubs, not to be confused with the Verdun of World War I, I took over, Eunice tended the sternline, and Armand clambered up the ladder to show our papers. It started to rain.

As we neared the junction with the Canal du Centre, we ran into a big, black squall accompanied by a downpour and strong winds. Fortunately it was over quickly, and at 1930 we arrived at the Chantier Naval. We talked with a barge woman who told us we were welcome to tie up, but that there was no transportation into town. Thanking her, we moved on down into Chalon-sur-Sâone, where we came alongside our friend *Lucitania,* which was tied up to another barge, which in turn was made fast to a mammoth set of stone steps that rise splendiferously from the river's edge to a beautiful plaza. We had had a successful, wonderful day and had made a good 107 kilometers, or about 65 miles, without a mishap. Maybe Eunice should take over from here on!

We got cleaned up and then excitedly stepped aboard *Lucitania* and over to the next barge. The plank from here to the steps was narrow and springy, a real old-fashioned "tickly-bender." In the dim light it almost frightened poor Lil to the point of staying aboard. With some coaxing and my holding her hand, she finally made it.

On top of the plaza facing the river was a statue of Joseph Nicéphore Niepce, the father of photography, né 3/7/1765. None of us had ever heard of him, but there he was and is! Past the statue is the Royal Hotel but we were told that no meals were served on Tuesday. A taxi recommended and drove us to the Hotel Terminus. We had an excellent dinner — good white wine Montagny '66, dinner for three (potage to *fraises* with vintage) for $18 — not bad! The service was good, friendly — we recommend it. Back to *Hebe* by taxi. *Bonne nuit!*

Armand and I kept our promise to *Lucitania* and got up at the crack of dawn. We slipped our lines and moved out into the river so that the inside barge could get free and be on her way. This accomplished we moved back in and alongside *Lucitania* again.

The good smells of coffee and bacon awakened the girls. It was a beautiful, clear day. Later, Eunice gathered the dirty laundry and we helped her and Lil across the barge and up the steps. It had been decided that the girls would rent a car, get the laundry done, sightsee, and do all the things women like to do. We would take *Hebe* back up the river to Chantier Naval.

Looking across the river from the foot of the statue, we could see an interesting group of buildings, a domed edifice (possibly a church), and three tall ancient Roman columns from Caesar's day. Abutting this to the south was a green grassy slope down to a low stone wall at the river's edge. Set into the green was a huge garden of closely planted red and white flowers — the white spelling out in bold Roman type NIEPCE against the red background — most effective. Coming down the river and passing before us was a spanking new power cruiser, followed by an old cutter about 40 feet overall.

So *ta-ta* to the girls and up river to Chantier Naval where we lay alongside a barge. The yard was impressive, with a large modern machine shop and all necessary equipment. There were three railways that took in a wide swath of real estate, inasmuch as they haul the barges sideways. Armand and I proceeded to the modern, brick office building where I asked for M. Dumont. He was out, but they were expecting us — please wait aboard and an engineer would come to inspect us. Some hours later, a man came aboard with an attractive interpreter. He wanted to see our plans and hear a description of what had happened. Luckily we had all the blueprints with us, including a docking plan that the engineer studied closely. The young lady told me that they would take the plans, and please, wait aboard until she returned with some word. And so we waited and waited. Several beers later, the young lady returned with the request that I come to the office.

I was shown into a well-appointed room in which I met M. Dumont and the gentleman who had been aboard. The girl remained. I was told that they had studied our plans, that they could be ready to haul us at seven in the morning. How long it would take for repairs depended, of course, on what they discovered. This seemed to make sense, but the idea of waiting until tomorrow to get hauled was somewhat irksome. I asked how much it would cost to haul us. They gave me a figure in francs that was beyond my ken. The girl succeeded finally in explaining that this came to $343.00. I started as if jabbed with a hat pin. The Frenchmen were imperturbably, quietly silent. "Surely, you must be kidding!" I exclaimed. "No, monsieur, this is so!" Holy smoke, I could haul her myself for that kind of dough and put on a sideshow to boot. So, thanking them for their good offices, I declined. They permitted me to phone the insurance people in Rotterdam who thanked me for being so considerate, and gave us permission to proceed to Lyon.

Returning to *Hebe* I found Eunice and Lil waiting. I gave them a report. They were in a fine fettle and had been having a wonderful time in Chalon-sur-Saône, a really interesting city, and couldn't care less about my woes. Back to the steps, each our separate ways. The gals gave me a quick tour of the town, and we had dinner at the Hotel Royal. Armand almost always ate aboard — he hated to spend money . . . on account of watching us pour it down the drain, I guess.

Lillian was disappointed that we were moving on. She said she loved the delays and hated getting places too fast. Eunice phoned Ivan (Hasslocker, that is), to bring him up to date. He reported that Dave had cabled, canceling out. We were sorry about that, but couldn't blame him.

The weather the next day was made to order — the air cool, the sky clear, and the river smooth. The Saône is a beautiful river with the hills forming a gorgeous background the entire way. It was so clear that we could see the snow-covered Alps miles away to the east and south. We should be in Lyon tonight. Ivan had said they would meet us and give us all the news then.

Hebe purred along happily, giving no trouble. All of us spent the morning on deck drinking in the sunshine and the scenery, remarking now and then about a church, a bird or even the many neat *"Zone D'Evolution de Sports Nautiques"* along the way. About noontime, we passed St. Martin Belle Roche, where the St. Martin winery can be seen close to the river. It would have been fun to stop, but we moved on. About five miles below we arrived at Macon on our right and lovely St. Laurent to our left. It took willpower to keep going, for here is one of the most famous names in the world when it comes to wine. The city is easy to look at — it was begging us to stop — and there are good facilities for mooring alongside. Also, there are some good places to eat, but we kept going, damn it. I wanted to say it was all Eunice's fault—alas, it was mine.

Early in the afternoon it clouded up and we went through a downpour. The visibility was almost nil. Will there ever be a day, I wondered, without rain?

The river meanders quite a bit below Macon and the character of the countryside changes subtly. The river majestically winds its way through the Burgundy country and into the Beaujolais mountains. As we came out of a big meander we could see a lock with much activity going on. We slowed down, we were coming to barrage Écluse de Bernalin in the Beaujolais. As we got closer, it was apparent that something was awry, but we were beckoned to enter, regardless. There was a barge forward to starboard and to port was a small boat. We were moved along on the port side. From this point, we could see that the gate was being repaired, and it was obvious that no one was going anywhere until this job was completed. In the meantime, the lockkeeper decided to admit as many boats as he could squeeze in—it was a large lock.

Eunice was holding the two champs, ready to leap ashore. Armand and I made lines secure. Then a most charming woman in grey slacks moved from a small group of spectators and marched alongside as if to inspect. Eunice asked her if she would take the pooches, please, and let them run. This started an animated conversation that was a pleasure to watch. The two gals apparently exchanged all kinds of views and/or opinions, the two dogs romped with abandon, and Lil, Armand, and I watched with amusement. This went on for some time until the forward gate was fixed. The lock was closed, and we started to descend. The lovely Madame ashore gathered the two dogs, handed them to Eunice, and then blew a kiss to all of us. When the gate opened there was an orderly exodus. But excitement with us was on the rise, for now we were moving down into Lyon, its hills, its bridges, its charm.

Eunice filled us in on her chat with the lady at the lock. She and her husband and some guests were spending the weekend at their cabin in the Beaujolais above the river. Espying an American yacht going by, they, knowing that the lock was under repair, decided to walk down to look us over, and also it seemed like a novel way to entertain their guests.

Exactly two miles downriver there is the Yacht Club du Rhône situated on the right bank behind a small island. Directly opposite is a *"Zone D'Evolution de Sports Nautiques."* The club offers moorings, good food, and fellowship. Just what the Yacht Club du Rhône is doing on the Saône we cannot explain—just lay it to French logic. If you don't stop here, you're nuts. We were nuts! A short taxi ride away there is the world-renowned restaurant run by the incomparable Paul Bocuse.

From the club to the center of Lyon is about eight miles. There are three locks. At the first one, L'Écluse de Rochetaille, we were given a paper with a suggestion to stop at Port du Plaisance, together with a rough chart indicating its position. The current picked up to about four knots—the river becomes fairly narrow here, the meanders more frequent, and the hills rise steeply. As a result, the sensation of speed becomes exaggerated and exciting. After going through the last lock, L'Ile Barbe, we seemed to fly as we hurtled under eight bridges, and wondered how we were going to stop. We passed under the Passerelle du Palais de Justice, and there to our right was a cathedral, and high up on a mountaintop directly above was the basilica. Over to our left was a large sign painted on the stone retaining wall *"Port du Plaisance"!* We made a wide swing to port just above the next bridge, Pont Tilsitt, turned into the current, and came alongside the *quai* easily as the dockmaster, M. Bonjour, took our lines. Hurrah, hurrah, and drinks all around.

This is a unique spot. There is a roadway that goes along the river's edge for two miles. The retaining wall is about fifteen or twenty feet back from the river and is some twelve or fifteen feet high. Stone steps are in the wall at intervals, and above is a well-cultivated park with large plane trees that extends up and down the river as far as you can see. The port is almost in the center of the city with the Farmers' Market only two bridges (about two city blocks) away, upstream. The hotels are only a block or two in from the river, and, just across town, an easy walk, is the Rhône. From the basilica, which can be reached by cable car, the view is vast, and on a clear day you can almost see Geneva nestled in the Alps.

We got ourselves prettied up, and just as I was chopping ice, who should step aboard—none other than our Listening Post and his bride, Sheila. What timing! How pleasant to see them!

After a couple of bombs, the five of us repaired to a saloon recommended by Madame of the Beaujolais. Dinner was excellent — the name of the place, La Mère Brasier.

Ivan brought us up to date on all the news and everybody's whereabouts. The Kellys were in Dortrecht, Dave had cancelled out as had Gould. We would check Poste Restante in the morning. And so to bed — late.

15

Lyon

When we arrived last evening, there was a cutter named *Blue Days* tied up a few rods ahead of us. This morning the owner walked back to inspect us. He introduced himself as a Mr. Rutherford, out of England. He and his wife had decided to pack it up and get away from the ghastly taxes and all, and were on their way to Malta. He had had some beastly rudder trouble as a result of some careless barge chap, snapped his rudderpost, you know. I asked if he were the cutter I had seen in Chalon coming down behind a new cruiser. Aye, he was. He explained that he had stopped at Chantier Naval, but was shocked at their prices. He and a carpenter he found over at the Yacht Club had made the repairs for a mere pittance. We showed him about the *Hebe* after which he invited Eunice and me over to meet his wife. We found them both delightful and had a couple of cups of Nestle's coffee and a pleasant chat. They were leaving just as soon as their pilot arrived. We wished them Godspeed. They left shortly after. We never did see them again, but often wondered about them — a nice couple.

The dockmaster had arranged to get us a frogman who made his appearance about mid-morning. He was a little fellow about 5'5" and apparently had been afflicted with polio at one time, but this didn't seem to bother him once he got into his wet suit. Down and under he went and in about fifteen minutes he came out to confirm that the propeller was like a pretzel and that the rudderpost was bent at the collar. We must have crashed with some power because that post is a good three inches plus of steel. But then forty-plus tons of boat can have quite a kick. He suggested pulling the propeller underwater. This didn't reason too well with me. I asked if he could cut a wedge from the top of the rudder so that it could pass the fairing piece. He took another dive and reported that he could and would return in the morning.

The dockmaster had another idea in the form of a contractor friend of his who owned some cranes. The friend came to see me with his proposal — he would bring his biggest portable crane down on the quay, lift us out, etc. For the life of me I could not see us swinging from one of his cranes. To begin with, he was inexperienced with marine work. The whole thing was just too hairy.

There were no yards in Lyon, nor, to our knowledge, are there any today, so we had no choice but to go along with M. Guy, the frogman. The insurance company in Rotterdam thought well of our plan and gave us their approval to proceed on whatever decision I made. They gave me the name and address of their agent in Marseille whom we should contact when, as, and if we got there.

Two more yachts came down this morning and tied up. One was the new power cruiser from England. She evidently had been having all kinds of trouble from the day she left the yard. The guests aboard were terribly aloof. The other boat was a yawl from Germany chartered by Herr Nierich, an automobile dealer in Hanau near Frankfurt. Accompanying him were a divorced photographer and a rather large scientist. The two men were very talkative, the divorcée was very quiet and quite obviously more interested, for the moment at least, in her camera.

Our friend from the Beaujolais came down the steps to visit us with her cute little grandson. She was even more attractive than I had thought. Maybe I had too much rainwater in my eyes up there in the hills. Anyhow, she was stunning and modishly arrayed in excellent taste. This time we got her name — Mme. Raymond Dechelette. Her given name was Nicole. She and her grandson thoroughly enjoyed a tour of *Hebe* and all of us enjoyed Nicole. She gave us many suggestions as to where to eat, where to shop, and things to do. She left with a promise to come back again.

Sheila and Ivan are late sleepers, and we did not expect them until around cocktail time. We had done all we could about the boat for the time being, so Lil, Eunice, and I took the cable car up to the basilica. It's quite a ride, popular with tourists and natives alike. The basilica is an attraction in itself. It is huge, fairly new, and with a tremendous bluestone gravel plaza overlooking the city, from which you can see forty or fifty miles in every direction. Below was *Hebe* looking like a toy. Down the hill to the south about half a mile, there are fabulous Roman ruins with two amphitheatres in amazingly good condition. One is so good that it is being used regularly for the theater festival held each year that packs in crowds from far and near. We took the cable car back down and then did a small tour of the old city, which is on the west bank. Fabulous old homes, tenements, and artists' flats everywhere, with little cafes or bistros here and there. Some of this old architecture is beautiful. What a shame we have so many glass cubicles in our modern cities today—even in France. So back to *Hebe* for a bath and into our drinking shoes.

When our friends arrived it was decided that we would go to La Mère Guy for dinner, a restaurant recommended by Mme. Dechelette. Ivan had heard good things about this place, too, but had never had the opportunity to go there. So off we went up the steps and over the bridge to get a taxi. The place is situated downriver on the west bank almost at the confluence with the Rhône. One taxi would not take five people so Ivan and Eunice went ahead and Lil, Sheila, and I followed soon after. The driver seemed to understand our directions and hustled us down the river, ultimately pulling into a rather seedy-looking place. Lil suggested that she and Sheila go in to see about our table while I paid the cabbie. I got out and looked about. Surely, I thought, something is amiss. As I entered the place I knew right away. Lil was remonstrating with the madam that there was a table reserved for Monsieur Latham—and getting nowhere. I interrupted to inform Lil and Sheila that this was a whorehouse and suggested that we get our fannies out of there. The madam smiled in agreement, and we walked out. A patron of the place came charging out and offered to drive us to La Mère Guy. We accepted.

When offered some money for the ride, the gentleman declined and apologized for our embarrassment—a pretty nifty touch, I thought.

La Mère Guy is elegant, with flowered borders around the lawn, the immaculate kitchen is on the ground floor, and the dining room above is posh. Ivan and Eunice were sitting at our table and were convulsed when they learned why we were delayed. Come to think of it, we were convulsed, too. Everybody laughed and laughed and laughed. The food here was absolutely tops—delicious—the service exquisite, but maybe just a shade under Paul Bocuse. When you get up to this level of excellence, it is really nit-picking. Bocuse's place probably has a little more going for it in atmosphere and personal flair. The wine selection in either place is nonpareil. We had a most delightful dinner. The check we will not discuss, advertise, or release.

As we were settling up, Ivan asked the maître d' if he knew of any hot spots. We got a car to take us to the recommended spot, but we were early. This place did not open until 2:00 A.M. A clique of customers was lined up, all in their fanciest finery.

In the still of the morning (after all, it was past midnight), some of the tones I heard sounded spooky to me. The characters at the door were like horses champing at the gate waiting for the bell. And when the door opened, they charged in just like horses. When the excitement subsided, we walked in. It was a typical "joint," a bar to one side, a few booths opposite and a dance floor to the rear with a phonograph bleating away with discordant music. The lighting, of course, was dim, but not dim enough to hide the truth—there wasn't a true female in the whole g.d. joint except my bride, Sheila, and Lil. Some people find this fun, but not Eunice, Lil, or I. There is no use in describing some of the conversation or demonstrations that occurred; it would add nothing to our lives. We knew that Ivan would not be offended, and so we departed, waving to him wrapped in the arms of Sheila as they danced in the dark. Outside I felt cleaner and better and so did two lovely women. We marched through the narrow streets, steering for a bright loom of light, and finally found a taxi.

At breakfast the next day, a rather nice-looking young man came aboard and introduced himself as Bill. He was well turned out in blue slacks and short-sleeved clean white shirt. He spoke with a cultivated accent, obviously a product of English public schools. He had our name down pat and seemed to know something about us, which I thought strange. He said he was in the yacht-ferrying business and was looking for a boat to take either north or south. I asked if he was a Rhône pilot. He answered he was not qualified. We offered him some breakfast, which he politely turned down. He wondered if he could be of any assistance. We explained that we were expecting a diver and could not determine our next move until he completed his work. Just then M. Guy arrived with all his gear, air tanks, underwater light, hacksaw, and a coil of nylon rope. All of us went out on the *quai* to watch. He got into his wet suit, strapped on his air tank, fashioned a bridle out of the nylon, which, he explained, he would use to hold him against the current as he worked. The light was plugged into shore current and taken below with him. We could not see much of the action, just a blur of light. He was under for three hours with only an occasional respite. But he did the job, by gosh, and I let go a big sigh of relief—not just because the job was done but also because that nice little guy was out from under and out of that strong current.

Lil and Eunice had decided to go to Paul Bocuse's for lunch. I figured I had better stick around. With the rudder now free, Armand went below to recouple it with the port rudder. Looking at our topsides, I noticed some pretty bad black spots, evidently oil or tar smears. Bill said Shell sold a good product for this kind of job and took off to get some. Damn good stuff, too. Armand, Bill, and I did the topsides all around and the *Hebe* looked lovely. Nicole stopped by and said she'd be back later when I told her the girls were off to Bocuse's. The dockmaster came to tell me I had a phone call. It was Kelly calling from Dordrecht. It seemed that *Andiamo* had had an engine breakdown, hence they did not meet us in Nancy as we had anticipated. Some barge offered to tow them down the Rhine to the yard at Dordrecht. That must have been a hairy ride! Well, anyway, Kelly wanted to know if it would delay us too much if we lay over another day until he and his bride could get to Lyon. "Tom" I said, "what the hell is another day. Come ahead."

Late in the afternoon the girls returned raving about their lunch and making comparisons with La Mère Guy. Paul seemed to be the winner by one *Ah!* Then Nicole stopped by with her *mari*, Raymond. He remained on the *quai*. He said that if he as much as put his hand on our rail he would get seasick. So we passed the drinks ashore and I joined him — a very nice fellow. Sheila and Ivan arrived wearing two tremendous heads and gasping for medical aid, which was administered immediately. We had quite a party going. Nicole and Raymond asked us for dinner at their home tomorrow evening. This was a most unusual compliment coming from French people so soon after meeting. We were honored and accepted. Sheila and Ivan planned to return to Geneva in the morning, that is, if they could make it.

The best laid schemes o' mice and men gang aft a-gley, so they say. Ours certainly did. Bill had gone off, the Dechelettes had gone home, and we were discussing plans for dinner when I received another phone call. It was Kelly again. It was just too much trouble getting their schedule readjusted and they had decided to visit locally where they were, okay? What could I say, but okay, Tom, we'll see you back in New York. This put everything into focus for me. I asked our dockmaster to call Madame who was in charge of the Rhône pilots to send a pilot over for interview — we could leave early in the morning. Then I paid our bill. Back aboard I announced the change in plans and poured a drink and said that just as soon as we settled on a pilot we could go to dinner. Eunice telephoned Nicole to give her the change in plans and apologize about dinner tomorrow. Nicole was so sorry but understood, perhaps we should stop in St. Tropez where they would be vacationing. Just then two pilots appeared, one the husband of the Madame boss and the other Robert Boudrant, who claimed he had been Irving Johnson's pilot. He seemed pleasant enough, talked knowingly, and if he was good enough for Irving Johnson he was good enough for us. I explained that we wished to go only as far as Avignon. This was all right with him. We made a deal and he was to be aboard at 4:30 tomorrow morning.

Why a pilot? The Rhône is a wild, rough, and powerful river, particularly at this time of the year when the rains from the Saône watershed are swelling the river and the melting snow and ice are still coming down the Rhône and the Isere. Altogether, currents as high as ten knots can be encountered. A novice can do it, but it is not advisable. The pilots know where the rapids occur and the changes that take place with respect to shoals and currents. Going downriver with the current under the boat plus the speed of the boat for steerageway, even an auxiliary sailboat attains fantastic speeds. Coming the other way, north, presents another problem, that of breasting against the current. A boat must be able to do ten knots or better. Of course, later in the year when the river usually is lower and the currents less, it is a mite easier, but the shallows become an increasing hazard. The French have been working on this for some time, dredging and constructing huge modern locks and hydroelectric dams (barrages) all of which are helping to make the Rhône more manageable. At this particular time in 1969, three of these locks had been completed, with two more planned and under construction. Today, these have been completed and the river should be considerably easier to navigate in either direction, but a pilot is recommended for those who are making a first trip. Oddly enough our insurance rates were not affected whether we used a pilot or not. It would be advisable to check this out.

Eunice, God bless her, got Armand and me up at 4:00. We did not disturb Lil. It was pouring. We had breakfast and waited, and waited. I was about to give up and proceed alone when Robert made his appearance at 4:45. It was still raining but had let up somewhat. Robert was dressed in a brownish lightweight suit and had no foul-weather gear, not even a hat. Had he eaten? Yes, some bread. Would he like eggs, coffee? *Oui,* he would have eggs, bread, and wine. Eunice was startled about the latter. I reminded her that he was French and it was not up to us to change his morals, mores, or what have you, so long as they did not put us in jeopardy. We outfitted him in my foul-weather gear. Armand had his set, and I only a thin raincoat. So we took off in the dim light. When all the lines were in and the fenders pulled aboard, I went below to the saloon to watch and wait for any calls from the bridge. We were moving along at a great pace, going under the many bridges at what seemed like breakneck speed. Of course, this was exaggerated — we were doing maybe seven to eight knots actually.

We would pass through five locks before reaching Avignon. The first two, La Mulatiere and Valence, are relatively commonplace and so we will not comment further on them.

In almost no time at all, we passed La Mère Guy's and Eunice and I salaamed. Under the railroad bridge at La Mulatiere where we joined the Rhône, and then under several bridges and past four ferry stations. The rain stopped and we went on deck just as we came to Vienne where there was a boat tied up to the *quai* on the east bank. Robert called attention to it—she was Irving Johnson's *Yankee*—with her masts nestled down similar to ours. It was too early to visit—6:45 A.M. It reminded us, though, that we had missed that well-known restaurant, La Pyramide. On we rushed past the confluence with l'Isere at Bourg-les-Valanece, past Valence to Le Pouzin where there is a large dam *"barrage de Lorio"* and the entrance to the *"Deviation la chute de Baix-Logis-Neuf,"* a canalized section of the river leading to our first of the new, big locks. It was 2:12 and we had covered 90 miles in nine hours. It had been raining off and on, but now was only misting. Robert beckoned for me to take the wheel. After some difficult explanation, I understood that the pilot is not responsible for a yacht while entering, in, or leaving a lock. I wondered if any pilot would accept full responsibility for damage at any other time when a boat was under his con. We entered the lock, which was open and displaying the green light. This was the newest of the three locks we would go through today, and it is worthy of some description. It is 195 yards long, 13 yards wide and the fall of the lock is 14 + yards. It can be compartmented into three sections and, like the next two, there is absolutely no turbulence on rise or fall. The bollards fall or rise with the level of the water in the lock. We made fast to a bollard with one spring line. Incidentally, yachts are allowed to use these locks provided they are in company with a commercial vessel. We were alone, but allowed to enter because there was a commercial boat below wishing to come up—fair enough. As we started down, I noticed we were developing a list. Looking about I saw that the "floating bollard" was stuck. I yelled at Armand and pointed. He quickly cast loose, and we straightened out and dropped down with no fuss whatsoever and with no line—very impressive—a neat piece of engineering.

Robert took over as soon as we were out of the lock. It is 13 miles to the next lock at Teil (de Châteauneuf). The rains came with a vengeance. Robert would not eat, except hunks of cheese, a piece of bread, and wine. It wasn't long before he called for brandy. In spite of the foul-weather gear, sou'wester, and a towel around his neck, he got soaked and, I would think, blinded—also cold. Eunice disapproved, but I gave him brandy anyway and stayed on deck to keep him company if nothing else.

It was impossible to see any scenery, but he saw whatever he needed to see and was able to get us to the next lock, which is longer than the first and has a drop of over 60 feet. Again, I was given the con. This time the bollard floated down with us. It was as smooth as silk.

From Teil to the next and last lock de St. Pierre at Bollene is twenty-two kilometers or a mere fourteen miles. We made this trip with no incident.

Many of the boat people refer to this last lock in awe as "the cathedral," and when you get down in it, you'll see why. You can damn near hear the organ music as you look up the nave. As an integral part of this, there is a large dam that provides water for the Donzere-Mondragon hydroelectric power station. The approach is made through the feeder canal, which is 390 feet in width and has a depth of 18 to 22 feet. The lock itself is 633.75 feet long and 37 feet wide. The drop or fall is 26 meters or 83 feet, which is made in just a little over six minutes, and you don't feel a ripple! At the time of our visit, this was the deepest single-lift lock in the world. Up till now the weather had been so lousy that the girls stayed below, but they came on deck to get a better view of this wonder. The weather was trying to cooperate as if to celebrate our arrival. So down we went just as advertised, and when out and clear Robert took over the wheel.

From here to Avignon is just under thirty-three miles. With the current under us it should not take too long. The girls stayed on deck drinking in clean, fresh air, while Armand and I had a couple of beers and Robert took a "sip" or two of wine. Occasionally we would pass ferry stations. It must be great sport steering one of those across against this current. Just above Avignon, there is a big bend in the river and I thought for sure we were going to hit the bricks as we came slewing around, but Robert knew what he was doing and straightened the boat out nicely. We went boiling down and, just above the bridge at Avignon, he turned *Hebe* in a sharp swing to port and brought her alongside a large white barge that had been converted into a restaurant. He held her ahead breasting the current until Armand and I could make her secure with our new mooring lines. He explained that the proprietors were friends of his and he would arrange for us to stay here for a few days. It was now 8:50 P.M. and he was in a hurry, he wanted to catch the next train back to Lyon for another job he had signed up.

Ahead of us a few yards, there was a new town *quai* or dock under construction. Across the river was a small restaurant set in a grove of trees. It looked like a hamburger or pizza joint. What to do now? First things first, I said, and we all had a snort. Then we tidied up and had dinner. It had been a long day. No one had trouble sleeping. The noise of the rushing river and some of the debris such as uprooted trees clunking against our hull was bothersome at times.

16

Avignon to the Med

The noises of the river against the hull awakened me early. I got dressed as quietly as possible, but, I thought, if everybody could sleep with all the banging I heard, my little rustling in the galley and on deck could hardly disturb them.

Everything looked in good shape on deck. We had double springs and double bowlines and sternlines out, and they were okay. The fenders were in good position and were not working or chafing. All the disturbance was from the river, swollen by the tremendous amount of rain over the past several days plus the usual runoff from the mountains. Evidently, there had been flooding in many areas, for the river was full of broken and twisted trees with some part of a barn or shed roaring by now and then. When any of this hit, it caused a helluva clatter and, from below, it seemed we would break loose at any moment. With everything in good order, I went over the rail to the barge and down the gangplank to shore. The day was clear, but it looked as if it would be a hot one. Walking downriver I noticed to my surprise that Avignon is a walled city. On the way, nestled against the wall, was a wine shop looking somewhat like a cave, but it was not open. Just below the famous bridge, I found an open gate into the city and entered. It was early, but people were beginning to emerge here and there to start the day's routine. It was fascinating. After about an hour of rubbernecking, I retraced my way to the gate and back up the river and found the wine shop open. I had had some Nescafe, but nothing else, and so seized upon this opportunity to have my "juice." It was delightful and cool inside, and the couple in attendance was cheerful and attractive. I was proffered a sip of this and a sip of that—what a beautiful way to start the day! I bought a couple of bottles of a very good Côte du Rhône and returned to *Hebe*. Everyone was up and Eunice was making breakfast—a red-letter experience for me in itself. Lil was looking like a morning glory as usual and all ready to pack for the Prieuré, a resort across the river. After breakfast, Armand and I went on deck to sit and look around when, lo and behold, who should swing a leg over the rail but Bill in his usual spotless white shirt and blue slacks. He said he had been to Marseille and had made a date for us at the Chantier de St. Nicolas. I asked him how he had found us. He said that he knew we had to stop here to let Mrs. Clarin ashore. This bird was a puzzlement to me. I thanked him and said he could stay aboard and proceed with us but with no pay. This was okay with him.

Inasmuch as Bill seemed to know his way around, we sent him off to fetch a taxi for Lil. While he was doing this, Armand and I tried to find a pilot for the trip down to the sea. There was none to be found, maybe tomorrow the head pilot would be back.

Bill returned with a cab and we loaded Lil's gear aboard and then helped her up and over the rails. What a great sport she was! We made our sad *adieus* and off she went to the Prieuré across the river. We would miss her.

Eunice, Bill, and I had lunch aboard the barge. It was clean and pleasant, but did not offer too much in the way of food—sort of like a high-class pizza joint. However, it is a good spot to be when you are forced to wait for a pilot or for the river to subside. By now, the new town dock must be in operation providing more accommodations for yachts.

After lunch, Eunice and I strolled into town to inspect the palace of the popes and all the other beautiful old buildings of the Holy Roman Empire and the very extensive and beautiful gardens. This whole setup, however, is most interesting and, judging from the throngs and tourist buses, a very profitable attraction.

Above and beyond the palazzi, there is a tract referred to as the gardens. My God, it's mammoth, beautifully tended, and with little chapels here and there. Eunice had a romp with her camera. We continued on up until we arrived at a low wall. From here it was a sheer drop down to the street below. We could see the bridge pushing out into the river as far as it goes, the barge restaurant moored along the shore, and behind it hidden from view was the *Hebe*. We probably could see the Prieuré if we knew where to look. Looking up river along the wall I noticed an aperture that turned out to be the entrance to some old, uneven, stone steps that dropped into nowhere. We decided to explore them. The steps go down at a very steep angle and at irregular intervals there are switchbacks or zigzags in directions. It seemed we never would reach bottom. When we did, surprise! We came out of the wall just a few rods from the barge.

Back aboard, I got out the charts of the river and studied and restudied them. If we couldn't get a pilot I figured I'd better get to know this river, at least on paper.

In the morning, Eunice and Bill went to inquire about a pilot at the navigation office. The pilot had returned, but he would not work for us because we had used a Lyon pilot. Eunice tried to explain in her best French that we would have been happy to use an Avignon pilot but they were not available in Lyon. Here in Avignon, she would not think of a Lyon pilot but only an Avignon pilot. On and on to no avail. Her French was impeccable, but she could not break through French logic.

It was blowing like mad today, and the sky was a beautiful clear blue—not a cloud to be seen. A mistral was blowing down its favorite route, the Rhône valley. The air was dry, a great day to do some varnishing. Bill thought this was a good idea, too, and, to my surprise, he pitched in with gusto. We were doing a big job in the saloon on the bar and cupboards when we heard a familiar voice say cheerily, "Good morning, everybody!" It was Lil. "What a pleasant surprise," I said, "did you get a little homesick?" She squiggled up her nose at me as if to say nonsense. "Okay, lads," I announced, "you don't need me, I'll be off with the girls." And off we went.

We pointed out to Lil the steps we discovered, but advised against our making the climb. Instead, we walked on down to the little wine shop where we did a little tasting, then on down and through the gate into the city. We ambled over to the museum, lovely. Then up into the large and charming square opposite the Hotel de Ville. There were many pruned plane trees under which tables and chairs were arranged, with people sitting, chatting, drinking, and generally enjoying life. It was very picturesque. We selected a table and melded into the scene. In the background, above the babble, we could hear a pleasant soprano singing a French ballad to the accompaniment of an accordion. The voice made its appearance from behind a kiosk, all contained in about a 5'2" strolling chanteuse with long dark hair, dark eyes, wearing a long striped, pleated skirt, and playing her accordion. How lucky can a guy get, sitting in the midst of all this *and* in the company of two lovelies! We broke the spell and ordered a double, extra dry with a twist, "One each, all around." Following this we ordered lunch, a salade Niçoise, and, of course, a spot of wine. Lillian told us about the virtues of the Prieuré, how magnificent it was and how delightful the clientele—how prominent some of them are. She invited us to dinner and, would we please, bring Bill along, "He's such a nice boy." This seemed like a good idea. Later we broke away reluctantly from our relaxing surroundings, and continued with a tour of sweet Avignon. Lil had been here years before and wished to refresh her memories. We went past the popes' palace safely; that is, no one grabbed her physically, or even spiritually, insofar as we could notice. Maybe it happened up in the gardens to which we repaired. Wherever we stopped, Lil seemed as happy as an expectant mother. Her eyes sparkled at every little step. It must have been a remarkable experience she was reliving and "he" must have been someone special. But you don't intrude on this kind of thing.

We moved on up through the gardens to show Lil the view from the wall. She pointed to where the Prieuré was snugly nestled. Back on down to town where we got a cab to the barge. Lil dropped us off and we promised to be on time and properly attired.

Stepping aboard *Hebe,* I looked up river. Coming around the bend, roaring down on us was a flotilla of small yachts being led by Robert, our pilot! He shouted "You still here?" and laughed as they went tearing by. Judging from the size of the craft he was steering, he wasn't getting much wine or brandy, I thought. This was my only consolation.

Bill said he could not join us for dinner because he did not have a tie or jacket. I offered to equip him. He laughed, saying that he was much too large. However, my jackets fit him to a T.

The Prieuré is a beautiful hideaway. The buildings date back at least 400–500 years. The clientele evidently is loyal and returns every year as faithfully as the swallows of Capistrano. There is a large swimming pool, there are at least six excellent tennis courts. It is possible to rent horses for trail riding. Aside from this, you sit on your duff and wait for the dining room to open. Dinner itself was ordinary. The wine, of course, could not be tampered with in the kitchen and was excellent. Bill seemed to have a pretty good knowledge of wines, which is a common trait of the English public-school product. And speaking about Bill, he revealed that he was hoping for a ten percent cut on our yard bill in Marseille. This really was no surprise to me, but I said nothing. I wondered what else he was up to. Openly, I wished him well in his project. Everything considered, we had a delightful evening. We left at a proper hour, thanked Lil profusely, and wished her a happy stay at the Prieuré. I did not think she was too happy to see us leave.

Eunice, Armand, and I breakfasted the next morning a bit latish. Bill was not aboard as usual. He always was up and away early, and when he returned he never wished breakfast, maybe a cup of tea on occasion. He certainly kept me guessing.

Armand said that he had been talking to the ferryman yesterday, and there was a chance he might pilot us downriver. This seemed encouraging and we asked Armand to seek him out. With Armand gone and Eunice doing the dishes, I got out the Rhône river charts again and pored over every legend and mark carefully until I thought I had them clear in my mind. Armand returned to report no success. Bill appeared about mid-morning with no comment with respect to his activities. I announced that *Hebe* was going downriver tomorrow at five A.M. and that any and all who wished to leave were free to do so. They looked at me in wonderment, not believing me at all. I repeated the edict. Slowly, they began to sense that I was in earnest. When Lil made her appearance and I told her the news, they got the message. The two boys started to grin and then said "Okay, cap, we go." Poor Eunice looked somewhat alarmed, but she married me for better or worse and decided on the latter. Lil said she would miss us. So we checked everything out. We had plenty of everything aboard. Our batteries were up, the generator was functioning. Now it was just a question of waiting. Bill had heard that a boat without a pilot had gone aground. I retorted that I had heard the same report, and if true we would wave at them as we went by.

Eunice, Lil, and I took off, first for a bite aboard the barge, and then for a last tour of the town. We ended up in the gardens and this time we introduced Lil to the steps. Back at the barge we said goodbye again—this time for real. We promised to give Lil a call when we got back to New York.

Morpheus dashed my good intentions: instead of waking before five we slept until seven. What the devil, we didn't have too far to go anyway. We started breakfast and got the boys up and about. Armand started our engine. We wanted it to warm up a bit to lessen any chance for it to stall, which would be disastrous in the strong current against us. Armand went aboard the barge and handed over the sternlines and stern spring. We singled up on the bowline and doubled back so we could slip it as we moved ahead. The mistral was still with us, which insured a clear day. "Okay, gang, here we go!" I put her ahead and she started to move as Armand released the forward spring. He jumped aboard and ran to the bow as Bill took in the spring. We gave her a little more throttle and *Hebe* moved with power.

Armand slipped the bowline, and we advanced the throttle to full. All hands were ready to leap into action if need be, and as we came abreast of the new *quai* I yelled, "Hard aport" and prayed. The current grabbed *Hebe*'s bow and swung us around heading downstream as I pulled back on the throttle and brought the rudders amidships. We all let out a big sigh of relief; the first maneuver was successful. Dead ahead to port was the bridge, we were tearing along at a tremendous pace. With the engine slow ahead, we must have been doing ten to twelve knots. Armand stationed himself ahead of the wheel to port, and Bill took a similar station to starboard. Even though I had memorized the charts, Eunice was with me to check off the various landmarks as we passed and to check the chart if I had any question. The bridge de Beaucaire at Tarascon, where the canal du Rhône à Sète meets the river, is seventeen miles below Avignon. We made it in just under an hour! There were occasions on the passage between Avignon and Arles when we had to be making eighteen to twenty knots over the bottom. It was hairy, and there was not much time to remark on the scenery. Traffic was not too heavy, thank the Lord. What there was helped us, particularly the big oil tankers coming up river, which gave us a good fix on the channel. Occasionally we would encounter rapids, and we would steer for the big, black eddies. There was a lot of steering to do, but it worked. The two lookouts were a great help in pointing to obstructions or white water ahead. The chart indicated construction work on another big chute, lock, and hydroelectric barrage similar to that at St. Pierre. When we espied it, I was confused because it was so huge and seemed to reach everywhere. The boys found the buoys for the chute and directed me to them. Giant dredges were at work in the dam area, and mountains of sand and earth from the bottom were being piled up on the west bank. Nowhere, thank heavens, did we see the boat that was reported to have gone aground. It must have been a rumor. As we came around a slight bend, we could see Arles silhouetted against the sky, a pretty sight. We passed the yacht club and went under the bridge. Below this point, the river widens and the current lessens. Off to our left immediately below Arles is the canal d'Arles à Bouc, which is another route to Marseille. We opted for Port-St-Louis-du-Rhône, twenty-five miles below. Eunice took the wheel from here on down to the port. There were whitecaps everywhere as the wind piped up. Off to our right was the Camargue, famous for its white horses, a special breed of small bulls that takes part in the Provincial bull fights, and the annual pilgrimages to Les-Saintes-Maries-de-la-Mer in honor of the gypsy patroness Sara. Off the mouth of Port-St-Louis I took the wheel again. We made a wide turn a little below so that we could come in against the wind. Inside the small harbor, we tried to come alongside a small blue boat on the east side of the basin. I could not manage and asked Armand to take over. He went outside, made a turn, and came back in alongside the *Pharo,* an ex–British Admiralty pinnace built in 1947, and we made fast. The trip downriver had taken 4½ hours. We had averaged better than eleven knots. It was 12:48.

Our bow pulpit extended over the stone *quai* and made a very convenient platform for going ashore or coming on board. Bill went ashore to get information, Armand tidied up the cupboards in the saloon, and I prepared lunch. At 1:30, Bill was back and we sat down to eat, or rather, they sat down to eat. I had prepared a tremendous salad full of fresh greens, tomatoes, etc., that Eunice had purchased in Avignon, and, on the side, there was a basketful of French bread, lots of butter, cheese, and wine. I never saw food disappear so fast. They asked for more before I sat down. Fortunately, Eunice had some "Laughing Cow" cheese aboard, that's France's answer to Elsie — *"La vache qui rit."*

We left the boys with the dishes and foraged into town with the dogs. The wind was blowing so hard it straightened the curly hair on our poodles. Dust was flying everywhere. The lower part of town offered nothing attractive in the way of victuals or wine, and everything was expensive. In the upper town, conditions were somewhat better but still not attractive. The restaurants were not at all inviting. Back we went to the lock area to speak with the lockkeeper. There was someone on duty twenty-four hours a day; but it was blowing so hard they would let no vessels through until tomorrow at the earliest. The drop here, incidentally, is between fourteen to sixteen inches, the difference between the sea level and the river at this point.

There were a couple of stores on the side of the harbor opposite from where we were moored. We inspected them with little satisfaction. We did get some bread though. I told Eunice we would have to smuggle it aboard or Armand would have it gone before breakfast. Back at the harbor side we inspected the little blue boat we tried to moor close to on our first try. Close up, we discovered it was a jousting boat with a platform in the bow for the contestant and colorful designs painted along the gunwales. Gee, this took me back to my early teens when we used to joust standing on the gunwales of a canoe. Jousting is a popular sport in the area. Over near the entrance to the lock, there was a man casting his net, with admirers looking on. We joined the coterie. This fellow was a big Corsican, judging by his accent, and he was a pro with that net. It would go out over the water in a perfect circle, drop flat, and go under. Slowly, carefully he gathered it in and up, and after each cast, he had a catch — flounder, it looked like. Tiring of this, we crossed the lock and ran into our German friend Nierich who had just arrived. He had left Lyon ahead of us with a flotilla and one pilot. We had not seen him on our journey downriver. He explained that they had holed up a few times, and altogether it was not too good an experience. The divorcée was still with them but evidently not very happy about her lot from what Eunice gleaned from her. As I recall, I never did see that gal smile. For her future happiness, I sure hoped she was more attractive to mankind on her skis. Nierich wanted us to go to dinner with him. We thanked him, but said we had toured the area and found nothing enticing. We went back aboard, and I prepared dinner, which was good, I thought. Bill and Armand devoured everything in sight which was not necessarily a compliment. Bill was wound up tonight—perhaps he was excited over the approaching kill—I didn't know, didn't care, and went to bed to escape.

In the morning, it was still blowing but it seemed to have abated somewhat. At least the lockkeeper thought so and opened the gates. Some vessels moved in including *Hebe*. Trailing us was Nierich, and all of us had to wait until he got his papers cleared.

The gates opened, and we paraded out single file. Eunice was on the wheel. When clear of the canal we gave her compass courses to steer and this seemed to please her. This also freed us to test our gear. First, the compass seemed to read "good" on all bearings. Next, the centerboard. It was jammed, probably the cable was crossed. We would pull the coverplate in Marseille and take a look. Then we tried the Penta Autopilot—the clutch slipped. Everything considered, we were in good shape, we had a good helmsman, the weather was good, the wind was dropping, and the sea was beginning to take on gorgeous color. We had passed Port-de-Bouc, that huge, smelly Shell refinery, and the world looked pretty good. The coast looked good, too. There were beaches here and there and little inlets which the railroad leaped across on arched bridges to disappear into tunnels to prepare for the next leap. To seaward, we could see small islands and an occasional freighter making its way to port.

Nierich, who was attempting to follow us, signaled on his horn for us to slow down. We were down to 1150 rpm, and he still could not keep up. We dropped astern, threw him a line, and towed him the rest of the way at between four and five knots, which reminds me that we also tested our Harrier speed log—the batteries were dead. You can't win them all, so they say.

We were closing in on Marseille. Off to starboard were several small islands and rocks. Ahead, high on a mountain, we could espy what looked like a glistening tower. Then to our right, we saw the Château d'If made famous by the Count of Monte Cristo. Ahead of us now, the breakwater brimmed into view, behind which we could see the cathedral and the huge shipyard. As we approached the entrance we noticed an attractive beach tucked back in a small bay beyond the eastern point. This disappeared from view as we made our way in. We passed a small boatyard on our right. Bill said that this was not where we were going to be hauled. We kept on. To our left was the entrance to the commercial harbor and yards. Up on a promontory to our right was the Institut Pasteur, beneath which was a yacht club followed by the Chantier St. Nicolas, a very compact yard. Overlooking this, facing seaward, high on another promontory, were the pink barracks of the famed Foreign Legion. Directly opposite to our left was the Fort St. Jacques. High on the mountain top, the glistening tower we had seen at sea was the Basilica de Notre Dame de la Garde, the patron saint of seamen. This is the entrance to the old harbor, our destination. Strewn on the rocks along the shore were nearly naked women, looking for all the world like a herd of seals basking in the sun. Ahead of us, all I could see were boats. Never have I seen so many clustered together. Bill said, "Wait till you get to Cannes." We slowed down, moved on in past the fishing fleet, and then to the Société Nautique Marseille, the yacht club. Boats everywhere, how in the hell do we move in. We cast Nierich adrift, and I asked Armand to take over from Eunice. A man was signaling frantically from the end of an outside slip. Armand and I said nuts to that and we moved closer to the clubhouse. Armand spotted a hole and made for it. You have to give the devil his due. This guy was just great when it came to power. He knew every trick, even though he could rack the bejesus out of an engine. He moved steadfastly in and when we reached the last line of yachts moored stern-to against the *quai*—he spun *Hebe* around and started back in between a large 72-foot "starboat" and another hull. The crews of the two yachts couldn't believe their eyes, but they sprang into action, eased off on their bowlines, and fended off as we came in. Bill tossed a sternline ashore, which was caught and made fast. Armand then moved ahead slowly as we payed out the sternline. He gave me the wheel and ran forward to the pulpit, signaling me to stop. Bill made the sternline secure, I kept it taut with the engine. Armand dropped down, slipped a bowline into a mooring buoy, came back up, and made fast. We eased astern slowly and made fast, this time with two sternlines. The dockmaster had made his way back from his original station on the outside and was not at all pleased. Armand was indifferent to his cries, and he and Bill put out fenders on both sides. Everyone about cheered *Bravo!* I, too, congratulated Armand. We put our gangplank ashore and made peace with the dockmaster. Across the harbor was the Hotel de Ville, a magnificent piece of work and the only building along the waterfront on that side of the harbor not destroyed by bombing in World War II. Except for the clubhouse we could see nothing on either side except yachts and masts. It was 2:00 P.M., Friday, June 27. We had covered a lot of miles since leaving Amsterdam, almost an even thousand, but like the Argonauts, we were not quite halfway there. About 1,200 miles separated us from our goal, Piraeus, the port of Athens. We had come "overland" through congested rivers and canals and had passed through 186 locks. Ahead lay open sea and the chance to do some sailing along the French and Italian coasts and across the open sea from Sicily to Greece.

17

Marseille

Originally it had not been our intent to stop at Marseille or even come this way. Eunice and all our friends told me that this was a horrible place, full of sin, vice, and shocking underground machinations. Never having been to any of these parts, it was easy to accept their opinions and, consequently, I was prepared to dislike the city.

Friends who had been in and out of here during World War II for the most part had nothing good to report. It should be obvious, therefore, that I was not in a receptive attitude upon arrival.

Frankly, Marseille attracted me from the first day to the last. The streets were well paved, which is more than can be said of New York City, for example. There were many parks and gardens, well tended, the city transportation was well organized, buildings were in good repair, commerce evidently was active, and, above all, the people we saw were active, content, and pleasant. As with any large city, I am sure that vice abounded, but it certainly was not overt to us or the casual tourist.

My first impressions were good and remain so. The white-slave traffic is controlled from here so they say, and 40,000 girls are shipped out of here annually, mostly to Arabic and North African countries. It may be so, but neither I nor any of us saw anything to support this supposition. Marseille reputedly is also a focal point of the drug or dope trade. Maybe so, but we were not accosted or approached in this connection, nor did we ever see anything suspicious relating to this kind of traffic. Mind you, I am not saying that it is not so, merely, that neither I nor Eunice nor our friends ever saw anything related to this.

The city had suffered from World War II, but most of the important landmarks had survived. It was strange that the entire waterfront of the west side of the Vieux Port had been bombed out with the exception of the Hotel de Ville. On the other hand, the east side of the port was not harmed at all.

Eunice went ashore to shop, but all stores were closed until 4:00. From now on, we'll have to get used to this siesta time. Bill went to the Chantier. I stepped on the gangplank, which was not secure, and I went ass-over-teakettle into the drink and came up underneath an open sewer. My glasses broke in two, but I was able to catch one half of them. Armand was on the *quai* in hysterical laughter, and this undoubtedly was the highlight of the trip for him. A crew member from *Attila,* the "starboat," reached in, and, with some help from Armand, fished the gangplank out and then me. I was covered with slime to put it politely and could not pull myself out. I stood on the *quai,* sodden and dripping and smelling something awful. "That was pretty funny, wasn't it, Armand?" This set him off in giggles again, and I joined him. With the gangplank back in place and *secure* I got back aboard and rushed for the shower. About a half hour later, I thought it was safe to come out. It was like skunk piss, all-pervasive. I could smell myself for days in spite of after shave, cologne, and everything else I could find.

Bill returned and told us we were to be in the yard at 7:30 A.M., July 3. I finished a "straight-boy," a neat shot of whiskey, and made lunch with what we had left — bread, butter, cheese, salad, and wine. Customs came aboard to inspect our papers and passports. He hadn't seen a *triptyque* in two years, and said we would have to go to the Custom Centrale to get a "Green Card." Noting that our destination was Greece, he told us we could buy duty-free ship's stores in transit and consume them aboard. Scotch, for example, was only 80¢ a bottle. He would send a friend to take our order.

At four, Eunice and I went ashore on separate errands. Eunice wanted to go to Havas Voyage, our mail drop here, then to a bakery, butcher, and Farmers' Market if she could find one. I had to find some thin sheet metal, bronze, brass, or copper. We had inspected the main and mizzen, and the sheaves, or pulleys, were "frozen" against the masts. We figured to remove them, grind them down a shade, then to open the mast slots a little, and to face the inside surfaces with metal. Seemed to me this should have been done in the first place. I scoured around with no luck. Eunice fared better. She found an excellent butcher where she bought pork chops. In the same area, there are many shops and a couple of blocks away there was the open market. Of passing interest, the whorehouses abut this area. I guess they feel they must be near a market. Sort of reminded me of Amsterdam, where they operate just a couple of blocks from the stock market. This area is located a few blocks back in from the head of the harbor on the east side, if you are taking notes.

We had a very late dinner for us. Hundreds of people paraded by along the iron fence to see the boats. Heaven knows there were many to look at. I fell asleep.

Evidently our conversation of the last couple of evenings began to sink in, for Armand was up early to hose and scrub the deck, his first offense since leaving Amsterdam. Bill went to get bread and milk. Everybody sat down to breakfast at 8:00. The bread was disappearing rapidly. Armand said, "Mrs. Latham, you want some bread?" "Some, Armand, I haven't had any." For the rest of the day, each of us did his own thing. Armand worked on the generator and later got all the rigging up on deck. Bill sanded and varnished. Eunice went to market and purchased one leg of lamb (*gigot*) at $4.60. per kilo (not cheap), two kilos of *boeuf* for *Bourguignon* from her new butcher, who fed the pups some scraps. At the market, she got fruit, lettuce, carrots, potatoes, and string beans. I found a chandlery up the street and made a friend of Juaneda, who attended me. He was able to direct me to a machine shop where I finally got some sheet brass that filled the bill.

On the way back, I passed a sidewalk café beyond the chandler's, about two blocks from the Société, and heard someone hailing me. Turning about I saw Nierich drinking at a table with a group. I joined them. His wife had arrived last evening, and she was there — quite nice — along with other members of his crew. Eunice came by loaded down like a peon's burro, net bags hanging from each shoulder and one in each hand. I went to help and introduced her to the group. It turned out that the divorcée photographer and Eunice were taught by the same English teacher in Hamburg. The two of them took off for some sight-seeing and picture-taking. Eunice got some very good pictures of the Saturday afternoon jousting. There is a special lagoon for this off the harbor between the Chantier and the Société Nautique. Nierich was going to have his masts stepped tomorrow, using the club's crane, and suggested that we do the same. We would use our own wishbone I informed him.

There had been a lot of guys promenading dressed in sailor's white. On the way back to the boat I asked a group of them where they were from. They were from the *Empire State IV,* the New York State Maritime training ship on its annual summer cruise. Some of them had been racing with the French using French sailboats. There would be another race tomorrow. I never did hear how they made out, but I do know they banged up one of the boats pretty much.

That night after a hefty *boeuf Bourguignon,* Armand was in an expansive mood and prated on for hours. I fell asleep.

The next morning, Bill slept late. He must have felt secure in the belief that his prey was ready for the kill.

Armand and I sorted out and inspected all our rigging and prepared all the gear for stepping the masts. Bill never had any experience with sailboats and was intrigued with the whole operation. When everything was all set, I went to Rafael, captain of the *Attila,* who recruited three hefty Frenchmen to help us lift the mainmast off the chocks and into the tabernacle. Even though it was a hollow spruce stick, it took five of us to lift and set it in place. I fastened all the shrouds to the mast and, when all this was done, we hooked up the jib stay with the wishbone. Armand started to crank in on the windlass. Our audience watched intensely and with some bewilderment as the mast slowly started to rise from the dead. It only took a few minutes and as soon as it was erect I coupled the head stay in place and then Armand and I set to on the shrouds. All hands sent up a cheer. Then we passed the beer. Next the mizzen, which was easy, and then the booms — by gar, she was beginning to look like a boat! We needed some sheaves for the backstays, but this could wait until the chandler opened tomorrow.

The rest of the day was spent visiting and drinking. Nierich stopped by to say that *Sigrid* was all rigged. He was flabbergasted at the progress we had made. Paul Demergy, radio officer from the *Empire State,* came aboard for two or three snorts — seemed like a good guy. Beef stew again, better the second night. Conversation got onto white slavery and dope. I fell asleep.

The next few days were almost phantasmagorical — everybody was doing something, and there was so much to be done in preparation for the haul out come the third. Looking back, it all seems unreal.

Armand had got the word — he was up-and-at-'em early every day with the hose and scrub brush, but forgot to close the ports on one occasion and caught me square in the puss as I was shaving.

We had to get our "green card" and Eunice and I took the ferry across the harbor, walked past the cathedral, and into the city where we found the Customs House. It was beautifully situated with lots of green grass and planting along the way. Getting the card was no fuss once we found the right window. The card is good for six months and if your boat is in French waters beyond this period you are liable for a substantial tax. Then we had to go to the insurance office at Rue de la République 21 where we told our story to a bald woman. I had a helluva time keeping a straight face — try it sometime! She told us to come back at 3:30 P.M. All this time Eunice had been my "seeing eye," so now to the glass place — the glasses were ready and cost seventy-seven francs, not bad. We went to see our friend Juaneda and got a coil of flag halyard and four sheaves for the backstays at $15.40 — not too bad, really. We went to the Chantier to look it over. There was one railway with a 55-foot English power yacht hauled at the head of it.

The owners were aboard and invited us up the ladder. Their names were Joan and Jim Nolan. We liked them immediately, and they seemed to respond. Jim knew something about us and had heard we were coming in. They were living aboard but he advised us to get a room for Eunice at some nearby hotel because the facilities are neither convenient nor pleasant. After looking over the facilities, Eunice took off in a hurry to find something, anything. The toilets were stand-up jobs. I never could master the technique of these torture chambers, and there was no need for Eunice to learn. After shopping around, Eunice reserved a room at the Pharo up the hill from the Chantier across from the Institut. It was a pleasant white stucco job with green trim and a terrazzo terrace. The propriétaire was a jolly fellow, whose usual attire was shorts and sandals, no top. He was quite a character with the unusual name of Théâtre.

Joan was a most attractive Canadian and Jim was a Royal Naval reserve from Liverpool, where he had been quite prominent politically. They had decided to "pack it up," bought the *Mynonie* and were on their way to Malta. They had two English lads aboard who were working their way "out" for food and smokes. The *Mynonie* had had a brush with a barge and a lock and suffered rudder and propeller damage. They were running low on money. I assured them they were not alone.

We called on the manager at the Chantier, a M. Henri Porta, one of the most dapper men we had met. To the day of our departure, I never saw this guy in the same outfit except once — different cuff links every day, clean shirt, polished shoes, immaculate hands. I watched him climb over boats, dash here, there, and everywhere about the yard — he never seemed to get soiled. He told us (in French, he could speak no English) that Irving Johnson had been in the yard a couple of times.

Bill had called Dartmouth and got a job to take a boat to Mallorca via the outside route. He would leave us after we got back in the water. In between times, he did some neat splicing aboard the *Hebe*.

We went back to the insurance office, this time sans bald-headed woman. A Mr. Couture, a Lloyds inspector, would be at the yard July 3 when we got hauled. Now to Havas for mail.

Eunice discovered some Greek ruins and that made her happy. She also took me one gray, muggy day to prowl around the ruins of Abbaye St. Victor high on a hill overlooking the port. This is worth a visit. It goes back to the second century.

Late in the afternoon of July 2, the rigging was complete and Eunice ran up the Storm Trysail burgee and then our house flag. It was a great occasion. Bill prepared dinner, *poulet provençal,* and served a Château Mouton Rothschild '55. Either he was closing in on us fast, or he was going to get a fat fee on his new job!

Came the dawn July 3. We were up early and raring to go. From the waterline up we looked like a million dollars. Word came from the yard to delay our arrival until 9:00. We prolonged breakfast. Finally we three men got the *Hebe* out from the snarl of boats and clear in the channel. We were off the entrance to the Chantier at 9:15. There a couple of men in a rowboat guided us into the cradle, which had been let down. They took great pains not to bang the hull. Methodically they got all the legs locked and braced against us, using pads between us and the legs. They gave the ready signal ashore, and we started to move in jerks. Eunice said, "My God, they'll shake us out of the cradle." Everything went well, and in a few minutes we were high and dry with our pulpit protruding over *Mynonie's* stern. Porta and Couture were watching from the office steps, both of them immaculate, looking more like bank officers than what they were. A ladder was placed against our rail, and one of the yardmen clambered up and made it secure. He smiled at us but offered no comment. I scampered down to get a look. The yard foreman was a good-looking Maltese, who was as strong as an ox. He offered his hand as big as a prosciutto and smiled a golden grin as he greeted me with *"Bonjour, monsieur."* His crew sprang into action immediately, washing the bottom, which was quite foul — with bare spots showing here and there. The starboard propeller looked like a pretzel, the shaft support was askew, and obviously this meant our shaft was bent. No wonder we made a clatter and shook. The rudder post was bent at the collar where it emerged from the hull. What a whack we must have taken.

Eunice tossed down *Hebe's* plans and I went to join Messrs. Porta and Couture, who had signaled for me. We went into Porta's office. Couture introduced himself in English. He was affable and outgoing. "The first thing," he said to Porta, "is to have a drink. *Monsieur,* break out the Scotch!" Porta obeyed and produced an almost-empty bottle for which Couture chided him in a very friendly fashion. He turned to me and remarked that conditions must be better aboard the *Hebe.* I called out to our boat and asked for a bottle.

Marseille 153

After a drink, Couture talked in French with Porta. Evidently everything was arranged, and he then addressed me in English. Repairs would cost somewhere between $900-$1100, the yard would work all night, and we should be back in the water on the fifth. In Europe, insurance claims are not paid until both the yard and adjustor make their reports. They would expedite their reports. In the meantime, *monsieur,* you pay in cash. All very good, but how do I know the claim will be honored. Please sir, have no fear, I have ordered M. Porta to proceed. Next, Porta wanted money. I said that I would cable our bank Monday. Porta wanted me to use his TWX now! I explained it was too late. Then tomorrow. No, tomorrow is a holiday — the fourth of July. *Qu'est ce que c'est,* fourth of July? All this through Couture as interpreter. What a shame we didn't have a tape. It was agreed that I would TWX the bank now so that it would be there first thing Monday. Couture had to go. We all shook hands and I went back to the *Hebe* to find that Eunice had gone aboard *Mynonie* via the pulpit. I joined her there and reported the events to all. There was nothing to do now but sit and wait.

Back aboard the *Hebe,* Porta climbed up for a visit. Eunice gave him the $2.00 tour. He was very impressed with the joiner work and the condition of the boat throughout. He couldn't believe she was eleven years old. He clued us in on Couture. He had been the Commodore of the Esso tanker fleet, was now retired doing insurance inspections and adjustments for Lloyds, and was highly respected. His wife had a ship-chandlery business handling all the needs of the big ships in the commercial harbor. Not a bad combination. Porta invited us and the Nolans to be his guest for lunch on the fifth at the Société Nautique. He then went over the side looking just as immaculate as when he arrived in the yard that morning.

We had lunch aboard. Then I helped Eunice move up to the Pharo, where I met the owner who was working with his flowers. It looked like a pretty nifty spot, but not the George V, mind you. After some errands in town, I stopped at Le Bon Vin located diagonally across from the Société. This had been recommended by the Nolans. I bought some thirteen percent table red. We had it for dinner. Le Bon Vin had our business for the duration!

A message was delivered from the office, which read that a Mrs.

Clareen had called asking us to call back that evening. Eunice phoned after dinner and came back with a big grin. Lil was homesick and was arriving via train on Monday! She would have come immediately, but she had paid up till then.

July 4th was spent leisurely by us, but not the yard workers. Everything was hustle and bustle. After all, what did this day mean to them. Couture stopped by to say all was going well. Porta was in a new outfit. We had a snort. The Nolans came aboard for a holiday drink. Eunice had arrived with a funny story to relate — a Koenigsburg beer truck could not get by on a turn in the road in front of the Pharo because a parked car was in the way. Four Legionnaires spotted the situation and lifted the car out of the way!

Bill scrubbed fenders, while Armand and I started to sort sails. Armand's hands were covered with oil and grease. I dressed him down for this, and he took off in a pet and went swimming.

Zamit, the Maltese foreman, was exhorting his crew to get on with the job. New cutlass bearings had been installed for the shaft, which, together with the prop, were still in the machine shop. The rudderpost had been straightened and this was being installed. Everyone was impressed with the rudder construction and assembly. It certainly was a unique piece of design, machine work, and assembly. The bottom had been scrubbed, sanded, and painted. We had discovered a leak in the cabin top over the saloon, and a man was busy removing the old covering and preparing the subsurface for new material.

An English cruiser about 45-50 feet had arrived with a crew of two Englishmen. They had an exclusive on some kind of stabilizer for medium-sized craft that they planned to demonstrate along the Med coast. Bill announced that he was joining them in the venture and moved aboard. It was evident to me, then, that his scheme of getting ten percent out of Porta had failed, and that his job of taking a boat outside all the way to Mallorca was a phony. We thanked him for all his help and wished him well in his new undertaking. He did have dinner with us that day, however. I cannot quite describe the feeling, but somehow I felt much better after that.

Saturday was a beautiful day weatherwise from dawn to sunset. It was clear, not too hot, and with a little breeze. All the work except the saloon top had been completed and we were ready to be launched on schedule at eleven. Eunice arrived with our mascots about fifteen minutes earlier. Launching was fun—the usual slow start, then the sudden rush ending with a big splash. Two men in a rowboat came out, picked up our trailing lines and rowed them to the outer *quai* only a few rods away. We were pulled over and made fast. All very neat!

Porta, natty as ever, drove the Nolans and us to the Société where we met Mme. Porta, a charming and vivacious hostess. There was a very pleasant guy by the name of George in attendance as interpreter. They thought of everything. We had an aperitif in the lounge after which we repaired to the dining room, which affords a magnificent view of Vieux Port. Our hosts suggested *loup* as a first course. This is the best fish in the Med as far as we are concerned, except swordfish, which can be found only on occasion. We had a delightful white wine with this. Steak was our main course with a good red wine. Altogether it was an excellent meal and the conversation, in spite of a language barrier, was stimulating. Coffee and a very heady liqueur were served in the lounge. Porta told us that his company had designed and built the interior. They did a good job. All of a sudden it occurred to me that Porta really was Alec Guinness playing a well-rehearsed part.

We were whisked back to the Chantier for a sea trial. Our host had to stay in the office, and Couture was not on hand. Mme. Porta, Joan and Jim, George, Zamit and another worker, Armand, and even Bill climbed aboard. We tooled out past Château d'If and around the islands and back. The trial was most unsatisfactory. The starboard engine vibrated like a maiden's heartthrob. I told George we would not accept the job or pay. Socially, however, the day was a huge success. *Hebe,* in spite of the vibration, nicely conveyed the sea's motion, and Jim, who steered her back into the Chantier, was surprised at how well she responded to throttle and rudder.

That evening Eunice and I went to a seafood restaurant opposite the *quai* at the head of the harbor. It is called Deux Soeurs. It is good and not too expensive. Eunice had *bouillabaisse* and I had *crevettes* with spaghetti on the side—$8.50. Incidentally, I cannot take raw garlic at all and only a little of it cooked. Here and at all the restaurants we sampled, unlike American-French and American-Italian saloons at home, the garlic was subtle. Much to my astonishment the *bouillabaisse* here is made without garlic. The garlic is served in a kind of roux, more like mayonnaise, in a small dish with a warning that it is *"très formidable!"*

The following day was stinking hot. Eunice moved back aboard. The Legionnaires whistled at her from up on the cliff, which, I'm sure, was good for her ego. Armand came down with the "bug." Bill was now installed aboard the demonstrator with his compatriots. I went to visit the Nolans to copy their weather-station list. At about 4:00, we got a wind shift and the temperature dropped. Joan and Jim want us to go to Malta. They're going broke. "Cheer up, friends, we're getting there fast."

Monday, July 7, broke cold, gray, and raining. Our prodigal guest was due to arrive today. Porta sent word for me to come to the office. As usual, he was in another outfit. I wondered if he were like my late grandpa who always had his complete attire labeled for each day of the week. He was not too happy looking. With the help of a secretary I soon learned why—it was Monday morning and he had received no money from my bank. I was astonished at first and then broke into laughter. "They're not even out of bed yet," I said. Porta smiled sheepishly—he had forgotten about the difference in time.

The weather cleared in the middle of the day and Eunice made her way to the Gare St. Charles and met Lil. Armand was delighted to see her; now he could fold the flag with her every sunset. The Nolans came over to meet Lil and have a few bombs. She was ecstatic to be back aboard *Hebe* and was thrilled to see her rigged and ready to sail.

The eighth was a traumatic day. Couture, a mechanic from Lloyds, a compass adjuster and his two boys, and the impeccable Porta stormed aboard for a second trial at 8:00 A.M. We went out near the islands and tried the engines at various rpm. Couture and his mechanic agreed that the vibration was excessive. Porta was unhappy about this and also because the money had not yet arrived. We returned to the yard, dropped Porta, Couture, and mechanics and went back out to work on the compasses. I couldn't understand a damn word but they put on a great show. The adjuster used only the sun. He gave us deviation cards on all three compasses. The steering compass was damn good, but the one in the saloon sure had a wacky card. It was pretty near the bar so I guess that explained it. With this work completed we returned to the Société Nautique alongside *Attila* and received a warm welcome from the dockmaster, Rafael Navarro and his crew, and others. Things at the yard were humming—there was no more room for us or the Nolans who had been launched and were tied up near the fishing fleet halfway in toward the club. It was cheaper for them there.

After lunch, we were boarded by two burly men with huge tool boxes. They informed Eunice that they were from Perkins and had been requested to examine our starboard engine by their boss, a buddy of Porta's. There was too much going on around here, so the girls fled. When the maulers got all through they tried to explain something to me. All I could say was, *"No comprendez vous."* We were at an impasse. Suddenly I got an idea. I walked down the gangplank, gave them the international "come-with-me signal" with the index finger, and led them into the office of the Société where there was a very attractive chick who could speak my language. I explained the problem to her. She got the gist and discussed the situation with the two mechanics and broke into laughter. She turned her pretty face to me to say that there is nothing wrong with our engine, these men think somebody is playing funny with them. That's what I told everybody in the first place, I said. We shook hands and left the office. Eunice, who had returned, went with me to see Porta down on the outer *quai* at the yard. The former director was there, *ancien directeur,* who understood English. In plain words, I told Porta his g.d. scheme didn't work. This upset him visibly, and he took the offensive and said my money had not yet arrived. Furthermore, he went on, after figuring everything out we owed him an additional $1500.00. At this point, if there had been a ceiling, I would have hit it. I stared at him in cold anger, inwardly wanting to punch the bejesus out of him. Finally, I blew! I ranted and roared, stomped my feet, and fanned my arms—"By God," I said, "You pulled one tooth pretty easy, and so you figured you could extract a couple more. How in Christ's name, in one day, with all the figures before you, can you calmly change your price one and a half times!!? All I'm getting around here is a royal Bulgarian screwing!" With that I turned to Eunice and said if Porta wanted any pictures, I'd draw them. I disappeared up the hill, out of the yard and back to the boat. Porta said to Eunice *"Mari* is very stern." Eunice replied, "So am I," and left.

The *ancien directeur* came aboard not long after to express concern about the whole situation. He did not like Porta's approach, but did try to explain that there had been considerable overtime in getting us out. The starboard-engine affair he would discuss with Porta. He invited me to the club for an aperitif. Perhaps some other time, I said. The wind had started to blow and I wished to check our lines.

During the night all the boats moved and strained as the wind held. Eunice woke me to say someone was aboard. I got up and found the biggest damn cat you ever saw prowling around the saloon looking for food. He sprang up the companionway before I could get to him. I closed the companionway, which I should have done in the first place. Cats are a problem at night in this area and in many other ports in the Med.

In the morning it was blowing a full mistral. The boats were riding well and all lines about us seemed secure. I asked Rafael how long. He gave a noncommital, Gallic shrug and guessed maybe three days, six days, nine days.

That afternoon Eunice and I went to see M. Théâtre at the Pharo and told him we wanted to call my office in New York. He was delighted to be of service and got on the horn. The French telephone service is beyond description. If *I* had tried to put the call through, undoubtedly I would still be there. Théâtre had a way with him, and in five minutes he announced with a moonlike grin that my secretary was on the line. I asked her to go downstairs to the bank to find out what had happened re our message and I would hold. It was a good connection. She was back within five minutes and reported that the bank had received the TWX first thing Monday morning and had cabled the money immediately to the bank and account number specified. I told her we were moving with the speed of the Argonauts, to give everybody a fond cheerio, and that maybe Ulysses would get home yet.

We walked down to the Chantier and announced ourselves at the office. Porta and I were cool. Eunice explained about the money.

She suggested that perhaps he should check with his parent company and we left.

The next day it was blowing harder, too hard to go outside the harbor. Our scheduled trial was postponed. Porta sheepishly reported that our money had been received on schedule but that the cashier had not credited the proper account. We shook hands.

Hippies from all lands seemed to be everywhere today, many of them traipsing by the fleet. An attractive girl from Short Hills, New Jersey—not a hippie—came aboard for a visit and a couple of drinks. Armand and I painted the lifeline stanchions and did a little varnishing. After colors and the ritual of folding the flag by Lil and Armand, the Nolans came aboard for a few drinks. They went back to *Mynonie* for dinner, and Lil, Eunice, and I went to the Calypso out on the *corniche* for dinner. This is an excellent restaurant and expensive. We had some hors d'oeuvres, *bouillabaisse,* and two bottles of rosé—$32.00. I fell asleep at dinner and it took an hour to wake me. The waiters and clientele apparently enjoyed the scene, I was told, and everybody had a chuckle. We had been in Marseille now for two weeks.

It was still blowing hard in the morning. Eunice took pictures of Rafael Navarro and his crew at their morning *casse-croûte,* best described as a Mediterranean coffee break. The poodles, of course, were there begging. Our Storm Trysail burgee was cut to ribbons and Lil was able to mend it, I don't know how. We decided not to fly any burgee until the wind let up. Nolan stopped by, and as we were chatting Porta came aboard with a Perkins mechanic. We started the engines, moved out into the waterway, and held a test inside the harbor. At 1500 rpm there was ten percent more vibration on the starboard engine and as the rpm was reduced the vibration abated, but there was still more than on the port engine. Perkins said it was not the motor. Finally, Porta said he would guarantee the job for as long as we were in French waters. It was his thought that the vibration was coming from the new bearings, and the vibration would reduce as they broke in. As we moved back into our slot, Porta was very impressed with the handling of the boat and remarked he would get no business if all yachts were so well handled. We went below for drinks during which Porta invited all of us to lunch for cous-cous, an Algerian specialty. That afternoon Lil and Eunice went off to see the Château d'If. They said it was terribly rough and wet outside. At 5:15 I got the weather report; seas 18 + feet, wind 45-50 knots.

We had dinner aboard with the Nolans as guests—roast chicken flambé in cognac—not bad for home cooking.

It was blowing like stink the next day.

The Penta man came aboard and fixed the clutch on the autopilot. He took the compass to fill it with fluid. Juaneda and his wife came to visit. Porta came by and said he would settle for another $560; this in addition to the $1,500 he already had. This was a damn sight better than his previous demand, and we gave him a check. Eunice gave him a Kennedy fifty-cent piece on a chain that pleased him. He would 'phone Couture about our settlement and come back.

At noon Porta picked us up, then to the Nolans, and away we went to Bosphore, a restaurant in a large new building facing the water on the other side of the harbor. Porta's wife was there and had obtained a table. She looked beautiful and had just come from a fresh *"coif."*

Cous-cous is difficult to describe. It has a semolina base but contains many ingredients. The way they make it here was indescribably delicious. We ate as if there were no tomorrow—róse with our lunch and Beaujolais with a delightful cheese to top it off.

After lunch, we went to see the Basilique Notre Dame de la Garde high on the mountain top. Eunice was in Mme.'s car, the rest of us went with Porta. It is an interesting climb up through the narrow, winding streets. The view from the top is magnificent and today you could see exactly what "seas, eighteen feet high" look like!

There are chapels around the compound in which sailors for centuries have placed votive offerings. The first church was Byzantine and was built in 1214. The huge present church was built around it and was started in 1864. Porta bought some candles and lit them. He knelt in a pew and prayed for our safe voyage. Outside we took pictures of everybody braced against the wind.

Mme. had to leave and she bade us all a friendly *adieu.* She drove Eunice back to the boat, and Porta drove the rest of us down to Société Nautique.

About five o'clock Porta returned to say that Couture must see me right away. Eunice and Lil had gone somewhere with Joan, so I told Armand I'd see him when I got back.

The drive out to Couture's was interesting to me from a sight-seeing point of view. Conversation was impossible. Porta smiled occasionally. The Couture place is on the eastern edge of the city. It is a stone building situated on a corner and built probably in the Victorian period. Inside it was cool. Couture was his usual ebullient self and led the way out into the back garden — a lovely spot, well landscaped. At the back of the garden there was a long, one-story building that served as his office and from which his wife ran her chandlery. I was introduced. She had an interesting, intelligent-looking face, a very pleasing personality, and her conformation was excellent, I thought privately. She assayed me quickly and evidently gave Couture a secret nod of approval. Obviously, this was the purpose of the visit. Mme. led us to a corner of the garden near the house where there was a flagged terrace with attractive wrought-iron furniture. We would have Scotch? *Oui!* Couture asked if I played bridge to which I said yes. Good, very good, we must play sometime. Mme. and Porta conversed in French, Couture and I in English. Another Scotch? *Oui, madame!* After some comment in French from Mme., Couture asked if we were free for dinner. Yes, we were available. Good, Mme. Couture and I will meet you at the boat at eight-thirty. Until then, *adieu*. So back into Porta's car and back to *Hebe*. I thanked Porta as best I could and said I'd see him tomorrow. We shook hands.

The girls and Armand were glad to see me back. I explained my absence and said we were going out to dinner and asked how much cash we could muster. Lil, Eunice, and I pooled our resources, which seemed to be enough. Also, I had some traveler's checks in reserve. As I was sitting on deck waiting, Rafael came to say good-bye. Good-bye? Where are you going?! A friend had phoned from Toulon to say the mistral had stopped over there. He was going to sail tonight at ten with some friends for a few days. His crew could take care of *Attila*, his boss was in Indianapolis, it would be okay. We shook hands, and I wished him well. I sent Armand over to *Mynonie* to tell them we were leaving for Saint-Tropez at 6:30 tomorrow and went below to announce the news to the girls, who were delighted.

Couture appeared promptly at 8:30. His wife would wait in the car; she did not like gangplanks. Yes, he would have a Scotch, which we had. Then to the car and the women hit it off beautifully from the start. We drove out the *corniche,* past the Calypso and just before the arched bridge over an inlet we turned off and dropped down into a quaint fishing village, Vallon des Auffes. Here at water's edge was the L'Épuisette, an elegant restaurant known especially for its seafood. Couture showed me around and, in particular, the wine cellar that was situated just above the high-water mark.

Dinner was very, very good, the service was pleasant, and the pace leisurely. The wine came at frequent intervals. We told the Coutures that we were departing at 6:30 tomorrow, and they were determined to make it a smashing going-away party. Both the Coutures were facile in either English or French and the two of them were full of the *joie de vivre*. At 68, he really was a hummer. We concluded dinner at about eleven-thirty and I was ready for the sack. The Coutures had other ideas. We were whisked off to a private, all-night drinking club, Chez Maurice, located somewhere in the heart of Marseille near the opera. There was a variety of entertainment, both professional and amateur, and everyone was obviously enjoying it. The Coutures had a regular table there. We entered into the spirit of things and contributed to the entertainment as well as the decibel level. Mme. not only was attractive but could sing and did. Couture knew everybody. We did not leave the place until after six that morning, and I had not fallen asleep! Back aboard *Hebe* about 6:30 A.M. Armand, who was on deck, looked somewhat relieved. He thought the underground had swallowed us.

The engines were warming up. We had said our good-byes to *madame* and thanked her for an exhilarating evening (they had paid for everything and would not accept a *centime* from me). Couture had left her in the car and was now aboard with the suggestion that we have a Scotch for the voyage, which we did. Jim sent one of his boys over to say they were leaving. We sent back word we would catch up with them outside.

Finally, Couture went down the gangplank and stood on the *quai* watching us as we eased off on our lines. Mme. joined him. As we moved out slowly through the mass of yachts, we waved back and forth until we turned into the waterway.

Gad, what an experience these past several days! I went below and got into my sailing togs. The girls changed also and prepared breakfast, which was served on deck. The day was pleasant, the wind had dropped out completely.

To this day, we exchange Christmas cards with the Coutures. We have not heard from the Portas. As to Bill, the last we heard, he had fleeced his compatriots of all their cash and jewelry and was on the "wanted" list in two countries.

Outside the breakwater, *Hebe* was skipping through the abating sea like a goddess.

As to my falling asleep, I discovered that, by reducing my daily prescription of digitalis one half, I could stay up with the best of them.

18

The Med

Past the Château d'If, around the point, and way up in to our left, we could see the arched bridge of the *corniche* below which we had had dinner last night. There was no wind, the sea was getting flatter and flatter, and assuming a glassy look. *Mynonie* was not in sight in the haze ahead, but she had a half-hour lead on us. Armand was at the wheel. With the point abeam, we laid a course to the Îlse de Hyères, which would put us well off Toulon and save some time. I flaked out on deck.

Some hours later, Armand awakened me; he had spotted *Mynonie* a couple of miles closer to shore than we. Her course indicated that she was making her way out and would meet us at about the Hyères. Abeam we could see Toulon, and sitting on the glassy sea like a bunch of ducks were the first French America's Cup challenger and her fleet. Obviously they were not going to get any experience here.

At about 11:30 we were abeam of *Mynonie,* but separated by about a half mile. The Hyères looked to be a very attractive and unspoiled group of islands. It would be fun to go back sometime for a closer inspection. One of these islands to the eastward is a famous nudist colony, Île d'Levant. At this time, at least, no one was permitted ashore unless starκ naked. Cameras were taboo. The reason for the latter, we discovered, was that the locals didn't want any competition with their postcard business. *Mynonie* and *Hebe* tooted in derision as we passed the island.

The day was hot. We had had some salad and beer for lunch, and now we were closing in on Saint-Tropez as we angled for the point. The harbor is around the point and a short way in. As you enter between the breakwaters there is a long *quai* to port leading all the way into the inner harbor, which is a fairly small circle and chock-a-block with yachts. Off to starboard, inside the entrance, there is a large marina. I chose the *quai* to port, and we made fast alongside about a quarter of the way in. *Mynonie* pulled in behind us. Our engines had run cool. The vibration in the starboard engine, we must confess, had improved but was still there. It was 5:00 P.M.

Eunice and Lil went ashore to the saloon Nicole had mentioned as a possible meeting place. The bartender said that the Dechelettes were at their cottage, "Les Carroufiers." Eunice telephoned. Nicole was delighted to hear from her and said they would be down as soon as possible. The poor souls looked for us in the inner harbor—no *Hebe;* then over to the marina, no *Hebe;* looking across the maze of boats one of their guests espied a ketch over at the *quai,* it was the *Hebe.* They had to backtrack all the way around. Nicole was so relieved to find us! Raymond, as usual, would not step aboard. We gave him a deck chair and passed the drinks over the side. Nicole was as charming as ever and her guests, M. and Mme. Gigou, were great fun. Monique spoke English, was from Marseille, and was a grandmother eleven times. It was hard to believe. John was a silk merchant from Lyon. He couldn't speak a word of English, but he and I had an intuitive understanding and got along magnificently. While we were reminiscing and chatting, Niarchos came in with his character boat (a boat with unusual features), *Kyma,* and requested us to move. This I refused to do. Jim Nolan did, though, and moved alongside us. There was plenty of room for *Kyma* ahead of us, but he wanted to be at the gate.

Nicole arranged with Eunice for the three of us to go to her place tomorrow for a swim and lunch. They left soon after, and the Nolans joined us for a quick tour of the immediate area.

On the surface Saint-Tropez is a posh place with many watering places around the inner circle of the harbor. The outdoor cafés were crowded with what appeared to be young dilettantes spoiled to the eyeballs. Their flashy and expensive runabouts were parked all over the place. I'm sure there must be some substance to this place, but it is not apparent to uninformed drop-ins such as we.

There was a big, good-looking, shiny black yawl in the inner harbor named *Illusion*. Shades of Vinny and Bus! They told us they were going to leave in the morning at seven. I wondered, what with all this ass-end mooring they do over here.

That night it was early to bed. There were at least three of us who couldn't wait!

The next day was one of those you read about—clear blue sky and beautiful Mediterranean Sea. There is no way to describe this blue. There is no color-card for it anywhere. Whatever the poets have said about it is true.

We ambled around a bit, saw a few topless gals at the yacht club, which did nothing for me. The *Illusion* was still there trying to get her hook up. It was entangled with a number of other anchor lines. A diver had been sent for, and Armand told us later that she finally got away at about two in the afternoon. In behind the waterfront, we came upon some very interesting fish markets but we made no purchases and after some picture-taking went back to *Hebe*.

The Nolans were up and about, and we gave them a rundown on our plans. We thought we could get away at three. They had no set plans and said they would wait for us.

The Dechelettes' cottage was delightful and Nicole was as cute and as excited as a bride preparing her first meal as she hustled about. A side porch covered with an arbor was set for lunch with shiny silver, beautiful china, and exquisite linen. We were getting red-carpet treatment, for sure. Nicole said we were to go to their daughter's home for a swim and then come back to lunch.

We walked up the road, maybe a half mile, to find a charming one-story mansard-roofed villa overlooking the bay. A large swimming pool adjoined the house on the bayside. The daughter was in her bikini and she was built like a slim Diana, goddess of the chase. Her husband, another silk merchant from Lyon, was in his shorts and greeted us with a smile and a wide open bar. What a paradise. We hustled into our swimsuits, and when I emerged from the house, there was Nicole in a green bikini as negligible as her daughter's, lying on her side wearing a mischievous grin. My bride is wonderfully endowed and I love her dearly, but this creature was built like a lithe Venus, and she knew it, and taunted me with her every gesture or move. I whispered to Eunice that I couldn't stand all these riches and temptations and dove straightaway into the cool water to slow me down! The others observed and smiled knowingly.

We enjoyed several dips, drinks enow, and fun conversation. It was as if we had known each other for years. At a signal from Nicole we got dressed, bade our hosts ta-ta and repaired to the Dechelette cottage.

Lunch consisted of the best *salade Niçoise* I ever have had, enough excellent wine until Bacchus himself wouldn't have it. There was fresh French bread, lots of rich butter, and finally we were served fraises, etc! I used my best and only French in praise of the repast — "c'est bon, c'est magnifique, tres bon" — which sent Nicole into gales of happy laughter. She knew what I was trying to say, but I guess it was my accent that tickled her. It must have sounded like some of our soldiers who returned from France and said such things as "Monsoor." What's the difference, so long as everybody is happy.

Time was flitting. Nicole suggested we stay in Saint-Tropez for a few days. Lil and Eunice looked at me hopefully. I hoped I did not offend and told Nicole that we had disappointed many people and that we must be going. However, I suggested, why don't all of you join us for a sail to Cannes. This fitted in admirably with everybody. Raymond had to meet their daughter Florence, a champion equestrienne on the French Riding Team, who was coming from Paris by train. Voilà, he would meet Florence at the Gare, and then they would meet us in Cannes. All of us pitched in with the dishes, got everything tidied up and then Raymond drove us to the *Hebe*.

We were late, and the Nolans were anxious. They said they would take off immediately and try to hold a place for us in Cannes.

There was a light breeze when we got outside the breakwater, and we made sail for the first time. Everyone, even Armand, was delighted — so was *Hebe* as she picked up speed and spanked her way along.

The lazy motion of *Hebe* soon got to Nicole and we bundled her up in a blanket in a prone position on deck. She was a great sport about it. Jean Gigou sat in a deck chair like an admiral on leave, enjoying every moment and casting a wink at me now and then. Monique, always with a cigarette hanging from her lips, marched to the bow and back several times to report we were doing well. We tried Mr. Moto, our automatic pilot, and he steered very well. It was too good to last. The wind pooped out and we had to drop sail and power the rest of the way.

There are two harbors in Cannes. The new one is very posh and expensive and too much exposed to the broiling sun. We entered the old harbor, which was just as crowded but more attractive. Jim Nolan was moored stern-to on St. Pierre *quai* just inside the breakwater to the left. We dropped our hook and backed in alongside. Raymond was there with Florence. She came aboard while he drove over to the Majestic Hotel where Ivan and Sheila were vacationing to report that *Hebe* had arrived. When he returned, we set up camp on the *quai* and staged a cocktail party with canapés served from our back porch. After an hour or so of fun and games, Jean and Raymond announced that they had reserved a table for dinner at a restaurant, La Voile aux Ventes, across the *quai*. How nice!

Our table was situated outside on the sidewalk facing the harbor and the outer breakwater. Raymond had selected the wine and the menu with great wisdom. It was a huge success. As our table was being prepared for coffee and liqueurs, a bomb burst somewhere out on the water and a beautiful array of colored stars appeared overhead. I said to Eunice across the table, "My God, they've thought of everything!" Nicole asked what I had said. She roared with laughter when she heard and passed the word to Jean, Raymond, and the others who thought it pretty funny, too, and they howled with glee. Raymond, through Eunice, thanked me for the compliment, but explained that this was Bastille Day!

The fireworks display went on for at least an hour. Crowds of people were assembled all along the shore and on the breakwaters. It was the most magnificent show of its kind we had ever seen.

When it was all over, Eunice noticed that Pompi had disappeared from his tote bag, and she became alarmed. Raymond said don't worry, we will find him. They were back in about fifteen minutes. There were three other restaurants on our strip. They went into each one to inquire and at the last stop found Pompi, strutting back and forth on the bar having a helluva time being fed and petted by the customers as he marched by. When he saw Eunice, he froze and then leaped into her arms in one grand swoop.

Parting is such sweet sorrow, but part we must. I attempted to get the check, but it had been paid. Raymond would not accept anything. He said we had paid too much in Marseille. And so, at 3:00 A.M. with warm embraces and handshaking we said, *"Adieu."* Wonderful people!

At about eleven in the morning Eunice and I stumbled over to Ivan's hotel. Evidently, Sheila and he had been on a binge too, and were just getting up. We had a pick-me-up on the terrace by the pool and arranged to take them and the kids out on the boat for a sail and a swim. There was no wind, but we did go out and tool around and had a magnificent time swimming, diving, drinking, and swapping stories about last night. Our swimming ladder was a bit too mobile for Lil but she managed. The Italian Line *Raffiello* cruise ship appeared and dropped anchor offshore to debark tourists and to take some away. There is no deep harbor at Cannes, so ships anchor off and use power barges to carry passengers to shore and back.

Back at the *quai*, Jim announced that they would leave for Malta via Corsica in the morning. I told him we had decided to stick to our original itinerary. We had a couple of snorts and wished them Godspeed.

That evening, Ivan drove us to a restaurant tucked away high in the mountains behind Cannes. It is called Georges Ullmer run by G. Ullmer, composer of the popular French song "Pigalle" and is a place most people never get to see. We suggest you try it. The drive is beautiful and "hairy" here and there; the view from the terrace is spectacular. The food is above average, worth the trip.

We tossed the sternlines to the Nolans as they took off in the morning and watched them leave. We hated to see them go; they were good folks.

Customs had left a message for us to appear at the office, so Eunice and I trundled over. They extracted a Custom's fee—for what we still don't know, a charge for water that we had not taken and a wharfage toll, altogether amounting to $20.

We got under way about noon, but not without mishap. Our anchor had caught on something big. We slowly winched it up and found a huge tractor tire wrapped around it. Passing a line through and around we were able to get free in about a half hour. Damned annoying.

There is an island off the eastern end of Cannes. It is possible to go between the island and shore, but we elected to go out and around it. There was no wind. It seemed strange after so much wind at Marseille. We steamed along the coast about a mile offshore, past Nice, and on to Villefranche, where the harbor is simply beautiful. Our navy was stationed here for some time. The backdrop of the snowcapped Alps makes this whole area a stunning picture of contrasts. We approached the shore to find the entrance to La Darse, the yacht harbor. It is distinguished by a high, massive, stone wall with a light on the end of it on the port hand and to starboard a mass of craggy rocks. This is set against a very steep hill with a few small houses tucked in here and there, all of which makes the hole or entrance difficult to find. At night it is easier because in the Mediterranean all lights at harbor entrance and/or channels are red to red and green to green; in other words the vessel's red port light will be matched with the harbor red light and the boat's green starboard light will be matched against the harbor green light.

La Darse is rather small and always crowded with yachts and fishing boats. A work boat for the Marine Laboratory is also located here. We moved in slowly looking for a spot to moor. At the head of the harbor we saw Errol Flynn's big schooner wasting away. We turned around and headed back out to tie up at the *quai* behind a barge immediately inside the harbor. As we sat down to enjoy our new surroundings the port captain, attired in spotless navy tropicals, came aboard and said we could not stay here. After some conversation in French with Eunice, he relented. He seated himself and said to me that he would enjoy a bourbon. I apologized and told him we were out of bourbon. What, an American boat with no bourbon! That's right, no bourbon, how about Scotch. Okay, Johnnie Walker Black. Sorry sir, we have only Johnnie Walker Red. *Mon Dieu,* we must correct this situation at once. We will drink it up, no? So, we had a few Scotches all around. He was a very entertaining man and full of information. We were expecting the

Hasslockers for dinner tomorrow, and I asked for a recommendation. He pointed across the harbor at the yacht club. For lunch he suggested the Âne Rouge at the old harbor in Nice. If we climbed the hill, we would find the bus stop. We could walk along the rocks to the hotel hidden from here by a small point of land. Another Scotch, please. No, he did not need to see our papers. We did not finish the Scotch, but we tried.

In the morning Lil, Eunice, and I climbed the hill and took the bus into Nice. We went to Dave's hotel to learn that he and his party never made it. Then we rented a car and toured the city, which to us was far more interesting than Cannes. The Russian church with its onion domes in gold leaf is very interesting and unusual for this part of the world. Eunice espied a Farmers' Market where we stopped for a tour of all the stalls. These markets are particularly interesting in France. After making a few purchases we tried the Red Ass for lunch—superb.

There are three roads along this coast, the lower or main road, the middle *corniche,* and the new upper *corniche.* We decided to go for a drive and took the lower road to Menton at the Italian border. On the way, we passed through Monaco. It was a good thing we did not come by boat because the tiny, picturesque harbor was chock-a-block. On the return we took the upper *corniche,* which is truly spectacular; not only the road itself with all its switchbacks but also the view in every direction.

Back aboard *Hebe,* we prepared for the Hasslockers who arrived almost on our heels. They were intrigued with La Darse and with the port captain who stopped by to reduce the supply of Johnnie Walker Red. Dinner at the yacht club was unusually good, especially for club food, and the wine cellar was complete. We planned to take off for Livorno tomorrow, so we lingered over dinner and after-dinner drinks. Sheila and Ivan left about 1:00. They would stay in Cannes until the end of the month and then return to Geneva.

According to my calculations we would arrive at Livorno at 6:30 A.M. if we took our departure at 3:00 from Cap Ferrat, which marks the eastern end of the bay in Villefranche. So after a lazy, late breakfast we drove into Nice and returned the car. Then we strolled along the promenade by the sea with Lil and Eunice regaling me with stories of their previous visit here. Rather nice, all this. Lunch was so good yesterday, we went back to the Red Ass and bumped into our port captain. He lived upstairs over the restaurant (probably owned a good hunk of it, too).

We took the bus back to La Darse. Armand was rested, had eaten lunch, and was ready. The captain came out for a good-bye sip and, after a few pleasantries, stepped ashore and tossed our lines to us. With a friendly wave, we disappeared behind the stone wall. At precisely 3:00 P.M. we took our departure from Cap Ferrat.

There was no wind; we would have to power all the way. The sea was flat, glassy. We let Mr. Moto do the steering as we sat in our deck chairs.

We went on watches at 8:00 with Armand taking the first watch. At midnight, when I took over, there was nothing to report. Weather conditions were unchanged and he had not seen any ships. He retired; all was quiet below except for the drone of the engines. All the dials read okay. Along around two, I spotted a light on the horizon off to starboard. It was a ship heading north according to my bearings. Our courses were converging. In a few minutes I could see through the glasses that it was a cruise ship ablaze with lights on every deck. She had the right of way, but I held course to get a better view and when we were about two hundred yards apart I took *Hebe* out of "auto" (Mr. Moto) and spun her in a big slow circle to port and passed under the stern of the cruise ship about fifty yards off. No crew members were in evidence anywhere. She probably was on "auto" and definitely was making for Genoa. Nothing else happened to relieve the monotony. At four Armand came on deck and I tumbled into the sack.

Eunice awakened me to report Armand had a lighthouse in view. I asked, "What time is it?" "It's 0630. He has another light off to port." "That's right," I shouted, "we are off the entrance to Livorno!"

Up on deck I looked about. There were fishermen all around us. The water looked dirty and soon, inside the harbor, the water was foul. There was a U.S. Army freighter being loaded. The crew waved when they saw our flag. We had run up the Q flag which drew no attention from anyone. We cruised slowly up to the head of the outer harbor looking everything over. It was a busy, commercial place, and filthy. We turned back and entered the inner harbor, past the yacht club on our right and halfway in we saw a man on the *quai* signal for us to come in. We dropped our hook, backed in, and threw him a line. When the gangplank was down and secure I went ashore and gave him a tip for which I received a smiling *"Gracia."* Lil got up and was amazed that we were in and secure; she had slept like a log.

After breakfast, no one had come near us; our Q flag was still up, and so I gathered our papers and passports and walked around the harbor to the Customs and Port headquarters. No one stopped me. An officer in his Sunday whites smiled a *"buon giorno,"* that was all. I noticed an officer in shirt sleeves sitting at a desk in a large office facing the harbor. When I asked for the port captain's office he said with a big grin, "You're in it, buddy." He went on to say that he had lived in New York City for twenty years and had come back to Livorno a year ago. The captain would not be in today, he went on. He turned off his shortwave radio and said, "Listen to those idiots, they yak all day saying nothing, just like the States." He looked across the harbor at the *Hebe* and said maybe somebody might stop by. What about our passports? Oh, those—well, I'll stamp them for you if it will make you feel better. He did and I trudged back and took in our Q flag.

Livorno is a big, bustling port and, in 1969, full of American troops. The buildings are typical Italian architecture, mustard yellow with white trim. It was Sunday but very busy "downtown." We took a cab, after some dickering, up along the coast beaches crowded with people, and then along the Arno to Pisa, which was loaded with tourists. I wore Bermuda shorts and so was not allowed to enter the cathedral, but the gals made it all right. Churches are not my long suit, so I had an "ice" while waiting. The area around the tower is interesting and worth a visit. After covering all the sights, we had a late lunch at a sidewalk café and then drove back to the harbor. The yacht club here is a "cute" place but offers no facilities other than very good showers. Eunice and the dogs had a great time in one of them. The water is hot, and the place clean. The drinking water in this area is not to be trusted. We took none on and stuck to bottled goods.

That evening we listened to the radio report of our astronauts landing on the moon—exciting.

In the morning, we went to a laundromat and did some shopping, then back to *Hebe* to get a quick lunch before departing for Elba. It was hot.

Elba is about eleven by twenty-five miles in size. It is mountainous, green, and fertile—beautiful. Napoleon should not have suffered here. The island lies a few miles off the coast of the mainland depending, of course, on which point you pick. From Livorno to Portoferraio, the spot we visited, is about fifty miles. There is an excellent white wine made in Elba, which until very recently was never exported. It is one of the best Italian wines we ever tasted.

We got away from Livorno about 1:00 P.M. Outside the breakwater a few freighters were lying-to waiting for pilots to take them in. The wind was WXN at about eight to ten knots. We made sail, mizzen, main, and forestay sail, and logged about seven knots on a broad reach. The wind did not hold its strength so we turned on the engines and ran along under both. The wind disappeared late in the afternoon, and we took in sail. There was a lot of traffic from the mainland to Elba. Hydrofoils, which move along at about thirty-five knots, and ferries run a frequent service from Piombino on the mainland, only twelve miles away. We learned that thousands of lower-middle-class Italians use these ferries regularly. The island offers many good beaches and camping areas. Throw all this in with a pleasant boat ride, and you have a pretty good deal.

We arrived at the gas dock outside the harbor at seven. Diesel was seventeen cents a gallon, plus a fee for Customs. I said the devil with it and we went inside—La Darsena—a big round harbor with many, many boats lying stern to. We backed in between a Dutchman to starboard and *Weekend II,* a blue ketch to our port. Alongside *Weekend II* was the *Fair Lady,* a large motor yacht owned by Bemberg, the Argentine textile baron. As soon as our sternlines were secure, a fat little man in white shorts and a T-shirt with the legend "Ormeggia Gori P. Ferrario" asked for our tonnage—we paid a 901-lira landing fee. The lira then was about 630 to the dollar. The Dutchman told us we should have gone to Porto Aburo—there is a good restaurant there. Behind us across the *quai* was a large imposing building, the Grand Hotel Darsena. We tried that but the *ristorante* was closed. Moving through the crowd we found an open-air restaurant on the *quai.*

Eunice had swordfish, Lil spaghetti, and I artichoke and green-bean salad—cost 2100 lira, about $3.50. The food was hardly worth it, the white wine was something else. We marched about a bit. The main streets are wide and go up the hill behind the harbor facade in long steps. These used to have open sewers running down the center but have been covered over. The side streets are narrow and dingy. Ice cream in Elba is a mania. Everybody, including ourselves, was licking an ice cream cone and there were vendors hawking their ices and *gelati* everywhere. Walking along the bay road beyond the harbor, we came upon a garden calendar that is replanted every morning, early, to indicate the day and date. It has been in use for 200 years.

Back aboard, we listened to Armstrong, Mike Collins, and Houston getting set for the moon lift-off. We could not find a public TV anywhere, but TV antennae were everywhere.

The following day we were awakened at 6:30 by a loud bang. Rushing up the companionway, we discovered that the *Alaciel* was leaving, and her hook was caught in our chain. We eased off our chain to give them some slack to play with. We got Armand up and went back to bed.

Later, Eunice, Lil, and I poked around the town. Napoleon souvenirs were on display in shops on almost every corner. Armand got a haircut for $1.10 and was tickled to death because they didn't scent him or try to "set" his hair as they did in Marseille. We took a load of that good wine aboard at about seventy cents a one-liter bottle. We noticed a surprising number of blond children, but never found out why. After lunch, Eunice and I had a wonderful swim at a beautiful beach on the north side facing the small island of Scoglietto. Unfortunately the beach was covered with globs of oil—some ship probably blew its bilges. The water was clean, blue, and very salty. On the walk back, we bought some round watermelons for twenty cents a kilo from a corner vendor. They were delicious. At 4:38 we left the harbor and set off for Civitavecchia, the commercial harbor for Rome. Pompi came up on deck to look around, then went below.

How did we know where we were going, some may ask. In the first place, my father always said if you don't know where you're going, don't go. In the second place, we had a complete set of charts from

Barcelona to Odessa in the Black Sea. They were U.S. charts, which I believe are superior and more up-to-date than others available. Also, we had a complete set of U.S. pilot books for the same area, brought up to current date. All of these are available through most any good shop. We got ours at New York Nautical Instrument.

At five the next morning we were in the harbor of Civitavecchia. It was full of ships. We headed for the *quai* at the head of the harbor beneath the mammoth fortress. A cop said we could not tie up here, too many ships, and sent us to the Darcena Romana, an old port built by Trajan, at the other end of the harbor. It was crowded with fishing boats and a few yachts. A fisherman caught our lines. At 5:58 we were all fast and tumbled into bed.

What a kaleidoscopic day! Eunice got up at 10:30 and went to the port captain's office to get information about fuel and the train schedule to Rome. She arranged for 2,500 liters of diesel at fifteen cents per gallon plus twelve dollars and seventy cents for a mobile pump. She gave the cop and the fuel man a pack of cigarettes each. They would come back in the afternoon, and Armand could move *Hebe* back into the harbor against the inner *quai*. There was a train at 12:35; round trip, second class, was $1.59 each. What a job Eunice did! Neither Lil nor I ever could have made ourselves understood, and certainly Armand couldn't have.

We caught the train, which did not go to the terminal. We could change or take a taxi. We elected the latter for 600 lira, about a dollar, and got a sight-seeing spiel along with it on our way to Hotel Mediterraneo—St. Peter's dome, the Arches of Constantine and Titus, Hadrian's Tomb, the Baths of Caracalla, the Via Veneto, and the Colosseum. At the hotel, Lil made a date with the hairdresser for 4:00, and she went off shopping. We were to meet at 6:30. Eunice and I went to Da Canepa across from the Grand Hotel for lunch. She had read in the *Herald-Tribune* about a big fashion show and went to the Grand Hotel. She came back with Eugenia Sheppard, an old friend. We had a nice visit. Jeannie didn't think much of the show. She had to go to Madrid and then to Athens for a cruise on Revson's yacht. We asked about Ted Kennedy and Chappaquiddick, which we had just heard about. She said all Europe was abuzz about it. She had to get back to write her column, and so we parted. Eunice and I went to the American Embassy to get some information about Malta and quarantine regulations for dogs. As usual, nothing but abuse there. Then down to the Poste to telephone. It was jammed mostly with American students with the same idea. One girl said she had been waiting for seven hours. We gave up that idea. Then to the Fontana di Trevi, where we took pictures of each other. Back at the hotel, Lil looked pretty spiffy in her new coiffure. We had a very good dinner in the hotel. Most of the clientele were Americans. We walked across the plaza to the Statione and just caught the 9:02 boat train, which was jammed to the guards. It was hot and dirty. Back at the boat now, just a short walk from the train, Armand told us that the Esso man did not make it but would be back tomorrow. He told us about a train that stopped that afternoon. The engineer and fireman got out, climbed over the wall, got some ice cream cones, finished them, and then got back in the locomotive to resume the trip. This seemed like a happy way to run a railroad, at least as far as the crew is concerned.

A harbor cop banged on our hull at 6:30 morning to tell us we had to move—a Spanish ship was coming in. We told him that we were here with the approval of the port captain and we were waiting for the fuel truck. We walked *Hebe* astern a few feet. He needed cigarettes. We gave him a pack. At 7:15 he was back, very angry. We did not move; he got no more cigarettes. At 7:30, the Esso truck drove alongside with a Customs inspector. In addition to fuel, we took on about 100 gallons of water, which is okay here, but chlorinated. We were charged $1.25 for the water, and after one pack of cigarettes, we were allowed as much as we wanted to wash down the boat. The Esso driver would not accept our credit card, nor would he wait until we got some lira. Eunice came up with $100, and this settled everything. We cast off at 11:40 and threaded our way through the very busy harbor—cruise ships, car ferries, and big island ferries everywhere. Outside we hugged the shore as closely as we could to take in the sights. There was a light breeze on the nose.

5:35 P.M.—still moving along the coast—sea calm with a gentle rock to the boat. Jacques content in Lillian's arms, Pompi resting below. Whole coast line being developed—looks like one continuous stretch of resort—not a wisp of smoke anywhere. All luxury hotels, apartment houses (condominiums?), villas, beaches, little houses, and hills behind. We were approximately 2½ to 3 miles offshore and heading southeast 137° doing 7½ knots over the bottom.

Light blue sky, faded a bit in the haze at the horizon, deeper blue water, white bow wave and sudsy wake in which our little white dinghy splashed along dutifully some 25 yards behind like an obedient white poodle, following in as straight a line as possible. The boom is swaying gently; the automatic pilot is doing the steering. We are flying four flags: CCA burgee flying from atop the main mast; the Italian courtesy flag—red, green, and white flapping from the spreader; our house flag flying from the mizzen; and the U.S. ensign on the staff at stern.

As we came abeam of Caldara, we thought of Betty Anne and Stu. We arrived off Anzio Point at 6:41 and stopped for a swim. It was good—beautiful blue, clean water, temperature just right. From out here, it is impossible to detect any signs of the devastation wrought during the famous battle of Anzio Beach in World War II. At 7:25 we rounded the point and turned north into the entrance. Behind the breakwater, we saw the masts of *Kyma* in position numero uno; Niarchos had beat us to it this time. We backed in between an Italian destroyer and a blue sloop named *Solaria*. Literally hundreds of people were on the *quai* watching us, cheering Bravo! Bravo!. We thought it was for us, but no, they had seen our American flag and were cheering it, because the astronauts had just splashed down.

We had dinner aboard and then joined the throngs on the *quai*. It was like a fiesta; everyone was in a gala mood. Along the way, there were vendors hawking oysters, cockles, mussels, and shrimp —*"fruti de Mare."* I tried some oysters, not bad, but not up to ours. Up in the town, everything was festive too, and the sidewalk cafés were buzzing with activity. We stopped at one and had a *limonada,* wicked ones, we.

Anzio today is both a populous and popular resort, within an easy drive or train ride from Rome. The beaches and swimming are good, the harbor is excellent for yachts. We liked it.

Eunice got up at six in the morning and went into the square to get bread, wine, and a paper. This is best described by an excerpt from Eunice's diary, which follows: (July 24—from Civitavecchia to Anzio).

"Before leaving any port, I did last-minute marketing and walking of dogs. No telling how long it will be or what we will find at our next port of call. A port, a city, a wilderness. Try not to buy too much that will spoil in the hot Mediterranean sun, but to have enough crackers, cans, and root vegetables and local wines to tide us over in case we can't find fresh food for a few days. All along the way the local food tastes better with the local wines—from the rivers —the Rhine, Mosel, Saône, Rhône—the cheeses (Camembert & red Rhônes!)—down to Provençe and the rosés of Provençe, which went well with the peaches and apricots—the tomatoes and veal in Italy taste just right with the local *vino bianco*. Our hold won't keep the vegetables fresh the way it did in the cold rivers and in the Med in Marseille, as the water is getting warmer below Rome."

The paper carried only two stories, the "splash down" of the astronauts and Chappaquiddick—Armstrong got top billing.

We got away at 7:30. The trip down the coast was pleasant, but without incident. We spent most of the day on deck so as not to miss any sights. Lil was mending flags off and on and then tried to read the newspaper. Eunice was at the wheel a good part of the time and attempted to translate the Kennedy story for her. We had some eighty-five miles to go and if we powered all the way we should be in at 5:30.

A few miles below Anzio, we passed Mt. Circeo, 1775 feet, which forms Cape Circeo. A yacht harbor is located at the base on the south side. Somewhere in here is where Circe kept Ulysses captive for so long a time. Some wind came in from the west at about eight knots so we cut the engines and put up every rag we owned and lowered ¼ board. We poked along at four to five knots for a while. The motion and the quiet were a treat. The wind, however, got tired, and at 5:15 we had to go back to power. We could see the island of Ischia and many ferries plying their way back and forth from Naples. At 7:00 we passed Castel dell 'Ovo to look in on the yacht basin Molosiglio and found it loaded with boats. The flattop *John F. Kennedy* was anchored out in the bay. We went back to Castel, where a rowboat came out to greet us. Eunice asked the price; it was too high. The owner came out, "Big Louie," and he talked it out with Eunice and would not budge on price. Finally in desperation, he asked for the *capitan*. During this tête-à-tête, Lillian chuckled throughout. "Big Louie" told me his price was eight dollars per day for me or Jesus Christ. I accepted the equal footing with grace, and we backed in. The water everywhere in this area is filthy, but the marina was neat, clean, and freshly painted in green and red. There were flower boxes of geraniums on every float. Next to us was a sailboat owned by a U.S. Navy man who was going to Anzio tonight. His crew, M. St. Jacques, was going too and would mail some film and letters for us through the fleet PO.

Dinner was on Lil on the terrace of the Vesuvio hotel which overlooks the Castel. We had an excellent meal for thirty dollars. The Vesuvio needs no introduction from us. The view from the terrace is beautiful. We could see *Hebe,* and Armand in the galley fixing his dinner. He almost always refused to eat ashore; it was too expensive.

Early in the morning I was walking the dogs when I heard a rhythmic slap behind me and coming closer. I turned around and saw a boy carrying a box of fruit on his head. The sole of one shoe was coming off and he had to slap it down so that he wouldn't trip. As he went by, I saw that he was holding his pants together in the rear where the seam had parted. Reminded me of that comical, pathetic tramp, Charlie Chaplin. As I watched him disappear down into the Castel, two big buses pulled up and disgorged a load of Yugoslavs on tour. They were well dressed and looked like a happy group. Either the publicity is wrong, or they are doing well.

Eunice, in her usual early morning shopping, found filth and squalor two blocks behind the American Express. There evidently is a lot of this in Naples.

Armand has started to chafe and act up. Instead of trying to phone home last night, he went off to do it this morning, all of which delayed our departure. I had chastised him for not washing the boat while he had plenty of water in the marina. While he and the gals were away I had a *limonada* with "Big Louie," and watched the fishermen bring in mussels for market. Just outside of the marina, they suspend hemp ropes and grow the mussels just like a stalk of bananas. I sure wouldn't eat any mussels grown in this water!

We finally got away a few minutes after noon. We were headed for Palinuro seventy-two miles away. Our ETA was approximately 9:00 P.M. Lil had told us she was going to Athens with us, and I was trying to make up lost time.

On the way out to Capri, the traffic was quite heavy with

hydrofoils, ferries, speedboats, and a few yachts. We went to within 100 yards of the beautiful island, took a few pictures, and then laid a course for Palinuro. The weather cleared somewhat, and Vesuvius was just barely visible. We won't be able to see the shore for a couple of hours as we make a straight line for Cape Palinuro. Along about 6:30 P.M. we came upon a cruiser anchored off a point. We passed under her stern and saw the name *Lucy Two*. She looked like a Mathews—no one was aboard, but tooling around in a rubber dinghy with outboard were a woman, man, and child. They waved. A few miles southeast of this point, there is a long ridge that rises to 3707 feet called Madonna della Stella (a good name!).

At 8:00 the sun was a huge red ball setting into the sea. Lil observed that this was the life, and within a few minutes we spotted Palinuro Light 677 feet atop a huge rock that juts out into the sea and drops sheer. In the daylight, it is a sight to see. It provides two excellent anchorages, depending on the wind. If it blows west to north, anchor to the south side, and vice versa. We put in on the north and anchored in eleven fathoms of crystal clear water. There was a yacht anchored ahead of us showing a red light (wrong!) that she changed to white as we anchored. Another yacht came in behind us. I dropped a small battery anchor light overboard and you could see the bottom where the light glowed.

The moon was bright, the night glorious. We could see a few lights ashore and hear an occasional voice. Dinner was late, 10:00, veal in Madeira, the red wine was lousy, the white wine from Naples good. Armand sulked. He rowed the dogs ashore at eleven and was gone for an hour.

Eunice stayed on deck for a spell. It was a romantic setting with the moon shining down over the shoulder of that massive rock called Palinuro.

The next day we got a better view; it was beautiful. Our little light was glowing from the bottom just where I dropped it. The shore, the yacht club, the few houses made you wish to stay—an unspoiled vacation spot. But, alas, all this has gone, so we have heard. A breakwater has been put in to the north side with a resulting development of the real estate. Looking at it another way, who can afford to get there these days—losers all around!

We awakened Armand at 7:30. He responded with the speed of a wounded tortoise and eventually rowed the two tigers ashore for a morning pee. Upon his leisurely return, we departed, for the record, at 8:00.

In the morning's light the rock of Palinuro possessed a majesty difficult to describe. It made you feel small, not in a demeaning way — you just looked at this sheer beauty in awe — sort of like going to church.

We moved around it slowly, looking into several grottoes at water level and ogling at three or four more higher up where the great, big, blue sea must have been at one time. On the south side of the rock, there is another beautiful anchorage to be used on calm days such as today, or when the blows from the north. The beaches were inviting, not a soul enjoying the attraction, not a house to spoil the scene. Again, alas, we hear this is no longer true.

Armand for some reason was flying the Storm Trysail burgee today. We took our departure from Palinuro at 8:09. Armand took the wheel with a course of 138°M for Capo Bonafati forty miles away, as we went below to prepare breakfast. Lil wanted to know where we were going. I told her that until I studied the pilot book we were crossing the Golfo di Policastro to Vaticano fifty-five miles beyond Capo Bonifati. She wanted to know if this was on the heel or toe — we said toe — she said, "Heel, toe, and away we go, doing the *Hebe* polka."

While the girls did the dishes I got out the pilot book and, after reading the descriptions of the various harbors available to us, it seemed that Vibo Valentia Marina on the south shore of Golfo di Sant' Eufemia should be our best bet. It is fifty-one miles from Bonifati. The wind was four to five knots ESE, on the nose, which meant power all the way and a run of about ninety miles. We were making fairly big jumps now, but limiting ourselves to day cruising only. With Armand getting a little sulky, it seemed best not to work either one of us too much.

All of us spent most of the day on deck. Our automatic pilot, Mr. Moto, did much of the steering, Lil groomed the dogs, Eunice worked on her diary. We were averaging about eight knots over the bottom. Eunice at one point was downwind of Armand and had to move. She suggested that we give him a cake of Dial and make him go for a swim.

At 12:30 we spotted Sera Dei Monaci, 3419 feet, and, a few minutes later, we were abeam of Bonifati where we changed our course for Vibo. The beaches along here are beautiful sand, good new roads followed the shore, and there was a modern hotel with an outside elevator going down to the beach. In France, we used to wonder where all the fifty million Frenchmen were. Here, it seemed that all the Italians were on the beach.

We are down to one bottle of Heineken's — Armand has switched to milk. Also, he doesn't seem to like the Italian bread as he did the French. You can't please everybody.

At 12:30, we were off Paola — Italy is only fifteen miles wide at this point. We could see olive trees everywhere — also flies and bugs.

At 6:55 we stopped for a swim, but could not get Armand in.

About a quarter to eight, we approached the breakwater at Vibo — there were two tankers lying outside, the sun was setting round and red. Inside we tied up to the *quai* nearest the outer end of the harbor. We were joined a little later by a Frenchman and his family who arrived in a small sloop. His name was Moreau; he worked for the World Bank in Versailles — a nice guy.

This place is dirty and buggy. There is a cement works here, too, which fills the air with a fine dust. We walked into town — nothing there except sullen people. There is another part of town up the mountain that must be better, but we didn't make it. Dinner aboard was good, pleasant.

At 6:30, we awakened the Frenchman and took off in the haze for the Messina Straits — hot and hazy all the way. On the way over, a couple of pipes in the cooling system of the starboard engine let go — rusted out. We proceeded on the port engine and pumped out the starboard engine room. We arrived at and passed between Scylla and Charybdis as if we had been doing it all of our lives. The whirlpool, currents, and wind lived up to the pilot-book description.

The wind was deceptive. Having traveled all the way from Vibo in "FAC," sailor's slang for calm, once into the straits we got a beautiful fair wind. Eunice suggested we put up some sail. The Pilot cautions against this, and pointing ahead, we could see where the wind stopped and the current fanned out into nothing.

The traffic was not heavy with the exception of the ferries that ply back and forth between Reggio di Calabria and Messina. The new "scenic railway" highway that we had seen all the way down the coast ends at Reggio, but looking over at Sicily, evidently a similar highway was being built around the island.

Messina harbor looked very busy, dirty, and noisy. The city itself, from our vantage point, was interesting architecturally, but I don't think we missed too much as we passed by.

A few miles below Messina, there is a beautiful tourist mecca known as Taormina. From *Hebe,* it looked most intriguing with its new hotels hanging onto the cliffs that drop into the sea, and the snowcapped Mt. Etna breathing heavily in the background.

Capo Schiso, at the southern end of Rada di Taormina, forms a fairly good yacht basin. Armand dropped our hook, and as I was backing in to the *quai* and just about to heave a sternline ashore, he put on the brakes of the windlass. I threw my arms in the air as if supplicating the good Lord above and roared a loud, "Jesus." Looking over the side, I noticed a scuba diver swimming unconcernedly between us and the *quai;* to port was a man fishing from a small boat. I decided to move out. When the hook was back aboard, Armand came aft and asked Eunice to count his money, he was quitting. He disappeared into his quarters. We moved out around Capo Schiso and set a course for Riposto, a few miles down the coast. Eunice pleaded with me to apologize to Armand. Finally, at six o'clock she effected a reconciliation.

At 6:30 we stopped for a wonderful swim just outside of Riposto. We entered the harbor at 7:00 and came alongside the wide *quai* inside the breakwater. The harbor master inspected our papers and requested us to move closer "uptown," ahead of the freighter *Andrea.* There were many people watching—sullen, pushy, sinister-looking. The city is noted for the dome on its cathedral—I could not see why. The many buildings clustered around the harbor make a beautiful sight of mixed colors—faded pastels of blue, rose, mustard. Looking about on the *quai* I spotted a taxi. The driver wanted $13 to drive us into town. Nuts to this! We walked, followed by the locals, who now broke into voice and agreed with me. When we got into the center of town, there was a total blackout. Armand decided to stay at a restaurant to eat in the dark (they must have had candles). I bickered with a cabdriver who took us to an open air restaurant up the coast. It was lousy looking, filthy—so back to *Hebe.* The driver tried to hold us up for a lot of dough. I gave him

1000 lira, about $1.60. A cop came along and said not to pay. As we approached *Hebe,* a figure leaped ashore and disappeared into the shadows. Nothing had been taken. We had potluck — pea soup, wurst, crackers, wine, and fresh plums.

The next morning we could see Mt. Etna smoking — like an angry bull, snorting through two nostrils.

After a quick breakfast, we left Riposto at 8:30 and headed for Catania. It was the clearest day yet in Italy, but there was a big swell running. Lil's ankles were swollen, so we got some seawater for her to soak her feet in, which seemed to help. Eunice was steering. A British helicopter followed us overhead.

At 9:40 we were abeam of Acireale, a bay where Ulysses' boats were pulled up; also the place where the Cyclopes lived. How do I know all this? Eunice told me, of course.

In a little while we could see Catania ahead, with big new apartment houses rising eight and twelve stories. Some years ago, Eunice and some pals had started out to see Greece. They stopped off in Sicily to see Syracuse and other historical spots. My bride was driving a rented Fiat and going along at about forty-five mph when the tie rod let go. The car plowed into a tree, and all the girls were hurt — Eunice and one other almost fatally. Some passing Italians got them into the U.S. Naval Hospital in Catania where Eunice spent the next six weeks. Between the U.S. Navy medics and an Italian plastic surgeon, they got her patched up pretty well. They told her she never would be able to play tennis again and that her right leg would never be the same. They didn't know my girl! Well, anyway, this is why Eunice knows so much about Catania, and one of the reasons why we were here.

At 10:58 we passed the outer breakwater and turned into the new yacht harbor to starboard. We backed in to the Nautica Italia Club. We were alongside a Dutch-built power yacht *Safari*. Armand had been on her shakedown trials two years ago. There was a big, black ketch there too, obviously an Alden design. Her name was *Lentini* and she reminded us of *Sea Gypsy,* a well-known Alden-designed schooner. Over in the old harbor we could see a U.S. destroyer.

Ashore in the club, Eunice called Ivan; then her old friend Signorella — gone; she tried some friends in Taormina — gone; also the Perkins dealer — he would send mechanics tomorrow.

A suave taxi driver came by and introduced himself, Giovanni di

Stafano. He knew many places. I asked him to stand by while we got ready. We got cleaned up and dressed in our shore finery. We climbed into his immaculate limousine and told him we would like a nice spot for lunch. The traffic in Catania is wild, but Giovanni got us through it nicely and up the coast on the outskirts of the city to a place called Costa Azura—a delightful old Italian *palazzo* overlooking the sea. We were ushered out onto a *terrazza* facing the sea. Lunch was superb, expensive. After lunch, we drove back into town to the Excelsior Hotel where I got a haircut and Lil had a coiffure. Eunice went to the Poste only to find that it and all the stores were closed. However, she and I were able to find a Standa (a large Italian supermarket chain) open, where there was a good selection of foods at not-too-expensive prices.

Dinner was on board—fried chicken and tomatoes, plus local wine.

The president of the "club" came aboard for a drink and a tip. It was terribly hot and raining. Later, a big white motor yacht came in loaded with pretty girls.

The following day we kept busy. Eunice went into the city to do laundry and to get everything we might need for our jump across the sea to Greece. I walked over to the U.S. destroyer to see if I could get an electrician and a mechanic to come over to check us out. Some junior officer haughtily advised me that this service was not available, and, furthermore, the ship was preparing to leave. Oh well, I thought, even the U.S. Navy has to get all kinds, so I said, "Thanks, Bub," and left.

Stafano was waiting for me back at the club—was there something he could do for us? I made a deal for him to take us to Taormina at 7:30 for a look-see and then to a good spot for dinner.

Walking along the *quai* I came upon a light blue power yacht getting ready to go somewhere. A very pleasant gentleman stepped ashore and introduced himself as Col. Profumo. He was English. Profumo—I wondered could it be the one and the same. Well, no matter, I introduced myself and told him we were leaving in the morning for Greece. He told me that his cruising range would not get him there—he was on his way to Syracuse and then Malta. He asked if he could come to see our boat and our charts. He came over later and was very complimentary about our "bucket." He looked at some of our charts and made some notes. Lil thought he was very handsome and a very polished gentleman. He was, too.

The Perkins men arrived, ripped out our rusty pipes on the starboard cooling system, and installed new ones—cost, 10,000 lira, or $65.00.

At 7:30 di Stafano arrived, the girls were ready, and off we went. Quite a ride. The traffic was immense—lemon groves all the way, with many flowers, terraced gardens, oleander, bougainvillea streaking by as we drove. Taormina itself is a tourist trap, but beautifully done. There are many narrow streets with enchanting shops—tourists everywhere—but you like it, at least we did. We went to the old hotel that Eunice had known and looked around. It had wonderful gardens and a beautiful view. The whole place seemed to have an aura all its own. With Mt. Etna in the background, and the sparkling sea many feet below, it's a most romantic spot. Back to our limousine. Stafano drove down through the throng carefully to the shore road and then into a drive that led to a restaurant tucked into the side of a cliff with a sheer drop to the sea. We were seated on a balcony. Below us were some islands with some lovely villas peeking up at us. Stafano was seated at another table behind us. This place specialized in seafood. It was good, delightful, and expensive.

Back at the club, Eunice would not let me pay Stafano because it was too much, she said. All of us went aboard *Hebe,* and Eunice started to haggle and bicker over the cab bill. Lil and I couldn't stand it so went to bed. The driver finally retreated from exhaustion along about three o'clock.

19

Greece

We were up and away at 6:30 that morning. How Eunice could do it with almost no sleep was a wonder to me. Our course was due east (90°), and Zákinthos was about 385 miles away. We were running at 1,500 rpm. Armand had run up the New York Yacht Club burgee. We passed through many, many fishing boats. Looking back we could see Mt. Etna with smoke curling out of some new holes that had broken through. About three miles offshore, we could smell garbage burning!

We had a light quartering sea with waves about 1½ feet. This was a little too much for Mr. Moto whose clutch was slipping. There was a slight breeze from the southwest. We set the main, and went to manual steering. An Italian coaster, *Gabriello,* passed us, a man on the bridge waving. Armand was feeling much better and was in pretty good spirits actually, and glad to get away from Italy, especially Sicily.

Having set up a system of watches (Swedish System), I hit the sack. Back up on deck at 12:00 with some drinks, I found the sea calm, no wind; Armand had dropped the main. At about three I tried the forestaysail, no help. We saw three ships; one Russian, one Italian, and one Don't Know.

At 1945 we spotted a tanker off to port heading for the Straits. At 2012 we took in colors; 2025 running lights on; 2030 dinner—veal roast, potatoes, green beans.

At midnight I was on watch and went below to make coffee. Mr. Moto was back on the wheel. It was a beautiful warm night with a big moon and a few stars, nary a ship in sight. A half hour later, back on deck, I realized that I did not hear the slap-slap of our dinghy. I turned around, it was gone. Making a big turn around to starboard, we started to make our way back. Eunice, sensing the motion from our turn, came flying on deck to find out what was going on. I explained that we had lost our dinghy and were going to run back for a half hour. She wakened Armand and the two of them began searching—Armand standing high on the main boom at the mast. We were just about to run out our time when both Eunice and Armand simultaneously spotted the dink in the moonlight straight ahead, a little to starboard. We came up to it easy, Armand got in and made the falls fast. We hoisted it up on the stern davits. Maybe next time, Armand, a bowline? Back to bed for Eunice and Armand.

Lil came on deck at about seven smelling like a rose. Eunice was in the galley fixing breakfast. Later, Armand said to her, "Mrs. Latham, do you believe in numbers?" "Why?" "I came to work for you on the 13th, I should have waited a day."

At 9:00 we spotted the only dolphin on the trip.

11:50 starboard engine springs a leak.

12:50 Eunice has a Cinzano.

2:00 it's sprinkling.

4:00 a red "Coaster" is heading south for Crete.

5:00 ship coming north from Crete.

7:20 sighted rocks—Nisoi Strofadis; land ahead—Katákolon.

This latter shook me up. We had not spotted the light on Zákinthos; maybe it was not functioning. Our course obviously erred to the south, so I adjusted a few degrees north. I supposed that our horsing around looking for the dink had something to do with it. At 8:30 it started to rain. At 9:02 we got a fix on Katákolon light and adjusted course to 320°M. At 10:34 we spotted the light on Killini and changed course to 255°M. The rain stopped about midnight. We had reduced speed because I had read about some dangerous rocks off the approach to Zákinthos. I need not have bothered, particularly on this course. As we approached the island, the shore lights were confusing, and we had a hell of a time finding the small green light at the entrance to the harbor. At 2:00 A.M. we slid past the breakwater and into a big, beautiful lagoon of a harbor. There was a happy party going on in the *taverna* on the outer end of the mole. The owner came to catch our lines as we came alongside the *quai* instead of backing in. He spoke good English and wondered if we had come for the race. What race? The annual race from Pátrai to Zákinthos to Kérkira. I thanked him for the compliment and said good night. It was 2:30 A.M., August 2, my mother's birthday.

The day was officially started by a taxi at 6:30 looking for a fare. Eunice told him to go away, come back some other day. I didn't stir. Then a lot of noise and conversation seemed to buzz all around us. Eunice said there was a big crowd. I told her to go back to sleep, we always draw big crowds. No, this was not for us. So we got up, and soon got the answer. The party had gone on and on. At about six, three of the guests got into their car to leave and had backed off right into the drink ahead of us. The people, fortunately, had opened the doors and swam out. The gang on the *quai* now were trying to pull the car out with ropes.

We were boarded by the doctor, the Coast Guard, Customs, the police; we had to show ship's papers, passports, health certificate for the dogs. Ultimately we got our "Transit Log," and broke out our Greek flag at the starboard spreader.

This island, sometimes called Zante, is one of the Ionians and is most attractive. It has lots of trees, much greenery, and many fertile spots, generally true of this group. There are many good bathing beaches. The local architecture is a mixture of Greek and Venetian. The beautiful church on the edge of the harbor is a perfect example of the Venetian influence. The city is clean, attractive, and growing. Many of the buildings have arcaded the sidewalks which is a treat on a hot day. As we were shopping for fruit (which is wonderful here), a little man came up to me and asked if I were English or American. I said, "American." Whereupon he flashed a big golden grin and said, "What the hell are you doing here this time of year. It's too damn hot." He had lived in the States for years and had returned to this, his native island, on Social Security only this year.

On the way back to the *Hebe*, we met a young New Zealander,

Peter Nightingale, carrying a knapsack and eating the wonderful white seedless grapes grown here. He was traveling all around the world on almost nothing and was going to catch the ferry here for Pátrai and then on to Kérkira — an attractive lad.

We loaded all our goodies aboard and got under way for Pátrai at 1:40. It was beautiful outside, but the wind was on the nose. You could see the mainland clearly and the island of Kefallinía to the north. Lil wanted to cruise all these islands, but we had to push on — we were overdue back at the office.

At 8:05 we were off the flashing green at the end of the mole at Pátrai — the air was laden with eucalyptus. Inside the harbor, there was a mass of yachts, all entrants in the race, among them, *Nefertiti,* the American 12 meter. A Greek destroyer, #54, one of Truman's gifts, was on hand to act as a committee boat. We tied up alongside the *quai* ahead of the destroyer and had dinner aboard, consisting of chicken from Zákinthos, rice from Italy, canned peas from Marseille plus some Sicilian wine, then some wine also from Zákinthos.

Lil and Eunice went ashore after dinner to look at the town. Walking up the main street that leads up a hill from a big, flowered park in front of the harbor, they were surprised to find so many restaurants, sidewalk cafes, and tourist shops open and doing a big business. The Greeks eat late and Pátrai is a big tourist center. The ferries from the islands and Italy move in and out of here many times a day. Also, this is the fourth largest city of Greece — over 100,000.

We stumbled out of the sack at seven. At eight, a bugle from the destroyer blew colors. After breakfast, Armand came out of the starboard engine room saying, "Surprise, surprise," and held two broken water pumps. Eunice and I stepped ashore, made arrangements for water, forty-five cents, and took off to see the town. On the other side of the lumber yard where we were tied up was the railroad depot where the funny, little, narrow gauge trains come and go with considerable frequency. We saw Peter Nightingale sitting on a spile at the head of the harbor. He explained that the ferry he was going to take yesterday was too expensive — he would get a cheaper one today. I wished it were that simple for us.

Through the flowered mall and up into the city, we saw many

hotels, shops selling tourist items, "worry-beads" and the like, and restaurants asleep from last night's vigors. We were impressed with the clean streets and the cool arcades. The air smelled of retsina. As a matter of fact, the people did, too. Flowers were everywhere, another nice Greek touch.

On the way back to the boat, we found a "deli" where we bought Greek beer called Fix. It is very good, but a little expensive. On board, we learned that a big ship was due in and we had to scoot. Too bad; we were going to fill our empty wine bottles from the public spring here.

We were out of the harbor at 11:37. In spite of the fact that the first gun for the race went off at 9:00, the fleet was still sitting outside with all sails hanging limp and useless.

To the north, the mountains were barren, forbidding; to the south were beaches, all crowded. Ferries were very busy in this area. Making our way eastward we could see the lighthouse that marks the narrows and the entrance to the Gulf of Corinth. At first glance, it looks as if it is out in the middle, but it is really at the end of a long sand spit. The water in the Gulf of Corinth is a deep, deep blue, darker than the Ionian or the Italian Med. Presently, we passed the attractive town of Návpaktos to our north. The south coast here, and almost all the way to Corinth, is covered with olive groves and vineyards. The gulf widens to about 4½ miles, that is if you don't include the Bay of Itea. It was too hazy to the north for us to see Itea, the port for Delphi. We had lunch with some Greek red wine—so-so. Moving along the shore of Pelopónnisos, we could see the coastal highway from Pátrai to Athens "littered" with buses going both ways. At 5:07 off Acra Likoporia we stopped for a swim—even Armand went in with soap. An outboard came roaring out from shore, and an old fisherman warned us with gestures to get out of the water—sharks. He may have been right but we didn't see any—then or ever. Regardless, it was good of him. Also, it should be known that when swimming we always have at least one person on board watching for boats and the swimmers. Back aboard we felt wonderfully refreshed. As I got out the Scotch and soda, Eunice said, "The pause that refreshes, the glass that cheers."

The sun was setting at 7:15 and, at 8:20 we saw the flashing green on the mole at Corinth. We were tied up to the *quai* behind the mole at 8:34.

At the head of the harbor, there was an open-air restaurant with some nice people who could understand English. Nothing ventured, nothing gained. We ordered small bottles of retsina all around. I spat it out immediately—it tasted like pure turpentine to me. Lil liked it and finished it, which proves that it's "to each his own." For appetizers, Eunice had octopus, while Lil and I had fried lamb's liver cut in strips; then broiled fish, good but bony, served with heads and tails attached. A Greek salad accompanied all this. It was pleasant, tasty, and fun. Armand went into town.

After dinner we walked around the city. There were many people about; some stores, such as confectioneries and wine shops, were open. We found the Roman Forum, which looked interesting, and then walked down the main stem to a hotel on a corner across from the harbor casino where we had an ouzo. Then to bed.

In the morning we got a map of the area and made a deal with the taxi to take us to Mycenae and back. The cabbie turned out to be a good guy as well as a good driver. The drive took us through a rich, cultivated plain with irrigation canals and pipes showing here and there. Peaches, pears, tobacco, citrus fruits, and tomatoes seemed to be thriving, all this in the same latitude as Wilmington, Del. Just below Mycenae we stopped at an attractive *taverna,* La Belle Hèléne, for a drink—*limonada* for us, Greek coffee for the driver. The ruins are most interesting—I finally got bitten with the archeology bug. How in the world this place was built was a marvel to me, perched as it is on top of a precipitous mountain.

On the way back we stopped for lunch at another *taverna,* Orestes, and got back to old Corinth in time to do the ruins there. These are fascinating. The layout of the streets, the shops, and temples are clearly defined, and the surviving ruins are in remarkable condition.

Eunice let loose in an area like this is like a rabbit in a lettuce patch—she won't leave until she has munched every succulent leaf. However, Lil and I were able to drag her away and back to *Hebe.* Armand told us we had to move to the head of the harbor because a ship was coming in. Eunice and I went for a swim first at a very good beach beyond the walled harbor. After a day of plodding around in the dust and ruins, this was most refreshing.

At the head of the harbor, we tied alongside the *quai.* There was an English sloop tied just astern of us. The owner, Roger Hayward, introduced himself, his wife Rachel, and his two children. They were a charming group. Roger told me that they had sailed from Benghazi in Libya, where he was employed. They were going to leave their boat in Piraeus, then fly to England to place their children in school. We told them about the open-air restaurant, and I invited them for an after-dinner drink on their return. We knocked off a bottle of Courvoisier before turning in at midnight.

The next morning, it was blowing madly, dust swirling everywhere, and our two boats were banging against the *quai*. Thank God for large fenders! The Haywards got away first. We backed out into the wind to give us turning room and then led the way to the small harbor at the end of the canal. The red flag, meaning "wait" was flying. They also fly flags to indicate the current in the canal; one white means the current is with you; two white, current is against you. A man on shore asked how fast we could go. We told him ten knots. Okay, up went the blue flag and we entered the canal. The Haywards had to wait because they were much slower and a freighter was coming in behind us.

The canal is fifty-eight feet wide and three miles long. The sides for the most part are sheer cliffs and they are covered with graffiti. There are two ferries to look out for, one at each end. About halfway through there is a railroad bridge over which a narrow-gauge train passed, loosing a lot of gravel as we approached. Next is a vehicular bridge that was crowded with spectators who cheered us as we passed beneath. We arrived in the harbor at the other end at 10:38; it had taken us 33 minutes. The pilot boat came alongside; we were boarded by an inspector. After looking at our papers, he asked for 12 drachmas ($16) toll.

Out into the blue Aegean, islands everywhere, Salamis ahead to port, we have twenty miles to go. *Hebe* is covered with salt and dust. There was a gorgeous sailing breeze (eighteen to twenty knots) but we didn't have the time. It was just as well for within fifteen minutes the wind dropped to nothing. Looking astern we could make out the Haywards coming out of the canal.

About noon we were below, with Armand at the wheel, when there was a loud bang and a shudder. I ran up on deck to discover that the main topping lift had parted, and the boom had fallen smack on top of the binnacle. Armand was unhurt; he had ducked, he said. We lifted the boom, placing it in the crutch where it should have been in the first place.

At 1:21 a modern passenger and car island ferry, the *Aphrodite,* coming out of Piraeus, passed us to port. The wind had returned, blowing twenty-five knots, right on the nose. We were taking a lot of spray and had to close all hatches and forward ports. We could see Aegina off to starboard. Ahead was Athens sprawling out along the coast for miles, it seemed. Above it all, we could see the Acropolis standing guard. Closer at hand we could see the headland of Piraeus covered with new, white apartments. Many, many tankers and freighters were anchored in the roads off the harbor entrance.

We passed the point and held fairly close to the shore. Soon we espied a bathing beach, then a high stone wall at the end of which was a light. We rounded a bell buoy and turned aport into Zea Marina, the new government-built marina for yachts—it was 2:46, Tuesday, August 5.

Zea is the outer harbor, not yet fully completed. It is a very large oval. Fronting on it are the administration offices including Coast Guard and Customs in one building. Off to the left almost in the center, set in a magnificent flower garden is the Marina *taverna* and restaurant. Through a narrow channel to the right is the inner harbor, Passalimáni, a huge oval surrounded almost completely by tall apartment houses. The harbor is a mass of boats, both power and sail. Open sewers empty into both harbors, which is not too pleasant at times.

We tied alongside a large empty *quai* but were told we would have to move because this was reserved for the *Meltemi,* an island cruise boat, due back in at 7:00. We promised to move after lunch. I made a large Athenian salad, and we sat down on deck for lunch at 3:20, a bit late. We were surrounded by huge yachts, most of which were flying the Panamanian flag—we called it the Panamanian navy. There were a few large British yachts, one flying the Blue Duster, which made it rather exclusive. There was a big American yacht, *Aventura,* which came in just ahead of us. We met the owner later, a nice chap from San Francisco. During the course of lunch an official asked for our papers—everything was in order.

At about 5:00 we moved over to the *quai* in front of the new restaurant alongside a big white yacht, *Mascot,* owned by an

American but flying the Panamanian flag. On the other side of us was a fancy-looking yawl with a gang of Italians aboard—some pretty good-looking women, I might add. Down the *quai* near the Coast Guard office was their big square-rigged training ship.

We were boarded by a Joan Keller, a girl from Brooklyn. She was working for one of the many yacht brokers and wanted us to consider her boss. I knew that most of them were crooks, but I figured we had a plus working for us with an American acting as a go-between. I promised to talk with her in the morning. She gave Eunice some advice on where to shop, etc., and told me about some of the restaurants over in Turkolímano.

Later, after a couple or three cocktails, we got a taxi and drove over. It's a fairly easy walk but we were tired. This harbor is almost a perfect circle. High on a promontory guarding the entrance is the Royal Greek Yacht Club. Ringing the harbor is a wide *quai* covered with tables and colorful awnings. Behind this is a roadway flanked on the inside by many restaurants. The idea is to select a table in front of the restaurant of your choice. A waiter will bring you wine immediately, and, when you get the urge, you walk across the street into the restaurant to make your selection, which is then prepared for you. I chose the Chanaris Restaurant, which is excellent. We had a wonderful spot at water's edge, the moon was up, there was accordion music coming from somewhere, there were many attractive people seated at the tables around us. We had a couple of bottles of Cambas Hymettus, a good white wine, for Greece. For dinner, we had shrimp as an appetizer and cold Langouste for our main course, with tomato-and-cucumber salad on the side. Very good; 500 drachmas, about $16.00, without tip.

I got up late even though there was plenty to do. After breakfast, Eunice and I went up to see the yacht broker and agent. Joan Keller was not there. Her boss, Mr. Y, was out, too. Back at the boat we collected Lil and took a bus into Athens, an interesting trip. It was crowded and the Greeks were yakking, laughing, having a fine time. The Greeks speak to everybody and not in whispers. We got off at the end of the line, Constitution Square, crowded with people and traffic. At American Express, we picked up some mail after pushing our way through all the American students. Out in front of the office, there are several rows of chairs where the customers, or anybody, sit and stare at the crowds or sip ouzo or some other drink. At KLM I made reservations for Eunice and me to leave on Sunday via Amsterdam, arriving in New York at 8:15 P.M. Lil and I went to TWA, but couldn't get anything for her for days. Just up the street is Olympic, and we put in there. Got first class for Monday. Then we picked up Eunice at American Express and walked over to the King George Hotel, the best, to see if we could get a room for Lil—today, but not tomorrow, they said. So we went next door to the Grande Bretagne and there, talking to the doorman, was my old friend Hap, an executive with Esso. He and I couldn't believe our eyes. I introduced him to Lil and Eunice and we repaired immediately to the bar where we had our first ouzo of the day. He was here on business for a few days. When we told him about ourselves, he said we should have a lawyer. He would talk to the general counsel over at Esso Pappas. Spyros Skouras was there and Hap introduced us. Through Hap's office, we got a room for Lil for tomorrow to Monday. We made a date for lunch tomorrow, then Hap had to go. After a quick lunch, we walked across the Square and caught a bus back to Piraeus. We passed the Roman ruins, a must, on the way down to the bay. The bay front was being developed by the National Tourist Organization, a branch of the government, for as far as the eye could see. The beaches were crowded; new buildings were going up everywhere. Flowers and gardens were profuse—the Greeks have a way with this kind of thing.

The streets are always clean in Greece, and the air in Athens is usually heavy with dust. Our bus took us along the bay up through the Kastella section of Piraeus overlooking Turkolimano, down around the inner harbor of Passalimani and let us off just above the Zea Marina restaurant. This is where the agent's office is, also.

Back on board, the girls started to sort things out and pack for departure. Later, I took the gals to dinner at the Zea restaurant, which was pretty good, fairly expensive. The decor was quite modern, but then so is everything else. Quite a contrast with the old. A good Greek wine is Boutari, we discovered.

Thursday morning we finally saw Mr. Y. He suggested that we open an account at a local bank, where he could deposit and charter money. He wanted to fire Armand and hire a Greek captain and mate. We told him to keep Armand. He took us to the First National City Bank branch down on the waterfront in the commercial harbor of Piraeus. We made a date with Mr. Y. for Saturday to be aboard *Hebe* to go over all details. He left. After opening a small account, we walked back to the boat. The noise and hustle in this city is almost incredible.

Back at the marina, Lil was ready. We got a cab, stowed all her luggage (this gal doesn't travel light), and drove off to the Grande Bretagne. If you think an Italian taxi driver is wild, try a Greek!

Hap was waiting for us with a friend, Angelos Billis, a movie director. The five of us had a couple in the bar and then into the Palm Court for lunch—something like the Plaza Hotel, in New York, only bigger. Hap informed us that a lawyer at Esso Pappas would be pleased to represent us. Also, Hap was leaving this afternoon for Salonika, but would be back tomorrow afternoon and would like to take us to dinner.

After lunch, I went over to see the lawyer. Seemed like a pleasant fellow. He studied law at New York University. He would be aboard Saturday with an agreement between us and Mr. Y. Back at the hotel I called the office—they couldn't believe the news.

Eunice and I returned to the boat, she to continue sorting and packing, I to work on the inventory with Armand. Eunice found time to go to the harbor office and paid our dues for the year. We got a twenty-five percent discount because the marina was unfinished. Our rate would go up on completion. The three of us, Eunice, Armand, and I went to dinner at the 7 Brothers Restaurant, an extremely popular eating place just off the plaza at the head of the inner harbor—sort of like Lindy's on Broadway.

These last few days were mad, mad. Friday morning I took a duffle bag up to the agents. He would ship it via surface for us. Eunice found a few things Lil had left and stuffed them in her reticule as we packed off for Athens. We had lunch with Lil, then walked over to "do" the Roman ruins. After trudging around here, very interesting, we got a cab and went up to the Acropolis. This is absolutely fascinating. We climbed over all the polished stones and steps, looked into the Treasury, the Porch of the Maidens, the museum, and the Parthenon. From the steps of this magnificent temple, you could see the Aegean through the haze. I couldn't tear

Eunice away, so, after a few hours, I walked back to the hotel to wait.

Hap arrived in the bar at about eight o'clock. After a couple of powders, we took a cab to Dionysus, a super restaurant at the base of the Acropolis. We had an excellent table on the terrace facing the "magnificent pile." Dinner was very, very good, the service pleasant despite the numerous guests. The evening show of lights and music was most interesting. They do this every evening at intervals until about eleven. This is hard to describe. Different parts of the Acropolis are lighted in color, and/or white in unison or in rhythm with classical music—it is both spectacular and dramatic. It was a delightful evening. We dropped Lil and Hap at the hotel and continued on to Piraeus. It was late.

Saturday morning, Hap showed up with his bathing suit. At noon the lawyer and his wife came aboard. We opened up the bar and had a drink while waiting for Mr. Y. When he arrived, we went over an agreement retaining him as our agent for charter and boat management, but with the stipulation that Armand be retained and that all charter agreements and major boat expense had to be approved by the lawyer. Our inventory was an integral part of the agreement. Everything was agreeable and a deal was made. Our lawyer agreed to hold some of our personal effects and the Mosel wine. Mr. Y. departed for another appointment; the lawyer and his wife took off with our goodies.

Alone at last, as they say, we had lunch—a Greek salad and white wine. Hap fell in love with *Hebe*.

We had a pleasant swim at the beach "over the wall." When we returned late in the afternoon who do you think was aboard—none other than Lil. It was nice! We chatted and had some drinks. Later, at the proper hour we had a farewell dinner aboard—baked ham, fluffy rice, petit peas (Marseille), zucchini, salad, and Mosel Kestner. *Voilà—Yassas!*

20

Epilogue

Pompi and Jacques were up early and off on their own. They had adopted this practice from the first day in Zea. They were back aboard as we sat down to breakfast, watching us intently, expectantly. At nine o'clock Armand got a taxi for us, which we loaded to the guards. I shook hands with him; Eunice gave him a kiss. We had done all we could.

At the airport we bumped into the Haywards who were on their way to London. We chatted, wished each other Godspeed, and parted.

Our flight was announced; we boarded the bus for the plane. It was a lovely day, great for flying and sailing, too. As we climbed the steps to our 707 I felt a tug on my sleeve. I looked, there was no one, just a gentle, warm breeze flowing. Funny. But I will swear that as we entered the aircraft I heard a lovely feminine laugh and the tinkle of a wine glass. *Hebe* was back with the gods.